W9-CFL-185

Capital Punishment

Recent Titles in
Historical Guides to Controversial Issues in America

Capital Punishment

Joseph A. Melusky and Keith Alan Pesto

Historical Guides to Controversial Issues in America

 GREENWOOD

AN IMPRINT OF ABC-CLIO, LLC
Santa Barbara, California • Denver, Colorado • Oxford, England

Library of Congress Cataloging-in-Publication Data

Melusky, Joseph Anthony.
  Capital punishment / Joseph A. Melusky and Keith Alan Pesto.
    p. cm. — (Historical guides to controversial issues in America)
  Includes bibliographical references and index.
    ISBN 978–0–313–33558–7 (hardback) — ISBN 978–1–4408–0057–3 (ebook)
  1. Capital punishment—United States. I. Pesto, Keith A. II. Title.
KF9227.C2M4158   2011
345.73'0773—dc23   2011022042

ISBN: 978–0–313–33558–7
EISBN: 978–1–4408–0057–3

15 14 13 12   2 3 4 5

This book is also available on the World Wide Web as an eBook.
Visit www.abc-clio.com for details.

Greenwood
An Imprint of ABC-CLIO, LLC

ABC-CLIO, LLC
130 Cremona Drive, P.O. Box 1911
Santa Barbara, California 93116-1911

This book is printed on acid-free paper ∞

Manufactured in the United States of America

To my children, Mike and Jessica,
to my wife, Marie,
and to the memory of my dad, George, and my mom, Eleanor.
—J.A.M.

To the memory of Richard F. Oles, who first sparked my interest in the
debate over the death penalty.
—K.A.P.

Contents

Preface

The debate about capital punishment is passionate and enduring. Context and circumstances matter. Who was the victim? What was done to him or her? Who was the perpetrator? Were there extenuating circumstances? Is he or she a sympathetic figure for some reason? Are we talking to the victim's family or the defendant's? What about contemporary mores and "evolving standards of decency"? This book examines the capital punishment debate. It raises questions and supplies few definitive answers. It does, however, attempt to provide a balanced and evenhanded analysis of the issues.

This book is written for patrons of public, high school, college, and university libraries. It is written for undergraduate students in American government, United States history, criminal justice, constitutional law, and civil rights and civil liberties classes. It is written for high school students in relevant advanced-placement classes. And it is written for citizens who are interested in the historical evolution and contemporary application of the death penalty.

This book combines analysis of important issues with references to landmark legal decisions, important documents, survey results, and empirical data. The book discusses the origins of the death penalty and traces its development from antiquity to more contemporary times. The opening historical chapter focuses on relatively recent history from the time of the founding of the American Republic to today. Next, in a fairly detailed chapter on "Facts, Figures, and Methods of Execution," statistical information about capital punishment is presented and discussed. In the third chapter, the death penalty is considered against a constitutional backdrop. Chapter 4 presents explicitly and systematically various arguments for and against the death penalty. Many of these arguments are embedded in historical treatments, statistical compilations, and cases throughout the book. We encourage you to reflect and decide for yourself which side you favor. We ask, however, that you read with an open mind the arguments on both sides before you reach your conclusion

The book concludes with three appendices. The first presents an annotated list of important capital-punishment cases. Landmark decisions and opinions are summarized, chronicling how the Supreme Court has assessed the constitutionality of the death penalty in light of contemporary mores and evolving standards of decency. The second appendix supplies a more general chronological treatment of capital punishment. The third appendix provides a bibliographical essay directing readers to other relevant sources of interest.

ACKNOWLEDGMENTS

Thanks to all of the people at Greenwood Press who worked to make this project a success. We want to thank our editors, Steven Vetrano, Suzanne Staszak-Silva, and Sarah Colwell, for their support throughout the early stages of this work. We want to thank our editor, Sandy Towers, for her encouragement and—most of all—her patience. Sandy, we hope you think this book was worth the wait! We also thank Jessica Ramsay, our editor during the final stages, for helping us, at long last, to finish this project!

—Joseph A. Melusky and Keith Alan Pesto

1

History

This is a book about the intellectual and legal history of the death penalty. It is not an attempt either to justify or condemn the death penalty, and unlike most of the literature published on the death penalty, this one does not attempt to change your position, whatever it is. We are attempting to present how the death penalty has been viewed throughout history, how it has been carried out, how criticism of the death penalty and justifications for its use have both remained the same and evolved over the centuries, and where the death penalty debate stands currently in the United States. We make some modest predictions about where it is likely to go in the future.

THREE PRELIMINARIES

The first point to note about the history of the death penalty debate before plunging into details is that although the death penalty itself has existed at least as long as there are historical records, the debate as it is currently framed is of relatively recent origin, stretching back approximately 300 years. Because that span of time coincides with the founding and settling of the American colonies and the independence and development of the government of the United States, there is a natural tendency to view the issues relevant to the death penalty as integral to our nation's history. To some extent, that is appropriate, because from the very beginning, the new United States of America was, both separately as states and collectively as a nation, at the forefront of dramatic changes in the way both crime and punishment were viewed. In the larger sense, however, this view overstates the importance of the death penalty to our ancestors and the relevance of their thoughts to our current situation. Though some of the issues surrounding the death penalty have persisted throughout history, and although the debates repeatedly use similar words and phrases, contemporary views of the death penalty might not even have been comprehensible to previous generations. We often assume that persons who supported our positions or took contrary ones in a previous era did so for the same reasons that we hold today. However, it is often the case that they paid little attention to the issues we believe to be crucial and looked at the same issues in quite different terms than we do. A simple example of this phenomenon is the movement to halt public executions.

Until the nineteenth century, the execution of a condemned criminal was a local and public ceremony, sometimes with political overtones, sometimes an almost quasireligious event in which the condemned man was expected to express his repentance and, in an early version of "Scared Straight," to admonish the children brought to witness the spectacle not to follow his path of crime.[1] From the late seventeenth century through the early nineteenth century, sermons preached at executions by ministers such as Cotton Mather, published together with farewell speeches of the condemned, were America's first popular literature. Those witnessing executions, like the 7,000 or 8,000 who watched the hanging of Levi Ames for burglary in Boston in October 1773, could purchase his final words of repentance almost at the foot of the gallows.[2]

Beginning in 1830 in Connecticut, there was a movement to abolish public executions. The period from 1833 through 1853 has been described as a "great reform era." Public executions were attacked as cruel spectacles. Cruel or not, by this time, they were certainly spectacles. Unlike in previous centuries, now the condemned rarely went contritely to his death. Tens of thousands of eager viewers still showed up to view hangings, but the popular execution literature became less about the sermon and repentance and more of a lurid account of the condemned man's crimes. Local merchants sold souvenirs and alcohol. Fights broke out as people jockeyed for the best view of the hanging or the corpse. Onlookers cursed the widow or the victim. They tried to tear down the scaffold or grab the rope for keepsakes. Mayhem and unruliness went on far into the night after "justice had been served." In response, some states enacted laws permitting private hangings, and Rhode Island (1833), Pennsylvania (1834), New York (1835), Massachusetts (1835), and New Jersey (1835) all followed Connecticut and abolished public hangings. Hangings were now carried out in correctional facilities. By 1849, 15 states were conducting hangings in prisons rather than in public. The same transformation was taking place in England. It seems counterintuitive at first glance, but this move away from public executions was *opposed* by

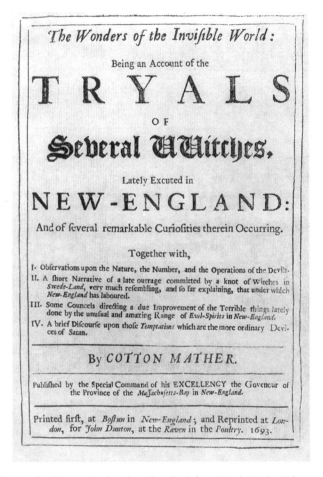

The Wonders of the Invisible World:

Being an Account of the

TRYALS

OF

Several Witches,

Lately Excuted in

NEW-ENGLAND:

And of several remarkable Curiosities therein Occurring.

Together with,

I. Observations upon the Nature, the Number, and the Operations of the Devils.

II. A short Narrative of a late outrage committed by a knot of Witches in Swede-Land, very much resembling, and so far explaining, that under which New-England has laboured.

III. Some Councels directing a due Improvement of the Terrible things lately done by the unusual and amazing Range of Evil-Spirits in New-England.

IV. A brief Discourse upon those Temptations which are the more ordinary Devices of Satan.

By COTTON MATHER.

Published by the Special Command of his EXCELLENCY the Govenour of the Province of the Massachusetts-Bay in New-England.

Printed first, at Boston in New-England; and Reprinted at London, for John Dunton, at the Raven in the Poultry. 1693.

A 1693 publication by Cotton Mather describes the Salem Witch Trials. (Library of Congress)

many death penalty abolitionists, who reasoned that public executions would eventually cause people to cry out against execution itself.[3] For their part, death penalty proponents wanted private executions because the circus atmosphere was eroding support for the death penalty.

A more subtle shift in the terms of the debate can be seen over the longer term. We are accustomed in the centuries since the founding of this country to think of government and law as entities that are independent of whoever happens to be president, legislator, or judge. The founders wrote of having "a government of laws, not of men." The novel idea that this is possible has also affected our view of crime and punishment: we can wage a "war on crime" because to us "crime" is almost personified (and in the popular media is a whole family of personalities, from the mildly offensive "victimless crime" to the sinister "organized crime"), and certainly seen as existing independently of particular crimes committed by particular criminals, much as the germs that cause an illness exist separately from a sick person. We can have a debate about "capital punishment" itself. But in an age of less detachment, when all government was personal and there was little distinction between crime and criminal or between a king and his kingdom,[4] any debate about the death penalty was more personalized, too. An example well known to the classically educated founders of this country was recounted by Thucydides in his history of the Peloponnesian War. When the city-state of Mitylene unsuccessfully revolted against Athenian rule in 427 BC, the debate in Athens between the pro–death penalty Cleon and the anti–death penalty Diodotus over whether to execute the rebels focused on proportionality and deterrence and does so in very modern language. With little editing, their speeches could be published as the majority and dissenting opinions of the Supreme Court. But this death penalty debate (Mitylene was spared, and the second ship carrying the pardon overtook the first ship carrying the death warrant because, according to Thucydides, of the reluctance of the first to carry out the sentence) focused on whether *particular* persons who had committed a *particular* crime deserved to be killed by a *particular method.* The broader question of whether the death penalty itself is justifiable did not arise and really could not arise until modern times. This may reflect progress, but we should not be smug: throughout most of history, our modern style of debating over capital punishment, often without reference to a particular crime, would be considered just as meaningful as the question of how many angels could dance on the head of a pin.

Second, although in today's rhetoric it is a popular axiom that "death is different" and a legal maxim endorsed by the Supreme Court that capital punishment needs special rules because it is different in kind from any other penalty, we have to make a conscious effort to realize that throughout history, death *was* different than it is now. Before the nineteenth-century development of the office of public prosecutor and the professional municipal police force, life-and-death decisions were much less the province of a professional elite and much more the business of every man. The lack of the cop on the corner[5] and a reliable prison system that routinely and securely incarcerated offenders undoubtedly meant there was more crime for every man to face. In the last decades of the twentieth century, thinking about the death penalty was driven by a widespread but mistaken belief that crime was increasing to unprecedented heights. That is an illusion caused by a lack of perspective. Estimates of the homicide rate in Western Europe from the last six centuries show that the risk of criminal homicide in the twentieth century was less than half the level of the eighteenth and nineteenth centuries. When the American colonies were being settled in the sixteenth and seventeenth centuries, the murder rate was at least five times higher than it is today.[6]

An additional source of disquiet unique to the American colonies was the frontier. Sometimes it was merely lawless, and sometimes it was the source of deadly attacks by Indians. It was always close at hand. When taking life without negotiation or hesitation might be necessary to keep oneself and one's family alive, there was little point in shrinking from imposing the death penalty on the deserving, especially after he received some form of trial.

This "shoot first, ask questions later" mindset did not apply only to the colonists' relations with Native Americans or to the settlement of the American West in the nineteenth century. Before modern technology made holding prisoners relatively safe for the captor, it was frequently the case that in war, captured soldiers were killed to the last man. Mass executions of prisoners by commanders regarded by their contemporaries as chivalrous, from Richard the Lion-hearted during the Crusades through Henry V at the battle of Agincourt, were considered the normal practice in war.

As often is the case, theory followed practice. As late as the seventeenth century, the Dutch jurist Hugo Grotius, whose writings were also known to and quoted by the founders of our country, wrote that it was part of the law of nature that the victor in war had the right to enslave or exterminate the vanquished.[7] With that view of the law of nature, the morally culpable criminal could hardly demand by right more lenient treatment than his judge and jury believed was owed to a defeated but not blameworthy soldier.

Until relatively recent times, any man of the upper classes in society who might have an influence on the criminal law faced violent death even when not defeated in battle or attacked by a highwayman. For more than a thousand years, from the settlement of the western Roman Empire by the barbarian tribes until after the Napoleonic Wars, combat to the death or at least to the shedding of blood was an expected part of the cultural world of any man of the upper class.[8] Through the fourteenth century at least, armed combat was a recreational sport used as training for real combat. Sometimes blunted spears and referees were employed. It its more extreme form, however, the contests were indistinguishable from all-out war, with death to some of the players a common occurrence and with only the code of chivalry to protect a surrendered combatant.[9] Politics, even in peacetime, was similarly a blood sport in England. Until the eighteenth century, losing one's allies at court or in Parliament could result in being attainted of treason.[10] Attainder was a legislative act requiring neither evidence nor trial that sentenced one's property to be seized and one's body to be hanged, drawn, and quartered. Telling an English judge, who might go from being a nobleman one day to being condemned to drawing and quartering the next, that death by hanging was a cruel punishment for crime would have gained bitter laughter at best.

The American colonies were mostly settled after the era of death by feudal war or religious crusade or bill of attainder had passed, and at least in the coastal cities men could afford to romanticize the risk of violent death. The new United States nevertheless acquired its own blood sports. Well into the nineteenth century, gentlemen continued to be expected to risk death in duels on obscure points of honor simply to maintain their reputations as gentlemen. This was so even after dueling had in most places been made a criminal offense. The most famous American duels are the fatal encounter in 1804 between Vice President Aaron Burr and former Secretary of the Treasury Alexander Hamilton, fought in New Jersey to avoid New York law, and the 1806 pistol duel in which future President Andrew Jackson killed Charles Dickinson, fought in Kentucky to avoid Tennessee law.[11] Until after the Civil War, the list of duelists killed, wounded, or unscathed, especially in the South, included congressmen, governors, and military men.[12] When members of the political elite were expected to voluntarily face death on a regular basis as the price of being considered gentlemen, they would scarcely have been expected to understand, much less to feel sympathy for, the view that death was too extreme a penalty for crime.[13]

Death was much more present even when not accompanied by war or violence. Until the twentieth century, the average family had a better-than-even chance of losing one or more family members to death in childbirth or by starvation, disease, or accident. In the seventeenth and eighteenth centuries, infant mortality in the colonies was at least 10 percent, and periodic epidemics of smallpox sometimes killed a fifth of the population.[14] Medical care was often unavailable, and in some eras it was incompetent. Death mostly took place at home, and if it held the same terror as it does for us, it was at least a less unfamiliar terror.[15]

The third preliminary point in considering the novelty of our contemporary viewpoint is that meaningful debate over the death penalty has, for the past 40 years, been chiefly conducted by judges and for judges. As popular polls confirm every year, many have opinions on the subject. It is an issue, however, that fortunately touches directly only a small percentage of society. Many people speak out forcefully on the death penalty precisely because they are secure in the knowledge that the topic, unlike other hot-button social issues like abortion or American military actions, will provoke only academic debate from holders of opposing views. Even for professional politicians, announcing a position on capital punishment is a covert way of signaling where one stands on other cultural issues without the risk of offending large blocs of constituents. After all, the average person is unlikely either to know a murder victim or to have a friend or relative on death row.

The consent of the governed, as expressed in the electoral process, is the foundation of the American tradition of government. Public opinion remains important to legislators considering death penalty laws in general and to governors considering the decision to sign an individual death warrant. Nevertheless, the electoral process, the weight of public opinion at large, and the views of prominent religious and political figures pale in comparison to the singular importance of judges.[16] To offer a simple illustration, in June 2008, Judge James Burge of the Lorain County Court of Common Pleas halted the executions of Ruben Rivera and Ronald McCloud by lethal injection in the state of Ohio because of his belief that Ohio's method of execution, by use of three drugs injected intravenously, could cause excessive pain and suffering. The state should use, he ruled, only one drug.[17] As you will read, the United States Supreme Court had considered virtually the identical question little more than a month earlier in *Baze v. Rees* (2008) and found that the same lethal injection method was *not* cruel and unusual punishment. Burge appeared to disregard the United States Supreme Court. And yet the Ohio case attracted nearly no attention. Why? In our times, we have come to expect that the validity of each aspect of the death penalty will be examined repeatedly and even repetitiously by lawyers and judges in each case.[18] As such, there is little reason to become upset with the decision of a state court trial judge. After all, his decision will be reviewed—by other judges. We rely heavily on the opinions of the United States Supreme Court in presenting current issues in the capital punishment debate because to understand the death penalty in America at this time is essentially to take a course in constitutional law.

IN THE BEGINNING

The first recorded execution in the American colonies occurred in Jamestown, Virginia, in 1608 when Captain George Kendall was shot by a firing squad. Kendall had been accused of sowing discord and mutiny and of spying for Spain against the British. Four years later, Virginia's governor, Sir Thomas Dale, implemented the Divine, Moral, and Martial Laws. These laws provided the death penalty for stealing grapes, killing chickens, or trading with Indians. Fearing that the threat of capital punishment for minor offenses would dissuade settlers from coming to Virginia, these laws were relaxed in 1619. The next known legal execution in the American colonies also took place in Virginia. Daniel Frank was put to death in 1622 for the crime of theft.

Since that time, the death penalty has been an almost constant feature of the American criminal justice system. But the death penalty had its origins many years earlier.

Death penalty laws date as far back as the Ancient Laws of China.[19] In the eighteenth century BC, the Code of King Hammurabi of Babylon codified the death penalty for 25 different crimes. Murder, however, was not one of them. The chief concern of the Code appears to be setting an appropriate measure of compensation for injuries to slaves, domestic animals, and property, with the death penalty serving as a back-up penalty for thieves without the ability to pay restitution and fines.[20] Michael H. Reggio notes that the first historically recorded death sentence occurred in Egypt in the sixteenth century BC. The wrongdoer, a member of nobility, was accused of magic. He was ordered to take his own life. During this period, nonnobles were usually killed with an ax.[21] The death penalty was also included in the fourteenth century BC's Hittite Code.

Many of the historical records of legal systems in the Middle East were unknown or at least untranslatable until well after our country was established and so had no effect on how Americans thought about the death penalty. The Framers, however, like educated Americans generally, were schooled in the classics and were familiar at least with the outlines of Greek and Roman history and laws. In about 621 BC, the Code of Athens attributed by legend to Draco reputedly made death the penalty for every crime and gave birth to the term "draconian" for inflexibly severe penalties.[22] According to Aristotle, a generation later, the lawgiver Solon reputedly retained Draco's laws for homicide but mitigated the severity of punishments for lesser offenses.[23]

The Twelve Tables, the first written laws in Rome, date from around 450 BC and include widespread use of the death penalty. As in Babylon and Egypt, the death penalty in Rome was different for nobility, freemen, and slaves and was the punishment for a wide variety of crimes including the publication of libels and insulting songs, the cutting or grazing of crops planted by a farmer, the burning of a house or a stack of corn near a house, cheating by a patron of his client, perjury, making disturbances at night in the city, willful murder of a freeman or a parent, and theft by a slave. Methods of execution were tailored to the crime (arsonists were burnt alive) and also included crucifixion, drowning at sea, burial alive, hanging, beating to death, and impalement. Imprisonment was prescribed for defaulting on a debt, but even there the death penalty remained a legal option:

When debt has been acknowledged or judgment about the matter pronounced in court, thirty days must be the time of grace. After that, then arrest of debtor may be made by laying on of hands. Bring him into court. If he does not satisfy the judgment or no one in court offers himself as surety on his behalf, the creditor may take the defaulter with him. He may bind him either in stocks or in chains; he may bind him with weight not less that fifteen pounds or with more if he shall so desire. . . . On the third market day, creditors shall cut pieces. Should they have cut more or less than their due it shall be with impunity.[24]

It is likely that enslavement of the debtor for debt was the normal penalty and that creditors rarely hacked a defaulter into pieces, but death remained as the ultimate sanction. Of course, at the founding of our country, educated Americans and Englishmen were familiar with the execution of Socrates in 399 BC, when the Greek philosopher was required to drink poison after his conviction for corrupting the youth of Athens by introducing heretical religious ideas.[25] One of the features of Athenian trials was the ability of the accused to propose his own penalty, and Socrates's refusal to propose his own exile as an alternative to death can be considered the first example of a prisoner volunteering for execution. Socrates was held up to the young as a classical model of virtue, and it surely would not have escaped notice that Socrates refused to condemn even an unjust death penalty.

Even more than the legacy of Greece and Rome, Christianity shaped the history of America and particularly its death penalty debate. The Bible is to this day the book most widely owned by Americans, and was often the only book owned or read by the generation of 1776 and the Framers of the Constitution. The Bible is often selectively quoted by death penalty proponents and opponents alike, but that is because there is such a wealth of good sound bites. The second chapter of Genesis can be said to begin the history of mankind with the warning by God to Adam that there is a death penalty: "In the day that you eat of [the tree of the knowledge of good and evil] you shall die."[26] Colonial readers would also consider the history of the great flood recounted in the sixth chapter of Genesis. In it, God decided to inflict the death penalty en masse, saying to Noah: "I have determined to make an end of all flesh for the earth is filled with violence through them; behold I will destroy them with the earth."[27] Moving from legendary into historic times, the eighteenth chapter of Genesis contains the first recorded debate on the death penalty in the plea of Abraham to spare the cities of Sodom and Gomorrah. Abraham anticipates the modern debate over the probability of an execution killing an innocent man, arguing that the destruction of the cities will cause the death of the righteous as well as the wicked.[28] From the beginning, the American settlers also were familiar with the law of Moses contained in the books of Exodus and Leviticus, which specified many capital offenses. Murder and some assaults, rape and unchastity, perjury, blasphemy and heresy, magic, and soothsaying were historically punished by one of four main methods of execution: stoning, burning, strangling, and beheading.[29] And of course, the most infamous execution in history is recorded in the Bible: in approximately AD 29, Jesus Christ was crucified outside Jerusalem on a charge of sedition. The accounts in all four Gospels refrain from any condemnation of capital punishment itself. The letters of St. Paul, himself a sentenced death row inmate, likewise avoid the negative commentary on capital punishment we would expect in a modern account.

Christianity began in a Roman Empire that had tempered the original severity of the Twelve Tables but still assumed the normalcy of capital punishment. By the end of the Roman Republic in the first century BC, the moderating influence of the Porcian and Valerian laws had extended some protection to Roman citizens, who ordinarily could not be subjected to capital punishment without an appeal.[30] Citizens like St. Paul who were sentenced to death could claim the right to the more merciful punishment of beheading. Those who were not Roman citizens were executed by crucifixion or died in the arena as popular entertainment.

Persecutions of Christians waxed and waned depending on the emperor, but by the third century AD, the position in society of the early Christians improved sufficiently that eventually the early Church Fathers had to consider the position of the Christian called upon to impose, not suffer, the death sentence. Tertullian, writing around AD 200, stated that "the servant of God should not pronounce capital sentences."[31] Church regulations from this time excommunicated magistrates who ordered executions.[32] Writing about 100 years later, Lactantius went even farther. In Book VI, chapter 20, of the Divine Institutes, after a discussion of the evils of being a spectator at gladiatorial slaughters, he continued:

When God forbade murder, this referred not only to killing in the process of robbery but also to the fact that one should not kill even in those cases in which it is considered just by men. . . . Thus the just man, whose task it is to administer justice, is not permitted even to charge anyone with a capital crime, since it makes no difference whether one kills with words or with the sword: killing as such is forbidden.[33]

In AD 313, the Emperor Constantine converted to Christianity. He abolished crucifixion and other cruel death penalties in the Roman Empire. The Church continued to consider participation in capital punishment a disqualification for any kind of clerical office.[34] Bishop Ambrose of Milan, in about the year AD 385, even requested civil officials involved in pronouncing death sentences to refrain from entering churches. Once Christians were legally part of society, however, theologians were increasingly obliged to face the fact that even if the *church* should not bear the sword, the *state* must. Without going so far as to approve of capital punishment, in AD 405, Pope

Innocent I lifted the sanction of excommunication for judges ordering executions.[35] Augustine of Hippo, one of the greatest of Christian writers of the age, assumed divine sanction for the death penalty early in his most famous work, *The City of God*:

There are some whose killing God orders, either by a law, or by an express command to a particular person at a particular time. In fact, one who owes a duty of obedience to the giver of the command does not himself 'kill'—he is an instrument, a sword in its user's hand. For this reason the commandment forbidding killing was not broken by those who have waged wars on the authority of God, or those who have imposed the death penalty on criminals when representing the authority of the State in accordance with the laws of the State, the justest and most reasonable source of power.

Augustine then recalled the account of Abraham and Isaac from the book of Genesis and the examples of Jephtha and Samson from the book of Judges, concluding:

With the exception of these killings prescribed generally by a just law, or specially commanded by God himself—the source of justice—anyone who kills a human being, whether himself or anyone else, is involved in a charge of murder.[36]

Because of St. Augustine's prestige as a theologian and philosopher, this portion of his work is often cited by death penalty proponents. But, to be fair, his writing must be placed in its context. Augustine gave no examples of a "just law" imposing the death penalty and only referred to capital punishment in the course of a larger argument against the Stoic philosophy that suicide was permissible. Augustine never authored any sustained analysis of capital punishment itself, and he personally wrote letters advocating commutation of the death penalty for individual condemned heretics. But there was no question in the Roman Empire, after Christianity became the established religion, about the lawfulness of the death penalty itself. The first major collection of Roman law in the Christian era, the Code of Theodosius in AD 438, made 120 crimes punishable by death.[37]

The Roman Empire was increasingly pressed in the West by immigration and invasion from Germanic tribes, and even before the last emperor in Rome was deposed in AD 476, the legal and cultural legacy of Rome passed to Constantinople. Between 529 and AD 534, the Emperor Justinian ordered a comprehensive compilation of the laws of Rome published in the thousand years since the Twelve Tables.[38] Justinian's Code preserved the death penalty for what we consider serious crimes but also for conduct that we would not consider criminal, such as holding heretical religious opinions. To avoid the shedding of blood, the prescribed method of death for heretics was burning at the stake.

Celtic Britain had a long record of punishment by death at least from about 450 BC, when the death penalty was often enforced by throwing the condemned into a quagmire. It became part of the Roman Empire in the first century AD. After four centuries of Roman occupation, the legions left Britain about AD 410, and the customary laws of the Angles, Saxons, and other Germanic tribes that migrated there took the place of Roman law. Throughout Britain and western Europe in the Dark Ages that followed the collapse of the Roman Empire, society reverted to the simpler tribal conception of law as the unvarying custom of real or mythical ancestors. This meant that the king and the ruling class were expected to be judges, but not in any sense legislators. Because the sole remaining force for civilization was the Church, the few attempts at the making of law codes practically ceased, except for imitative efforts such as the laws of King Alfred of Wessex, in about AD 890, who began his legal code with the Ten Commandments. Penalties, from fines to execution, were everywhere at the discretion of the king. Hand in hand with their more primitive concept of society, the new masters of the old Roman provinces considered crimes mostly to be personal offenses against the victim or the victim's family, not offenses against society, so what records of criminal legislation we do possess from this time often resemble a price list: a murderer, rapist, or thief could sometimes buy his freedom by paying sufficient were-gild, or compensation. Looking at ancient and medieval law codes with their schedules of compensation for murder should not mislead us into believing that life was literally for sale. It is almost certain that criminals caught red-handed were summarily executed; monetary penalties were more often used when a killing was committed without witnesses or in circumstances making proof of the crime difficult.[39] By the tenth century, hanging from gallows had become the most common method of execution when fines and other penalties were judged insufficient to maintain the peace.

When William the Conqueror brought Norman law to the British Isles after AD 1066, he would not allow any person to be killed or hanged for any crime, limiting the penalties to blinding or castration. William is credited with bringing another change to the law of England, trial by battle. Proving one's innocence by the sword or having one's champion do so became supplements to the existing practices of swearing to one's innocence under oath and trial by the ordeals of water or hot iron. Naturally, defendants often died during these "factfinding sessions," which neatly reversed the modern order of doing things, by inflicting the punishment first to obtain the verdict. Trial by battle at least appeared to guarantee a speedy resolution without any appeal.

In the latter half of the twelfth century, King Henry II began to centralize the hearing of criminal cases in England by establishing a system of royal courts with an appeal to the king's central court. King Henry's motivation seems to have been fiscal rather than judicial: by getting litigants to resort to the King's courts rather than use the older methods of trial, the Crown obtained the revenues from the trial, including the property of the defendant if he were convicted and condemned. In keeping with the political theory of feudal society, it was considered necessary for a defendant to admit that the king's courts had jurisdiction over his case. Royal efforts to obtain the formality of a plea of not guilty and the statement of the defendant that he chose to be tried "on his country" became an end in itself. Today, the entry of a "not guilty" plea is now an almost pointless formality, but in the Middle Ages, because a man could transmit his lands and goods to his family if he died unconvicted or in an old-fashioned trial and did not enter a plea in the royal courts, it was often the most significant step in the judicial process. Defendants could be and were tortured by starvation, thumbscrews, or *peine forte et dure*, that is, "punishment hard and long," by loading weights upon the spread-eagled defendant's chest until he should consent to a jury trial.[40] Some modern writers on the history of the death penalty miss the point when they talk about the punishment of pressing. Judges did not consider pressing a man to death cruel and unusual punishment because it was not punishment at all: to them, it was part of pretrial procedure. Attempts to abolish pressing in England in the 1650s were unsuccessful, and it remained a legal possibility to use pressing long after jury trials became the normal practice and trials by ordeal and by combat went out of use. Pressing was used as late as 1692 in Massachusetts during the Salem witch trials, and it was not formally abolished there until 1772.

Through the Middle Ages and into the Renaissance, capital punishment was accompanied by what we would consider torture. Most barons had drowning pits as well as gallows, and they were used for major as well as minor crimes. Men, like Llywelyn ap Gruffydd, who in 1401 misled an English army hunting Welsh rebels, were hanged, then taken down and drawn and quartered, whether dead or alive. Beheading was considered a merciful reduction of the penalty for the upper classes. The customary punishment for high treason by a woman was burning. One could be burned for marrying a Jew or other heretical offenses, like wearing a man's clothes, as Joan of Arc was charged with in 1431. When a woman was burned, the executioner tied a rope around her neck when she was tied to the stake. When the flames reached her, she could be strangled from outside the ring of fire. This "humanitarian" gesture sometimes failed, leaving the condemned literally to be burnt alive.[41]

In the sixteenth century, under the reign of Henry VIII, reportedly as many as 72,000 people were executed. Sometimes there was a grim humor in the sentence: a cook accused of poisoning was boiled for up to two hours before he died. In the following century in France, hundreds of persons were hanged, or in some cases broken on the wheel, for the crime of selling calico cloth in violation of guild rules.[42]

Torture, both in aid of capital punishment and as an independent tool of criminal law, had a long history of its own. Roman law forbade the torture of nobles but assumed that slaves would lie and so provided that they be tortured to assure that they gave reliable evidence. Naturally, the desire to avoid further torture meant that an intelligent slave who could figure out what testimony would spare him often gave the evidence desired by the torturer, whether true or not. We should not scoff at the naiveté of Roman practice when we consider contemporary controversies over waterboarding as an intelligence-gathering method. Indeed, there is no reliable way to test the accuracy of convictions obtained by torture with those obtained from 12 jurors hearing evidence, but since the mid-eighteenth century, society has generally disapproved torture regardless of its reliability, because it is brutal and has a way of growing to be an end in itself.[43]

The Roman use of torture died out in western Europe with the invasion of the Germanic tribes, not because the Goths and Franks were more humane, but because their factfinding methods were different. Trial by the ordeal of water—the pure element of water was thought to reject the guilty, thus leading to the obvious problem of proving one's innocence by sinking but being rescued before drowning—or by the ordeal of iron—walking a prescribed nine feet carrying a heated iron of various sizes depending on the charge and then waiting three days to see whether blisters or infection showed evidence of guilt—and trial by battle were considered to be valid ways to determine matters of guilt and innocence.[44] Obviously, judges could significantly control the outcome of a trial by ordeal by specifying how long the accused must remain under water or how hot an iron should be heated. An element of chance was always present, but there is evidence that in doubtful cases, ordeals were scaled down to give the accused more chance of acquittal.

The demand for more sophisticated legal tools in the urban civilization re-emerging in western Europe after the tenth century[45] and dissatisfaction with the superstitious relics of the pagan barbarian past led to the abolition of trial by ordeal by the early thirteenth century. In the Fourth Lateran Council of 1215, the Catholic Church forbade clerics to take part in trial by ordeal. Because the ordeal was deprived of any possible supernatural sanction, the ordeal was now seen as an ineffective way to determine guilt. Trial by battle was probably recognized as equally flawed, but it persisted for centuries because combat did not need clerics to bless it and still had deep roots in a violent world.[46] Nevertheless, civil society found it necessary to attempt to determine who was telling the truth and who was not in disputed cases involving crime. One experiment that survives today in greatly modified form is the jury trial system begun in England under King Henry II. Another option was the revival on the continent of Europe of the Roman practice of torture. Roman law, and Justinian's Code in particular, had been preserved in the Byzantine Empire and were rediscovered in the West in the later Middle Ages. They were enjoying a revival of interest and prestige at the new universities in Pisa, Bologna, and Paris. Despite an ineffectual protest by Pope Alexander in the twelfth century that confessions must not be obtained by torture, torture was embraced by rulers such as Alfonso X "the Wise" of Castile, St. Louis IX of France, and Frederick II of Sicily[47] just as readily as polygraph and fingerprint evidence were in later centuries. By the mid-thirteenth century, Pope Innocent IV confirmed that torture could be used to investigate those accused of heresy.[48] When modern nation-states formed in the following centuries, many of them codified the use of torture as an investigative tool. These "reforms" hardly made it to England. In one of the historic ironies of the death penalty, America's heritage from England of relatively humane criminal laws is mostly due to England being behind the times, not ahead of it. England's three oldest common law courts—King's Bench, Common Pleas, and Exchequer—never directly adopted the Roman-influenced civil law and therefore were not legally authorized to use torture. But the introduction of some parts of continental law in the fifteenth century to govern procedure in specialized royal courts called prerogative courts, such as the Court of High Commission and Court of Star Chamber, established torture as a possible tool of English government from about 1470 until about 1641.[49] The Tudor era was particularly savage in its use of torture, first under Henry VIII as he strove to liquidate Catholic opposition to royal control over the Church of England, next under Mary I as she attempted to recover England for Rome by executing Protestants, and then under Elizabeth I as she attempted to despoil upper-class Catholic resistance much as her father had despoiled the monasteries. If the accused heretic or traitor—the two were synonymous at this stage—confessed under torture, he was then subject to the death penalty for treason. The death penalty for common criminals could hardly receive much attention in an age that did not consider the drawing and quartering of heretics as evil, but only the drawing and quartering of the wrong heretics.[50]

Yet even in this era, there were serious writers who attempted to bring about changes in capital punishment. For arguments that might have been fresh centuries later, consider Sir Thomas More's *Utopia*, written in 1516. More, a lawyer, diplomat, and later Chancellor of England under Henry VIII, not only opposed imposing the death penalty for differences of religious opinion, but in *Utopia* offered what may be More's own argument against the death penalty for theft in the speech offered by Hythlodaeus ("Nonsenso"), a lawyer who has traveled to More's mythical land ruled by reason. Hythlodaeus argues that hanging thieves is immoral, because it treats all crimes the same and violates the commandment not to kill. It is also ineffective, not only because it gives a thief an incentive to kill his victim, but also because it fails to eliminate poverty, the root cause of theft. In More's Utopia, the normal penalty for major crime is slavery, "which is just as unpleasant for the criminals as capital punishment, and more useful to society." After many years, those prisoners who show signs of feeling sorry for what they have done earn the prospect of being released. Prisoners who refuse to accept their punishment are, however, "slaughtered like wild beasts."

Thomas More himself fell from office and was executed by Henry VIII for holding treasonous religious opinions. More certainly was centuries ahead of his time in advocating less-bloody criminal laws. Even notable religious reformers of the time such as Martin Luther and John Calvin did not call for any innovation in criminal law. Writing in 1523, Luther commented:

Here you inquire further whether constables, hangmen, jurists, lawyers and other of similar function can also be Christians and in a state of salvation. . . . There must be those who arrest, prosecute, execute, and destroy the wicked, and who protect, acquit, defend, and save the good.[51]

Calvin similarly accepted the death penalty as appropriate for criminals, and although he deplored the manner of execution, he accepted the necessity of the condemnation of Michael Servetus for heresy.[52] Servetus was burned at the stake in Calvin's Geneva in 1553.

In the century after More, there was condemnation of the death penalty inflicted in pursuit of religious persecution in England, but it was not condemnation of cruelty or executions in general. Rather, it was almost entirely Anglican condemnation of religious persecution of Anglicans by Queen Mary I, the Catholic daughter of Henry VIII and Catherine of Aragon. During her reign from 1553 to 1558, Mary brought back into use an obsolete medieval statute that called for the burning of heretics. Mary had perhaps 300 Protestants burned at the stake, much to the dismay of the Spanish ambassador, Simon Renard, who recommended more use of imprisonment and banishment and fewer executions because he correctly saw that Mary's capital punishment policy was making martyrs of those executed, not curbing heresy.[53] In large part, this was due to the success of the *Book of Martyrs*, written by John Foxe while he was in exile in Switzerland during the reign of Mary I, and published in England in 1563. For 200 years, Foxe's lurid descriptions of the burnings and tortures of saintly Protestants by Bloody Mary formed part of the childhood entertainment and moral education of Englishmen and later of the American colonists. Foxe's book was a partisan brief in favor of Elizabeth's church and against Mary's church, not a tract against the death penalty. Some readers undoubtedly drew the conclusion that burning people for heresy was a bad idea, but most were centuries away from objecting to the death penalty generally. Under Elizabeth I, who reigned from 1568 to 1603, the death penalty for treason was again used for Catholic heretics, and those who failed to keep up with the religion of the sovereign were hanged, drawn and quartered, and their entrails thrown into boiling water. Though revolting to many, these old-fashioned executions remained popular entertainment.[54]

The colonies brought England's capital punishment laws with them, and some colonies strove to keep up with modern times by permitting torture as an investigative tool. Massachusetts inherited this practice from the English Court of Star Chamber, which existed from 1487 to 1641. In 1641, the year that the Star Chamber was abolished in old England, the drafters of the Massachusetts Body of Liberties, the first Bill of Rights in the colonies, saw nothing incongruous in placing these two provisions in sequence:

45. No man shall be forced by Torture to confesse any Crime against himselfe nor any other unlesse it be in some Capitall case where he is first fullie convicted by clear and sufficient evidence to be guilty, After which if . . . it is very apparent there be other conspiratours . . . then he may be tortured, yet not with such tortures as be Barbarous and inhumane.

46. For bodilie punishments we allow amongst us none that are inhumane Barbarous or cruel.

Quite clearly, in Massachusetts torture was not always "barbarous or cruel," and the death penalty itself was not cruel at all.

The social dislocations caused in seventeenth- and eighteenth-century England by the enclosure of farm land for grazing of sheep and wool production, and later by the Industrial Revolution, displaced and impoverished the lower classes in England. Parliament responded to the resulting rise in begging and property crimes with the only tools it knew: harsher criminal laws. In 1723, the traditional common law felonies that bore the penalty of death in England were supplemented by the Black Act, so called because it was aimed against poachers and vandals who went in disguise or with their faces blacked. At a stroke, more than 50 new crimes punishable by death were added to the law, including the crimes of destroying orchards, breaching the mound of a fish pond, and setting fire to a haystack. To Englishmen who emigrated to the American colonies and whose descendants gathered to ratify the Constitution and the Bill of Rights, increased reliance on the death penalty was part of their recent history.

But even stark examples of unjust capital punishment did not call the legitimacy of the death penalty into question. In 1746, Scottish rebels supporting

Bonnie Prince Charlie in a quixotic attempt to overthrow King George II were defeated at the Battle of Culloden. Those not summarily executed or able to flee to America were taken to England and tried in Surrey before English juries, convicted, and executed by being hanged, drawn, and quartered. The well-known accounts of these legal proceedings were seen by American observers as the basis for the Constitution's requirement, in Article III and the Sixth Amendment, that a defendant's trial be held in the state where the crime was committed. It was not a motivation for questioning the death penalty itself.

Capital punishment was also divinely sanctioned. In case anyone in New England had missed the discussion of the death penalty in the book of Genesis, there were plenty of sermons to remedy the lack. One of the most famous sermons delivered in the colonies was "Sinners in the Hands of an Angry God," first delivered in Connecticut in 1741 by Jonathan Edwards, an important early American theologian who was also president of Princeton College and the grandfather of Aaron Burr. Edwards compared eternal justice to earthly justice:

When God beholds the ineffable extremity of your case . . . he will have no compassion upon you, he will not forbear the executions of his wrath, or in the least lighten his hand; there shall be no moderation or mercy, nor will God then at all stay his rough wind; he will have no regard to your welfare, nor be at all careful lest you suffer too much in any other sense, than only that you shall not suffer beyond what strict justice requires. Nothing shall be withheld because it is so hard for you to bear.

* * *

Thus it will be with you . . .

In our times, even pro–death penalty apologists are tempted to explain those passages away, but these exhortations were designed to convince, not appall. They would have filled most listeners in the generation just before the ratification of the Bill of Rights with dread for the state of their souls, not with disappointment at the bloodthirstiness of God. Edwards drove home the point that if they rejected their chance at repentance:

God will be so far from pitying you when you cry to him, that it is said he will only laugh and mock. [S]o far from pitying you . . . he will only tread you under foot. . . . [H]e will crush out your blood and make it fly, and it shall be sprinkled on his garments, so as to stain all his raiment.

Even if his listeners did not come away believing that God would enjoy their eternal torture, they certainly they would come away with the impression that their pastor did not think a quick death by hanging was cruel.

It should be easy for us to see that at the founding of this country, the insecurity caused by crime and the public need for final punishment of the criminal were issues much "closer to home," whether home was the colonies, England, or the Continent. Under conditions of insecurity and anxiety, the focus of the law is on simply maintaining public order. This is not to say that early Americans were semicivilized vigilantes. To the contrary, particularly in New England, they were uniquely conscious of their historical inheritance, if not positively proud of themselves as the high point in human progress. Like Governor John Winthrop, Increase Mather and Cotton Mather, and Jonathan Edwards, they saw America as the new Israel freed from the corrupting influences of recent history and harking back to an imagined pure state. Death penalty laws varied from colony to colony as a result of that vision. Some were very strict, while others were not, but all had the death penalty. Virginia has been mentioned. The Massachusetts Bay Colony held its first execution in 1630, even though the Capital Laws of New England, modeled in part on the book of Leviticus, did not go into effect until later (1636–1647). The death penalty was imposed for premeditated murder, sodomy, witchcraft, adultery, idolatry, blasphemy, assault in anger, rape, statutory rape, manstealing, perjury in a capital trial, rebellion, manslaughter, poisoning, and bestiality. By 1780, capital crimes recognized by the Commonwealth of Massachusetts were reduced to seven: murder, sodomy, burglary, buggery, arson, rape, and treason.[55]

Once acquired for England from the Dutch, the New York colony instituted the Duke's Laws of 1665. Under these laws, death was the prescribed penalty for denial of the "true God," premeditated murder, killing someone who was unarmed, killing by lying in wait or by poisoning, sodomy, buggery, kidnaping, perjury in a capital trial, denial of the king's rights or raising arms to resist his authority, conspiracy to invade towns or forts in the colony, and striking one's mother or father. South Jersey and Pennsylvania began with more lenient capital punishment laws, but under the direction of the Crown, harsher penal codes were enacted. North Carolina was relatively more severe, applying the death penalty to a wide variety of crimes. The fact that North Carolina had no state penitentiary probably contributed to its reliance on capital punishment.

By 1776, most of the colonies had roughly similar death statutes on their books. Capital crimes generally included arson, piracy, treason, murder, sodomy, burglary, robbery, rape, horse stealing, slave rebellion, and often counterfeiting. Hanging was the most common method of execution.[56]

So how did England and its American colonies move from history's apparently uniform record of bloodthirstiness to a relatively mild present? It helped that with fewer class distinctions, labor generally in short supply, and land available on the frontier, America did not have the same economic incentives for property crimes that made English law harsher in the century before the Revolution. It is also a matter of importance to the history of the death penalty that the American colonies were settled during the period known as the Enlightenment. After the bloody and passionate Reformation and Counter-reformation era of religious wars, the intellectual style of the era of the eighteenth and nineteenth centuries was cooler, almost mathematical: if you started from a blank slate, if you thought things through long enough, all your problems would be solvable. Scottish rebels still might be killed on the battlefield and African slaves might be taken in the triangle trade, but in the salons and coffeehouses, the intellectuals were beginning to debate refinements to the laws of war and the implications of man's universal right to liberty. In the era from Jonathan Edwards and Benjamin Franklin to Benjamin Rush and Thomas Jefferson, political and theological figures were apt to be well versed in the natural sciences, and politicians were expected to be accomplished in more than politics, and the mechanical scientific philosophy of the age of Isaac Newton eventually spilled over into political theory. Centuries earlier, Dante's cosmos required "love which moves the sun and other stars" and a personified Nature maintained at every point by a personal God. By the seventeenth and eighteenth centuries, philosophers who believed in God found it possible to give increasingly sophisticated explanations that could be written without reference to any religious ideas. To Descartes, Pascal, and Leibniz, "nature" was simply matter in motion. Because the world was obedient to a remote Creator's mathematical laws, it was best understood by calculus professors, not mystics or clergymen. Their heirs who shaped our political world, from Thomas Hobbes and John Locke to Thomas Paine and Thomas Jefferson, took from them the idea that the world is a mechanism and all we have to do to have harmony on Earth and goodwill among men is to keep the mainsprings of the mechanism in balance and repair or replace them if they no longer work. The Declaration of Independence practically reflects this principle, proclaiming that we can alter or abolish our forms of government without being bound by the way things were done in the past.

Historians of the death penalty can point to the dates of three key events from the Enlightenment as the start of the modern age.

1688

When we consider the death penalty in the United States, we start with the Eighth Amendment to the Constitution, part of the Bill of Rights ratified in 1791. But our Bill of Rights was named after and consciously modeled on the English Bill of Rights. The English Bill of Rights was presented by Parliament 100 years before the Constitution to William of Orange and Mary for their acquiescence as a prerequisite to assuming the English throne, after the ouster of James II by the British aristocracy in what is known as the Glorious Revolution. One of the proximate causes of that revolution was disgust at the excesses of the famous "Bloody Assizes."

In the 1640s, the religious conflicts between the Puritan faction and the Anglican hierarchy within the Church of England had combined with the political conflicts between Parliament and the Stuart kings to ignite the English Civil War. Parliament and Puritans won the military struggle, and Charles I was executed in 1649. In the 1650s, England was governed under the military Protectorate of Oliver Cromwell. After Oliver Cromwell's death in September 1658, his son and successor Richard Cromwell proved unable to maintain his father's control over religious and military factions. The anxiety of the public over an economic recession and the opposition of the gentry to centralized military rule caused Parliament in 1660 to invite Charles II to return to his father's throne. The Restoration of Charles II was conditioned on his declaration of amnesty for almost all those who had opposed Charles I in the civil war. A small number who had participated directly in the execution of Charles I received the traditional penalty for treason, to no great public outcry.

But despite Restoration, political and religious tensions between the king and his allies in Parliament and the remnant of the Commonwealth coalition and their allies in Parliament continued to plague England. Charles II's potential successors were his legitimate brother, James the Duke of York, and his illegitimate son, James Scott the Duke of Monmouth. The Duke of York, who wished to model his monarchy on the absolutist example of Louis XIV of France, ascended to the throne as James II in February 1685. This was obnoxious to Parliament, which since the English Civil War saw itself as the senior partner in the division of power between the King and the legislature. James II resembled Louis IV in another way obnoxious to Parliament: unlike Charles I and Charles II, James had been raised as a Catholic. Charles II had favored toleration for Catholics and dissenting Protestant sects (and granted Pennsylvania to a Quaker, William Penn), but only pushed as far as Parliament would allow. James II, however, claimed the power as King to make law and appeared to Parliament all too ready to use that power to dispense Catholics in England and Ireland from the legal penalties and disabilities imposed on them during the previous century. This outraged Parliament. To translate their conflict into modern terms, James II's attempt at religious toleration (or separation of church and state) was considered tyranny by Parliament, because it conflicted with Parliament's support for an established church and its claim to possess the law-making power in England.

The Duke of Monmouth, presenting himself rather unconvincingly as the champion of Anglican Establishment, began an uprising in southwest

England in June 1685, hoping that the gentry and nobles who opposed his uncle's partiality toward Catholics would rally to his standard. The Establishment was hoping for William of Orange, however, and few of them supported Monmouth's Rebellion. Almost immediately, the Duke's few troops were routed, and he was captured and beheaded in July 1685.

In the aftermath, James II sent Judge George Jeffreys to the Duke of Monmouth's landing site in Cornwall to punish anyone who had aided the rebellion. The result was the Bloody Assizes, in which Jeffreys had approximately 300 participants hanged for treason. As was traditional, many of the bodies of the dead were beheaded, quartered, covered in pitch, and exhibited on a gibbet. Several hundred more, including women and girls, were transported as slaves to the sugar plantations of the West Indies. While a few supporters of James II cheered the get-tough policy, most of England was disgusted by the heavy-handed retribution against fellow Englishmen.[57] In part this was because the trials and executions of rebels were delayed and could not be justified as the grim necessity of an ongoing war. The paradox persists today: cut off avenues of review for a condemned criminal and you run the risk of executing the innocent; hold the condemned in prison while reviewing the matter and you weaken any claim that the death penalty is necessary as a deterrent.

No doubt some of the Parliamentary allies of William of Orange in the winter of 1688 were zealous in support out of revulsion at the Bloody Assizes and also in fear of their fate if William failed. Therefore, one of the legal protections Parliament was careful to include in the Declaration of Rights presented to William as a condition of their support, and which was passed as a statute in 1689 as the Bill of Rights, was that "excessive Bail ought not to be required, nor excessive Fines imposed, nor cruel nor unusual Punishments afflicted." This precise language was in all likelihood due to the memory of Judge Jeffreys.

Judge Jeffreys had already distinguished himself as one of Charles II's judges in presiding over the prosecution of Algernon Sidney for treason. In a 1683 trial that even by the less-demanding standards of the day appeared to be more political than legal, Sidney was convicted and sentenced to death based on Sidney's assertion, in an unpublished manuscript taken from his house, that kings ruled with the consent of the governed. Jeffreys instructed the jury that such a statement was treason in itself.[58] Sidney's essay, posthumously published as *Thoughts on Government*, became a standard text in the libraries of educated Americans.[59]

Two years later, in 1685, Judge Jeffreys presided over the trial of a professional informant, one Titus Oates. In the power struggles between Charles II and Parliament, some aristocrats[60] found Titus Oates a handy tool who now had grown dangerous. In several trials conducted between 1679 and 1682,

Titus Oates stands in the pillory at the Temple gate after his convictions of slander and perjury for his multiple false testimonies, ca. 1685. His name later became synonymous with cruel and unusual punishment. (Hulton Archive/Getty Images)

Oates's false testimony that Catholic noblemen participated in supposed plots to overthrow Charles II had resulted in death sentences for 15 opponents of Parliamentary supremacy. When it became clear that the ultimate targets of Oates's testimony about a supposed plot to poison Charles II were Charles's wife, Queen Catherine, and his brother and successor, James the Duke of York, the royal judges could no longer continue to turn a blind eye to Oates's implausible testimony. Even opponents of the Crown who had encouraged Oates's perjury at first had begun to fear that he might turn on them for extortion. Oates was accordingly convicted in 1684 of slander and in 1685 of perjury. The punishment for perjury, a misdemeanor, was whatever sentence less than death the judge decreed. Jeffreys's lesser punishment of Oates was a fine, imprisonment for life, and an order that Oates be flogged twice by the hangman, once while walking while tied behind the hangman's cart on the road from Aldgate to Newgate and then from Newgate to Tyburn. At a walk, this two- to three-mile course gave a vigorous hangman the opportunity to lash Oates for approximately an hour. Jeffreys further ordered that Oates be held in the pillory on the five anniversaries of his perjured accusations, exposed to public ridicule at best and to crippling or fatal stoning at worst.[61]

In 1689, after four years of imprisonment interrupted by stretches at the pillory, Oates took advantage of James II's ouster to petition William and

Mary's first Parliament to set aside his sentence. The House of Lords denied the petition, but nine members dissented, writing that they believed that Oates's punishments were contrary to the Bill of Rights's prohibition of cruel and unusual punishments and that Jeffreys had given a "cruel, barbarous, and illegal judgement" in sentencing Oates.[62] After more several years, Oates was pardoned and released. Judge Jeffreys, meanwhile, had been arrested as the last official loyal to James II when he fled to France, and he died in the Tower of London.

It is a truism that history is written by the winners, and Judge Jeffreys and King James II were clearly the losers. Protestant dissenters who had supported Monmouth's Rebellion and the much more numerous advocates of Parliamentary supremacy who wished to put the judicial power under legislative and not royal control found common cause in blackening Jeffreys's reputation. A new round of pamphlets and books of martyrologies describing the victims of the Bloody Assizes and accusing Jeffreys of drunkenly presiding over sham trials was published and became popular in both English and colonial libraries. Titus Oates, though never respectable or able to regain the influence he had had at the height of political conflict, survived to proclaim his righteousness and Jeffreys's iniquity. Though from our century's perspective, Jeffreys's conduct was unexceptional and his real offense was being one of the last influential English jurists subservient to the Crown rather than to Parliament,[63] in the eighteenth century, his name became synonymous with cruel and unusual punishment.

And although the Bloody Assizes or the pillory for life were inconceivable in America, the abuses perpetrated in Sidney's trial were things the orators and pamphleteers of independence could present as a real possibility. The Stuart Kings, Judge Jeffreys, the Bloody Assizes, and Titus Oates remained in public memory through the eighteenth century. To many Americans in 1776, the reason for independence from England was their perception that the abuses of the Stuart kings were being replicated by King George's ministers. As a result, notwithstanding the lack of controversy in 1776, 1787, or 1791 over the severity of American criminal law, most of the new states imitated the English Bill of Rights's guarantee against cruel and unusual punishment as cheap insurance against would-be Jeffreys.

1748

Charles-Louis de Secondat, better known to history as Baron Montesquieu, published *Spirit of the Laws* in 1748, just in time to form the early reading of Thomas Jefferson, James Madison, and other colonial intellectuals. *Spirit of the Laws* was banned in France by the Catholic Church in 1751, which probably guaranteed its best-seller status in Protestant England and its colonies. There was much for an Englishman to like. Montesquieu looked at an ideal England and compared it favorably to other countries and particularly to France. Montesquieu theorized that it was England's mixed constitution—its balance of the legislative branch with the exclusive power to tax, an executive who could veto bad laws, and a judiciary independent of the other two branches—that was responsible for England's success. Montesquieu was as popular with the English as any admirer, and his assessment that the English constitution with its separation of powers and checks and balances was superior to the French gained credibility from England's repeated military success in wars with France during the latter half of the eighteenth century. In Book VI of *The Spirit of the Laws*, Montesquieu further compared the severity of punishment in England to other lands:

It is an essential point, that there should be a certain proportion in punishments, because it is essential that a great crime should be avoided rather than a smaller, and that which is more pernicious to society rather than that which is less.

* * *

It is a great abuse amongst us to condemn to the same punishment a person that only robs on the highway and another who robs and murders. Surely, for the public security, some difference should be made in the punishment.

In China, those who add murder to robbery are cut in pieces: but not so the others; to this difference it is owing that though they rob in that country they never murder.

In Russia, where the punishment of robbery and murder is the same, they always murder. The dead, say they, tell no tales.

Where there is no difference in the penalty, there should be some in the expectation of pardon. In England they never murder on the highway, because robbers have some hopes of transportation, which is not the case in respect to those that commit murder.

Montesquieu had first sounded this theme in the work that made him popular, his *Persian Letters*, printed anonymously in Holland in 1721. Using the literary fiction that he found the correspondence of Persian travelers in France and throughout Europe, Montesquieu used the perspective of a foreigner to comment on the merits of milder criminal laws:

[H]owever cruel the penalties are in a state, they do not make people more obedient to the law. In countries where punishments are moderate, they are as much feared as where they are despotic and terrible.

Whether the government acts with moderation or with cruelty, there are always different degrees of punishment; major or minor penalties are applied to major or minor crimes. The imagination adjusts itself automatically to the customs of the country that one is in. A week's imprisonment, or a small fine, impress the mind of a European who has been brought up in a humane country as greatly as the loss of an arm would intimidate an Asian.

* * *

Furthermore, I do not see that public order, justice, and equity are better preserved in Turkey or Persia or under the Mogul than in the republics of Holland, Venice, or even England. I do not see that fewer crimes are committed there, or that men are more law-abiding because they are intimidated by the magnitude of the penalties.[64]

Although Montesquieu saw things we probably would not and missed things he should have seen, like the increasing harshness of English law under the Black Act, after the Glorious Revolution and the end of widespread use of capital punishment for political purposes, there is no doubt that there was more mildness in criminal punishment in eighteenth-century England than there had been in previous centuries.

1764

In 1764, the Italian reformer Cesare Beccaria published his essay *On Crimes and Punishments*, forcefully condemning the use of torture in judicial proceedings and the widespread use of capital punishment. Written in Italian, it was quickly translated into French and English and spread throughout Europe. Like Thomas Paine's *Common Sense*, Beccaria's *On Crimes and Punishments* was instantly popular, not because it was a work of great scholarship but because it expressed succinctly ideas whose time had come. English translations of Beccaria's essay were published in Philadelphia and New York in the 1770s, and his thesis that perpetual imprisonment was a more effective deterrent to crime than capital punishment was well known to the Framers. John Adams quoted Beccaria to the jury when he defended Captain Preston and the British soldiers tried for murder after the 1770 Boston Massacre. Jefferson cited Beccaria in his work on revising the criminal code of Virginia.

Beccaria, a social contract theorist like Englishmen Thomas Hobbes and John Locke and Frenchman Jean Jacques Rousseau, started from the premise that laws received their power from the surrender of a portion of each citizen's private liberty, but "only the least possible portion, no more than suffices to induce others to defend it."[65] Beccaria added the point, later developed by promoters of the philosophy of utilitarianism, that the purpose of society was "the greatest happiness shared by the greatest number."[66]

From these two basics, in Chapter XVI of *On Crimes and Punishments*, Beccaria launched a purely logical assault[67] on all capital punishment. One

C. Rampoldi inc.

Cesare Beccaria

Cesare Beccaria published his *Essay On Crimes and Punishments* in 1764, in which he wrote that perpetual imprisonment was a greater deterrent to crime than capital punishment. (Cesare Beccaria, *Opere di Cesare Beccaria*, 1821)

by one, Beccaria set up his points: because no man has the right to take his own life, he cannot surrender a right to the state to take his life. Therefore, the state lacks the moral authority to take any life, and capital punishment, since it is "the war of a nation against a citizen whose destruction it judges to be necessary or useful,"[68] can only be justified by reasons of necessity.

However, Beccaria argued capital punishment was neither effective nor necessary in almost every case. Beccaria considered two possible exceptions. First, the death penalty might be necessary when the citizen, although imprisoned, "still has connections and power such as endanger the security of the nation" in a time of social upheaval or anarchy. Second, executing a criminal might be justified "if his death were the only real way of restraining others from committing crimes."[69]

Beccaria proceeded to show that this second case was illusory:

It is not the intensity of punishment that has the greatest effect on the human spirit, but its duration, for our sensibility is more easily and more permanently affected by slight but repeated impressions than by a powerful but momentary action. The sway of habit is universal over every sentient being; as man speaks and walks and satisfies his needs by its aid, so the ideas of morality come to be stamped upon the mind only by long and repeated impressions. It is not the terrible yet momentary spectacle of the death of a wretch, but the long and painful example of a man deprived of liberty, who having become a beast of burden, recompenses with his labors the society he has offended, which is the strongest curb against crimes. That efficacious idea—efficacious, because very often repeated to ourselves—"I myself shall be reduced to so long and miserable a condition if I commit a similar misdeed" is far more potent than the idea of death, which men envision always at an obscure distance.

* * *

The death penalty becomes for the majority a spectacle and for some others an object of compassion mixed with disdain; these two sentiments rather than the salutary fear which the laws pretend to inspire occupy the spirits of the spectators. But in moderate and prolonged punishments the dominant sentiment is the latter, because it is the only one. The limits which the legislator ought to fix on the rigor of punishments would seem to be determined by the sentiment of compassion itself, when it begins to prevail over every other in the hearts of those who are the witnesses of punishment, inflicted for their sake rather than for the criminal's.

For a punishment to be just it should consist of only such gradations of intensity as suffice to deter men from committing crimes. Now, the person does not exist who, reflecting upon it, could choose for himself total and perpetual loss of personal liberty, no matter how advantageous a crime might seem to be. Thus the intensity of the punishment of a life sentence of servitude, in place of the death penalty, has in it what suffices to deter any determined spirit. It has, let me add, even more. Many men are able to look calmly and with firmness upon death—some from fanaticism, some from vanity, which almost always accompanies man even beyond the tomb, some from a final and desperate attempt either to live no longer or to escape their misery. But neither fanaticism nor vanity can subsist among fetters or chains, under the rod, under the yoke, in a cage of iron, where the desperate wretch does not end his woes but merely begins them. Our spirit resists violence and extreme but momentary pains more easily than it does time and incessant weariness, for it can, so to speak, collect itself for a moment to repel the first, but the vigor of its elasticity does not suffice to resist the long and repeated action of the second.

* * *

But he who foresees a great number of years, or even a whole lifetime to be spent in servitude and pain, in sight of his fellow citizens with whom he lives in freedom and friendship, slave of the laws which once afforded him protection, makes a useful comparison of all this with the uncertainty of the result of his crimes, and the brevity of the time in which he would enjoy their fruits. The perpetual example of those whom he actually sees the victims of their own carelessness makes a much stronger impression upon him than the spectacle of a punishment that hardens more than it corrects him.

The death penalty cannot be useful, because of the example of barbarity it gives men. If the passions or the necessities of war have taught the shedding of human blood, the laws, moderators of the conduct of men, should not extend the beastly example, which becomes more pernicious since the inflicting of legal death is attended with much study and formality. It seems to be absurd that the laws, which are an expression of the public will, which detest and punish homicide, should themselves commit it, and that to deter citizens from murder, they order a public one.[70]

Beccaria's assumptions about what would deter the average criminal were sweeping generalizations and his logic was hardly impeccable. After all, if the basis of society's right to punish is the consent of the citizen, there is the obvious objection that no one consents to his own life imprisonment any more than to his own capital punishment. Even in Beccaria's own day, philosophers such as Immanuel Kant found Beccaria's justification of punishment by its deterrent effect to be immoral because it disregarded the punishment the criminal himself deserved in favor of the effect of the punishment on others. But there is no doubt about Beccaria's popularity. In addition to energizing opponents of capital punishment in America, Beccaria was praised by philosophers David Hume in England and Voltaire in France and monarchs Frederick II of Prussia and Catherine the Great of Russia. Empress Maria Teresa and Grand Duke Leopold publicly acknowledged Beccaria's influence on their respective decisions about the abolition of the death penalty in Austria and Tuscany.[71]

STIRRINGS OF CHANGE

Meanwhile, in England, the number of capital offenses peaked at 222 crimes by the mid-1700s. Crimes punishable by death included stealing from a house in the amount of 40 shillings, stealing from a shop to the value of 5 shillings, robbing a rabbit warren, cutting down a tree, and counterfeiting tax stamps. In part due to Beccaria and in part due to a general trend toward modernization and codification of the laws, reform eventually followed in England. In 1823, approximately 100 crimes were exempted from the death penalty. Between 1832 and 1837, many additional capital offenses were eliminated. In 1840, an attempt to abolish *all* capital punishment failed, but through the nineteenth and twentieth centuries, more capital punishments were abolished in Great Britain and throughout Europe.[72]

Just as the harsh penalties in Draco's Code and the Twelve Tables are unlikely to have been carried out in every or even most cases, even before the severe penalties prescribed in English law were formally repealed, they were often disregarded in practice. The records of proceedings in the Old Bailey, London's criminal court, by one scholar's estimate, show that by the late 1760s, 70 percent of defendants in English capital cases were transported to the American colonies, while others, though at first sentenced to death, were ultimately pardoned and whipped or jailed for short terms.[73] Transportation to America halted with the war for independence, but Australia became the destination for transportees from 1787 until 1857. By the early nineteenth century, well over 90 percent of death-eligible defendants were being pardoned.[74]

The changes taking place in English law and practice affected Americans both directly and indirectly through the end of the colonial era and into the nineteenth century. Politicians in the new country had undoubtedly read John Locke's thoughts on the proper scope of the criminal law as:

[A] power to make laws, and annex such penalties to them as may tend to the preservation of the whole, by cutting off those parts, and those only, which are so corrupt that they threaten the sound and healthy, without which no severity is lawful.[75]

More recently, lawyers in the newly independent United States were the students of William Blackstone's *Commentaries on the Laws of England*, published in four volumes between 1765 and 1769. Blackstone's *Commentaries* were sometimes the only law books in a colonial lawyer's office, and even after independence, Blackstone continued to influence nineteenth-century lawyers like Daniel Webster, Chancellor James Kent of New York, and Abraham Lincoln. Blackstone described the large number of crimes that remained capital offenses in English law at that time, including many petty property crimes, but noted several practices besides the royal pardon upon condition of transportation that eased the severity of the law. Often, juries would not convict regardless of the evidence when the penalty for a minor crime was great. One of the ways juries did this, Blackstone wrote, was "pious perjury." Theft above the value of 12 pence was grand larceny, a capital offense. The figure of 12 pence, according to Blackstone, had been set in the tenth century under the Saxon king Athelstan, and after eight centuries of inflation, even a minor theft could lead to a hanging. Therefore, Blackstone asserted, "the mercy of juries will often make them strain a point, and bring in larc[e]ny to be under the value of twelvepence, when it is really of much greater value."[76] Reduction in the penalty for crime would therefore make guilty verdicts easier to get and punish crime more effectively. Influenced by his reading of Beccaria,

Blackstone called for repeal of capital punishment for offenses "merely against the municipal law only, and not against the law of nature, since no individual has, naturally, a power of inflicting death upon himself or others for actions in themselves indifferent."[77] Blackstone approved of capital punishment in cases of murder and other serious offenses and for support quoted God's command to Noah in Genesis 9:6 that "whoso sheddeth man's blood, by man shall his blood be shed." But Blackstone obviously considered himself an advocate for leniency in sentencing:

We may further observe that sanguinary laws are a bad symptom of the distemper of any state, or at least a weak constitution . . . [t]he laws of the Roman kings, and the twelve tables of the decemviri, were full of cruel punishments . . . the Porcian law, which exempted all citizens from sentence of death, silently abrogated them all. In this period the republic flourished: under the emperors severe punishments were revived, and then the empire fell.[78]

After separating from England, the constitutions and criminal codes adopted by the American states tended to announce their adoption of the philosophies of Locke and Montesquieu, Blackstone and Beccaria. Pennsylvania, already influenced by the state's Quaker heritage, stated in its Constitution of 1776 that punishments should be "less sanguinary and in general more proportionate to the crime." The preamble to Pennsylvania's murder statute in 1794 proclaimed to the world:

[I]t is the duty of every government to endeavor to reform, rather than exterminate offenders, and the punishment of death ought never to be inflicted where it is not absolutely necessary to the public safety.

As this preamble implies, Pennsylvania still believed there was a place for the death penalty when absolutely necessary. All the states and the federal government retained the death penalty. This was not because the death penalty could have been overlooked. In addition to reading Beccaria and Blackstone, the signers of the Declaration of Independence in 1776 had personal reasons to study the death penalty. They knew their English law and history, and despite the high rate of royal pardons in lesser matters, they knew that if they had lost the war, they would have been lucky to be hanged as traitors, if lucky. If unlucky, they could have expected to hear the formula used by English judges for centuries, that:

you be drawn upon a hurdle to the place of execution; that you be there hanged by the neck, but not until you are dead; but that, being alive, you be cut down, and your bowels taken out and burnt before your face; that your head be severed from your body, and your body divided into four parts; and that your head and quarters be disposed of as the King shall think fit: and may the Lord have mercy on your soul.

If the new United States had abolished capital punishment, it might have been seen as an understandable reaction to its members' own experiences or at least their fears. However, the Articles of Confederation, the first Constitution of the United States in effect from 1781 to 1789, omitted any discussion of the subject. In 1787, the Articles of Confederation Congress passed an Ordinance for the Governance of the Northwest Territories. The Northwest Ordinance did address capital punishment in ways that were carried over into the Fifth Amendment and Eighth Amendment to the Constitution. First, the Northwest Ordinance stated the traditional prohibitions of the *Magna Carta* of 1215 against any person being fined excessively or being judged other than by one's peers or contrary to the law of the land. Second, persons charged with crimes were entitled to bail except "for capital offenses, where the proof shall be evident or the presumption great," and "no cruel or unusual punishments shall be inflicted."[79] There was no provision restricting what could be a capital offense, and the phrase "cruel or unusual" was left undefined.

After the drafting of the Constitution, the First Congress passed the first federal crime bill in 1790. It defined the federal offenses of treason and made treason "willful murder on federal property," piracy and other offenses on the high seas, and forgery subject to the mandatory penalty of death by hanging. There were only two substantial debates over the death penalty in the First Congress. One was whether counterfeiting deserved the death penalty. Following the English tradition of protecting commercial transactions, the House of Representatives decided it did. The other was whether the body of an executed criminal should be delivered to a doctor for dissection and study. Congress decided that it would.[80]

The few specific offenses made subject to capital punishment by Congress reflected a larger nineteenth-century movement taking place in the United States and in Great Britain toward making the criminal law more temperate without totally abolishing capital punishment. The abolitionists were influenced not only by the writings of Montesquieu, Voltaire, Beccaria, and Bentham but also by the English Quaker reformers, John Bellers and John Howard, who wished to improve prison conditions.[81] Dr. Benjamin Rush, a signer of the Declaration of Independence and founder of the Pennsylvania Prison Society, questioned the deterrent effects of capital punishment and regarded it as brutalizing. Following Beccaria, Rush urged its total abolition. Prominent figures supporting Rush included fellow Pennsylvanians Benjamin Franklin and Pennsylvania Attorney General William Bradford. In 1793, Bradford, who was later named Attorney General of the United States, published "An Enquiry How Far the Punishment of Death is Necessary in Pennsylvania." Although Bradford insisted that the death penalty be retained, he conceded it was ineffective in preventing certain crimes. Repeating Black-stone's observations, Bradford said that the death penalty made convictions harder to obtain and that a mandatory death penalty made juries even more reluctant to return guilty verdicts. As a result, in 1794, the Pennsylvania legisla-ture abolished capital punishment for all offenses except premeditated murder, that is "murder in the first degree." Unpremeditated murder and manslaughter were punishable by imprisonment only. This was the first time murder had been broken down into degrees.[82]

Other states followed Pennsylvania's lead, and in the first half of the nine-teenth century, almost every state passed statutes that reduced the number of capital offenses. Opposition to the death penalty mounted between 1776 and 1800. Thomas Jefferson recommended that the Virginia death penalty be reserved for only treason and murder. The legislature rejected Jefferson's proposal by a single vote.[83]

There were reforms in the *imposition* of the death penalty. As part of a larger trend toward centralization of state government, many states took the hangman's job away from county sheriffs or the wardens of the county jails and provided for execution in a state prison. The Supreme Court eventually was confronted with a challenge to this innovation and held that this change in execution practice was constitutional in *Holden v. Minnesota* (1890), although the last public executions in the United States did not come until the 1930s. In 1936, approximately 10,000 gathered to watch Rainey Bethea hanged in Owensboro, Kentucky; a year later, a crowd estimated at 1,500 watched the hanging of Roscoe Jackson for murder in Galena, Missouri.

Additional reforms were mixed. The federal crimes code permitted both whipping and standing in the pillory (for perjury). In 1796, the New York legislature authorized construction of the state's first penitentiary, abolished whipping, and reduced the number of capital offenses from 13 to 2. Similar reform measures were passed in Virginia and Kentucky. Four more states— Vermont, Maryland, New Hampshire and Ohio—reduced the number of crimes punishable by death. Each of these states also built penitentiaries. But a few states went in the opposite direction. Rhode Island restored the death penalty for rape and arson. Massachusetts, New Jersey, Connecticut, and several southern states increased the number of capital crimes, especially for offenses committed by slaves.[84]

In 1846, Michigan became the first state to abolish the death penalty. It repealed the death penalty for all crimes except treason, and there is no record of anyone being prosecuted for treason against a state. In 1852, Rhode Island abolished the death penalty. In the same year, Massachusetts limited its death penalty to first-degree murder. In 1853, Wisconsin abolished the death penalty for all crimes. The reported impetus was a gruesome execution in which the victim struggled for 5 minutes at the end of the rope, and a full 18 minutes passed before his heart finally stopped.[85]

Although most states did not abolish the death penalty, some states began to pass laws against mandatory death sentences. In 1838, Tennessee enacted a discretionary death penalty statute. Alabama followed suit. In 1872, Kansas passed a "Maine Law" mandating a delay between the imposition of sentence and the signing of the death warrant, a *de facto* abolition. Iowa, Maine, and Colorado repealed the death penalty in 1872, 1876, and 1897, and then reinstated it in 1878, 1883, and 1901, respectively.

Eighteen states had shifted from mandatory to discretionary capital punishment by 1895. This was perceived as a victory for abolitionists because prior to this reform, the states mandated the death penalty for anyone convicted of a capital crime, regardless of circumstances. The motivation behind discretionary capital sentencing, however, was not to encourage the jury to be merciful. As Blackstone and Bradford had observed, discretionary sentencing was an attempt to make the death penalty more acceptable to the jury in order to increase the conviction rate of capital defendants.[86]

The American Society for the Abolition of Capital Punishment was formed in 1845, with President James K. Polk's Vice President, George M. Dallas, as its first president, and with expressions of support from prominent federal politicians including former President John Quincy Adams.[87] Despite this, little attention was given to the death penalty at the federal level until almost the twentieth century. Not only was crime and punishment a peculiarly local concern, the nation's government was preoccupied throughout the century. At first, the very survival of the new nation was in doubt. Before the Civil War, westward migration and the social problems caused by economic expansion and an economy based on slavery in the South gripped the nation's attention. Imprisonment for debt, a legacy of English commercial law, was a far more pressing social concern than capital punishment. In some states, five-sixths of persons in jail were there for failure to pay debts, in some cases very small debts. Abolition of imprisonment for debt was the focus of debate through the 1820s. It was accomplished beginning with federal legislation passed in 1832; most states abolished imprisonment for debt in the next 10 years.[88]

After the Civil War, the nation's attention was briefly focused on the death penalty by the trial and execution of Mary Surratt for her role in the assassination of President Lincoln, and by a case with many modern features: the extended treason proceedings against Jefferson Davis, the President of the defeated Confederate States of America. Davis was captured in 1865 and held in a military prison while the government debated whether to hold trial before a military commission or in the civil court. In 1866, Davis was indicted for treason, a capital offense, but Davis's lawyers eventually obtained dismissal of the charge in President Andrew Johnson's general amnesty on Christmas Day 1868 after waging a publicity campaign intended to influence elite opinion that Davis's trial would be a political minefield whichever way the jury voted, and after Chief Justice Salmon P. Chase, who was assigned to try the matter, hinted to Davis's counsel what legal attack to make on the charges.[89] But the Davis case, with celebrity lawyers, newspaper debates, and judges making decisions based on their political calculations, was the exception for its time. The economic and social impact of mass industrialization and mass migration from Europe in the latter half of the nineteenth century claimed far more of the public's attention and therefore Congressional efforts than did further reform in what already seemed to be an adequate system.

Finally, in 1897, Congress passed a statute that drastically reduced the federal offenses subject to the death penalty to three: treason, murder, and rape. More significantly, at the urging of Civil War general and New York Representative Newton M. Curtis, the federal government joined the discretionary capital punishment states. For the three remaining federal death penalty offenses, the jury had the power to reach a verdict of guilty "without capital punishment," thus sentencing a defendant to life imprisonment instead.[90]

The states and Congress would continue to pass new capital punishment statutes into the twentieth century. There would be new issues affecting the death penalty, but mostly they were about how to carry it out efficiently and justly, not whether to abolish it. What would be different about the debate in the new century would be the role played by the hitherto unimportant Eighth Amendment and the hitherto uninvolved Supreme Court of the United States.

NOTES

1. Sometimes the crowd had an interest in making sure the hangman hanged the right man. Peter G. Fish, *Federal Justice in the Mid-Atlantic South* (Washington, D.C., 2002), 87, 282–83. For centuries, though, attendance was chiefly for the entertainment value. Crowds gathered in Paris in 1613, with children and picnic lunches, to watch four horses tear apart the assassin of Henry IV of France. In 1660, Samuel Pepys recorded in his diary that after he witnessed the public hanging, drawing, and quartering of Major-General Harrison in London, Harrison's "head and heart were shown to the people, at which there were great shouts of joy." Robert K. Massie, *Peter the Great: His Life and World* (New York: Alfred A. Knopf, 1980), 252. Things had not altered by the mid-eighteenth century: writing at midcentury, the Paris lawyer Barbier commented on the way the crowd applauded a cleanly

delivered decapitation and how women of the upper class reacted more favorably than men to the public torture and execution of Damiens, a servant who had stabbed Louis XV with a penknife. Damiens was finally torn into pieces by horses. In James Boswell's *Life of Samuel Johnson*, Boswell casually mentions in October 1769 that he had been down to the gallows in Tyburn to see the execution of several convicts and asks Johnson whether it would trouble him if a close friend were charged with a capital offence. Johnson replied that he would do what he could to comfort his friend, but "once [he was] fairly hanged I should not suffer."

There were signs of change. In 1775, Catherine II of Russia executed Pugachev and other leaders of a revolt against the Czarina, and although some of the minor participants had their noses torn off, Pugachev himself was decapitated before being quartered because Catherine, who was a patron of Diderot and Voltaire, wished to be seen as a more humane ruler than Louis XV. Henri Troyat, *Catherine the Great* (New York: Meridian, 1994), Joan Pinkham translation, 213–14.

2. Daniel E. Williams, *Pillars of Salt: An Anthology of Early American Criminal Narratives* (Madison, WI: Madison House Publishers, Inc., 1993), 23. Levi Ames's final words went through eighteen editions in the months just before the Boston Tea Party, making him, according to Williams, America's most celebrated criminal.

3. For example, in 1835, Maine enacted a moratorium on capital punishment after more than 10,000 people who watched a hanging had to be restrained by police after they became unruly and began fighting. No governor ordered an execution under the Maine Law for 27 years. Michael H. Reggio, "History of the Death Penalty," http://www.pbs.org/wgbh/pages/frontline/shows/execution/readings/history.html (6 November 2008); University of Alaska Anchorage Justice Center document, "History of the Death Penalty & Recent Developments,"http://justice.uaa.alaska.edu/death/history.html (15 November 2008); and Death Penalty Information Center document, "History of the Death Penalty," http://www.deathpenaltyinfo.org/part-i-history-death-penalty (15 November 2008). This history is based in part on annual capital punishment bulletins of the *Bureau of Justice Statistics*, U.S. Department of Justice, Reggio's "History of the Death Penalty," and the Death Penalty Information Center's *History of the Death Penalty*. For an additional discussion, see our earlier treatment of this subject in Joseph A. Melusky and Keith A. Pesto, *Cruel and Unusual Punishment: Rights and Liberties Under the Law* (Santa Barbara, CA: ABC-CLIO, 2003).

4. This personal tradition of government as the squire next door and law as the unvarying custom had its strongest theoretical support during feudalism but survived at least into the eighteenth century in England and the American colonies. Today, with few exceptions, only religious traditions preserve the idea that there are divinely ordered laws that are timeless and not subject to amendment. Classical philosophy held a similar concept of natural law at least since the first century BC, when Cicero wrote "True law is Reason . . . Its validity is universal; it is immutable and eternal." Since the founding of this country, however, the general trend in ideas has been toward increasing religious and philosophical skepticism. By the late nineteenth century, the habit of thought common to legislators and judges was uncomfortable with

or hostile to the idea that law was anything other than the command of a legislature or court. The sense that there was a higher law to which all law should conform was seen as superstitious attachment to the past. Justice Oliver Wendell Holmes, Jr., on the Supreme Court from 1902 to 1932, derided this in a 1917 legal opinion as the belief that law was a "brooding omnipresence in the sky."

5. As late as 1785, a proposal to establish a police force of 225 men for London was defeated. Roy Porter, *English Society in the Eighteenth Century* (London: Penguin Books, 1990), 119. There was historically a fear in England and its colonies of any body of men that remotely resembled a standing army.

6. Steven D. Levitt and Stephen J. Dubner, *Freakonomics: A Rogue Economist Explores the Hidden Side of Everything* (New York: HarperCollins Publishers, 2005), 22.

7. Although the idea of laws of war may seem an oxymoron, this harsh view was moderated in practice by intelligent self-interest and fear of retribution. In the next century, even the theory had changed: according to the Swiss lawyer Emmerich de Vattel, the rules of war forbade the execution of prisoners taken in a declared war. Emmerich de Vattel, *The Law of Nations or the Principles of Natural Law* (Washington, DC: Carnegic Institution of Washington, 1916 [1758]) Charles G. Fenwick translation, 258.

8. "Dueling was a point of honor in the nobility . . . it was difficult to get through a titled life without at least one puncture." Will Durant and Ariel Durant, *Rousseau and Revolution* (New York: Simon and Schuster, 1967), 732.

9. For a twelfth-century example, consider the early career of William Marshal, who rose from a landless knight to well-to-do baron on the strength of ransoms earned in tournaments and who took part as an elder statesman in negotiations leading up to the drafting of the *Magna Carta* in 1215. Sydney Painter, *William Marshal: Knight-Errant, Baron, and Regent of England* (Baltimore, MD: The Johns Hopkins Press, 1933). As the military importance of the armored knight declined, tournaments became less like combat, until by the fifteenth century jousting with artificial rules remained only as a spectacle or, occasionally, as a trial by combat between two litigants of noble birth. Maurice Keen, *Chivalry* (New Haven, NJ: Yale University Press, 1984), Chapter V, *passim*; 204.

10. During the War of the Roses from about 1455 to 1485, Desmond Seward estimates, "Out of 70 adult peers during this period, over 50 are known to have fought in battles they had to win if they wanted to stay alive." Desmond Seward, *The Wars of the Roses*. (London: Penguin Books, 1995), 8.

11. Jackson's strategy appears to have been to let Dickinson, the better marksman, have the first shot, and hope to stay alive long enough to aim carefully. Jackson was successful but carried Dickinson's bullet in his chest for the rest of his life. Robert V. Remini, *The Life of Andrew Jackson* (London: Penguin Books, 1988), 53–54.

12. Senator Henry Clay (wounded, 1809), Commodore Stephen Decatur (killed, 1820), Governor James Hamilton of South Carolina (14 successful duels). Ten duels were fought in New Orleans on one Sunday in 1839. Daniel J. Boorstin, *The Americans: The National Experience* (New York: Random House, 1965), 208–9.

13. Even recreations familiar to us such as boxing were often bare-knuckle brawls sometimes fatal to the participants. Samuel E. Morison, *The Oxford History of the American People, Volume Two: 1789 through Reconstruction* (New York: Meridian, 1994), 219.

14. David E. Stannard, *The Puritan Way of Death* (New York: Oxford University Press, 1977), 52–57.

15. If we judge by the percentage of books, letters, poems, and sermons devoted to the topic, dying a good death—the *ars moriendi*—was until after the American Civil War as much a popular theme of previous times as dieting is a preoccupation of ours. Drew Gilpin Faust, *This Republic of Suffering: Death and the American Civil War* (New York, Alfred A. Knopf, 2008). *passim.*

16. Whether this trend will continue into the twenty-first century is unsettled, but it was virtually a constant theme in the political life of the United States throughout the twentieth century. In a May 3, 1907, speech to the Elmira Chamber of Commerce, then New York Governor Charles Evans Hughes, later to be a Justice of the Supreme Court from 1910 to 1916, and later its Chief Justice from 1930 to 1941, remarked: "We are a nation under the Constitution, but the Constitution is what the judges say it is." At the close of the century, in November 1996, the monthly journal *First Things* conducted a widely read symposium on the proposition: "The government of the United States of America no longer governs by the consent of the governed;" most of the contributors echoed the position of former Court of Appeals Judge and Solicitor General Robert Bork that "the most important moral political and cultural decisions are steadily being removed from democratic control." Robert H. Bork, "Our Judicial Oligarchy," *First Things* 67 (November 1996): 21.

17. Karen. Farkas, "Judge Orders Change in Lethal Injection Drugs," *(Cleveland) Plain Dealer* (June 11, 2008): p. B1.

18. Later that year, Ohio executed two men who had not been covered by Judge Burge's decision despite last-minute attempts to benefit from that ruling. On October 14, 2008, Richard Cooey was executed by lethal injection. Cooey was 41, having been on death row for 22 years after he and Clint Dickens, a juvenile not eligible for the death penalty, were convicted of the kidnap, robbery, rape, and murder of two college students. Cooey went out in unusually undignified fashion, filing in addition to the ordinary appeals and requests for pardons two lawsuits that gained him little sympathy. Cooey, who had unsuccessfully attempted escape in 2005, claimed that the prescription medication he was taking for migraine headaches might interfere with the anesthetic administered during his execution. He also claimed that he had gained so much weight in prison that it might interfere with the effectiveness administration of the drugs. Michael McIntyre, "A pain lives on with appeals: Victim's family longs for relief in Cooey's execution," *(Cleveland) Plain Dealer* (October 12, 2008), p. B1.

A month later on November 19, 2008, Ohio executed Gregory Bryant-Bey for the 1992 murder of a coin-store owner. Bryant-Bey was also serving a life sentence for a murder he admitted committing, but he claimed he had been framed for the murder that led to his death sentence. A group of about 70 people protested outside the prison. Erica Blake, and Jim Provance, "Bryant-Bey put to death for 1992 North Toledo murder," *(Toledo, Ohio) Blade,* (November 20, 2008).

19. Reggio, *id.* 3–4. For an additional discussion of historical and contemporary methods of execution, see Melusky, "From Burning at the Stake to Lethal Injection: Evolving Standards of Decency and methods of Execution," a paper delivered at a meting of the national Social Science Association, Las Vegas, NV, April 17–19, 2011. See also, "The History of Execution Methods," *http://istina.rin.ru/eng/ufo/text/296.html* (April 2, 2011) and "Top 10 Gruesome Methods of Execution," *http://listverse.com/2007/09/12/top-10-gruesome-methods-of-execution/* (April 2, 2011).

20. Michael L. Rustad, "Happy No More: Federalism Derailed by the Court That Would be King of Punitive Damages." *Maryland Law Review* 64 (2005): 461–540, 519–18, 418.

21. Reggio, *id.*

22. According to Plutarch, who wrote in the first century AD, Draco explained that since minor offenses such as idleness and stealing an apple or a cabbage deserved death, there was nothing else but death for more serious offenses. Plutarch, *The Lives of the Noble Grecians and Romans,* (New York: The Modern Library, Random House, 1961), John Dryden translation revised by Arthur H. Clough (originally published 1864), *Solon,* 107.

23. Aristotle, *The Athenian Constitution* (c. 330 BC) (London: Penguin Books, 1984), P. J. Rhodes translation, 48.

24. Jayne S. Ressler, "Civil Contempt Confinement and the Bankruptcy Abuse Prevention and Consumer Protection Act of 2005: An Examination of Debtor Incarceration in the Modern Age." *Rutgers Law Journal* 37, Issue 2 (Winter 2006): 355–98, 359.

25. Plato's dialogues *Euthyphro, Apology, Crito,* and *Phaedo* are our sources for the trial and death of Socrates. Historians generally believe that the charge of heresy was a pretext and that Socrates was condemned for his real or imagined association with the antidemocratic faction known as the Thirty Tyrants, which had been ousted from Athens in 401 BC.

26. Genesis 2:17, RSV.

27. Genesis 6:13, RSV.

28. Genesis 18:25, RSV. Ultimately, there are not even 10 righteous to be found and both cities are destroyed.

29. Clemens Thoma, "The Death Penalty and Torture in the Jewish Tradition," from *The Death Penalty and Torture,* 64–74, Franz Bockle and Jacques Pohier, eds. (New York: The Seabury Press, 1979.) As was well known, Jewish practice came through the centuries to be strictly circumscribed by procedural protections built up in the Babylonian and Jerusalem Talmuds, to the point that a Sanhedrin that ordered capital punishment once in seven years (other versions say 70 years) was described as a murderous one. *Id.* at 66.

30. Roman law permitted executions without trial during emergencies threatening public order. In ordinary criminal cases not involving threats to public order, upper-class Romans believed their punishments to be quite mild. William M. Green,

"An Ancient Debate on Capital Punishment," from *Capital Punishment*, 46–54, Thorsten Sellin, ed. (New York: Harper & Row, 1967). In part, this was because death sentences could be imposed only after an appeal to an assembly dominated by nobles, and even then they were routinely stayed to allow the condemned, when a noble, to go into exile. Members of the lower class could expect slavery in the mines or gladiatorial schools as an alternative to execution. Lesley Adkins and Roy A. Adkins, *Handbook to Life in Ancient Rome* (New York: Oxford University Press, 1994), 39, 46–47, 353–54.

31. Francesco Compagnoni, "Capital Punishment and Torture in the Tradition of the Roman Catholic Church," from *The Death Penalty and Torture*, 39–53, Franz Bockle and Jacques Pohier, eds. (New York: The Seabury Press, 1979).

32. Henry Chadwick, "Envoi: On Taking Leave of Antiquity," from *The Oxford History of the Classical World*, 807–28, John Boardman, Jasper Griffin, and Oswyn Murray, eds. (New York: Oxford University Press, 1986), 824.

33. Compagnoni, *id.* at 46.

34. The Roman Catholic Church's canon law existed in various collections for well over 1,500 years before it was codified in 1917. Section 984 of the Code of 1917 expressly prohibited the ordination as a priest of any judge who had imposed the death sentence and anyone who had voluntarily accepted the office of public executioner, based on the idea that one who took part in the administering of the death penalty "has shown himself in some sense lacking in mercy." T. Lincoln Bouscarens, S. J. and Adam C. Ellis, S. J., *Canon Law: a Text and Commentary* (Milwaukee, WI: The Bruce Publishing Co., 1946), 376–77. In the general revision of canon law that was completed in 1983, these two disqualifications were eliminated. Canon 285 of the 1983 Code now prohibits anyone who is ordained from holding any civil office, even as a juror. James A. Coriden, Thomas J. Green, Donald E. Heintschel, eds. *The Code of Canon Law: a Text and Commentary* (New York: Paulist Press, 1985), 221.

35. Boardman, *id.* at 824.

36. St. Augustine of Hippo, *City of God, Book I, ch 21* (c. AD 413) (London: Penguin Books, 1984), Henry Bettenson translation, 32. In Book V, Augustine praised rulers who "are slow to punish but ready to pardon," take vengeance on wrong only "because of the necessity to direct and protect the state," and pardon "in the hope of amendment of the wrong-doer." *Id.*, 220.

37. Davison M. Douglas, "God and the Executioner: The Influence of Western Religion on the Use of the Death Penalty." *William & Mary Bill of Rights Journal* 9 (December 2000): 1, 37–170.

38. The resulting work, called the Corpus Juris (Body of Law), was in use in the Byzantine Empire for the next 900 years. It was rediscovered in the West in the eleventh century AD and significantly influenced the development of law on the continent and, to a lesser extent, in England.

39. This has its modern parallel in argument that the death penalty should not be imposed in cases where there can be some doubt about the identity of the murderer because proof has rested on circumstantial evidence or on disputable eyewitness identification.

40. George Fisher, "The Jury's Rise as Lie Detector," *Yale Law Journal*, 107 (December 1997): 575, 588–89.

41. Reggio, 1–2, DPIC, "History."

42. Robert L. Heilbroner, *The Worldly Philosophers* (New York: Simon and Schuster, Inc., 1961), 18.

43. Voltaire was widely admired in the generation that approved of the Eighth Amendment. In the 1769 edition of his *Dictionnaire Philosophique,* Voltaire added an entry for Torture, bitterly denouncing its retention in French law when the English and even the supposedly backward Russians had abolished it. Voltaire imagined the wife of a magistrate eagerly greeting him at the door with "My angel, did you give anyone the question today?" Voltaire (Francois Marie Arouet), *Philosophical Dictionary* (London: Penguin Books, 1972), Theodore Besterman translation, 394–96. The same controversy persists today over confessions obtained without *Miranda* warnings: they are suppressed not because they are unreliable, but because we see such confessions as the first descent down a slippery slope back to the age of the "third degree."

44. More than one modern critic of our system of public defenders has compared trial by champion to trial by lawyer, charging that the wealthiest defendants get the best justice because they buy a bigger champion.

45. Rodney Stark, *The Victory of Reason* (New York: Random House, 2005) Chapter 3, *passim.*

46. Trial by battle was used by all classes of society until it was restricted in the thirteenth century. Nobles continued to use the judicial duel for a few more centuries, in England into the reign of Henry VII. No one bothered formally to abolish trial by combat in England until 1819. H. L. Ho, "The Legitimacy of Medieval Proof," *Journal of Law & Religion* 19 (2003–2004): 259–98.

47. Frederick II, who readily used torture, criticized trial by ordeal because it was "not in accord with nature and does not lead to truth." Quote from Joseph Gies and Frances Gies, *Life in a Medieval City* (New York: Harper & Row, 1969), 205.

48. Compagnoni, *id.* at 42.

49. Christopher Hill, *The Century of Revolution* (New York: W.W. Norton & Co., Inc., 1961), 178. The end of legal torture was a byproduct of the English Civil War's general abolition of the powers of ecclesiastical courts and not due to specific opposition to torture itself. J. P. Kenyon, *The Stuart Constitution 1603–1688 Documents and Commentary* (London: Cambridge University Press, 1966), 223–26.

50. Thomas More, *Utopia* (London: Penguin Books, 1965 [1516]), Paul Turner translation, 49–54, 104–5.

51. Martin Luther, "Temporal Authority: To what Extent it Should be Obeyed," in *Selected Writings of Martin Luther 1520–1523*, Theodore G. Tappert, ed. (Philadelphia, PA: Fortress Press, 1967 [1523]), 293.

52. Owen Chadwick, *The Reformation* (London: Penguin Books, 1990 [1964]), 90.

53. Chadwick, *id.* at 127–28.

54. "The Elizabethan mob dearly loved a bloody execution, and any felon was the hero of a few hours, whatever his crimes." Evelyn Waugh, *Edmund Campion,* 3rd edition, (London: Longmans, Green and Co., 1961), 197.

55. Reggio, 2, DPIC, "History."

56. Reggio, 2–3, DPIC, "History."

57. Seymour Schofield, *Jeffreys of "The Bloody Assizes"* (London: Thornton Butterworth, Ltd., 1937), 162–201. Known for a rather grim sense of humor, Jeffreys had one rebel, who swore he would not go to church until Monmouth was King, flogged in front of his parish church. Alice Lisle, a woman more than 70 years old, was sentenced to be burnt at the stake for harboring rebels in her house; the sentence was commuted to beheading.

58. P. J. Helm, *Jeffreys: A New Portrait of England's "Hanging Judge"* (New York: Thomas Y. Crowell Co., 1966), 95–100. Sidney was sentenced to being hanged, drawn, and quartered; the sentence was commuted to beheading.

59. Bernard Bailyn, *The Ideological Origins of the American Revolution* (Cambridge, MA: The Belknap Press of Harvard University Press, 1992), 34–35.

60. Chief among them was the Earl of Shaftesbury, John Locke's patron.

61. Helm, P. J. *id.*, 13–14, 51, 119–23.

62. Neil H. Cogan, ed., *The Complete Bill of Rights* (New York: Oxford University Press, 1997), 625.

63. In 1701, Parliament enacted a statute providing that in England, judges served during good behavior in office rather than at the pleasure of the King. Colonial judges throughout the eighteenth century sometimes still found themselves removed or unpaid if they ruled against the Crown.

64. Montesquieu, *Persian Letters* (London: Penguin Books, 1993 [1721]), Christopher Betts translation, 158–59.

65. Cesare Beccaria, *On Crimes and Punishments* (Englewood Cliffs, NJ: Prentice Hall, Inc., 1963 [1764]), Henry Paolucci translation of Beccaria's *Dei Delitti e delle Pene*, 12–13. In eighteenth-century America, it was printed and sold by R. Bell, Philadelphia (1778), translated from the French by Edward D. Ingraham. A second American edition was published by Phillip H. Nicklin, Philadelphia (1819). http:// www.constitution.org/cb/crim_pun28.txt (15 November 2008).

66. Beccaria, *id.* at 9.

67. As Beccaria put it, "with geometric precision." Beccaria, *id.* at 10.

68. Beccaria, *id.* at 45.

69. Beccaria, *id.* at 46.

70. Beccaria, *id.* at 46–50.

71. Beccaria, *id.* at x (Translator's introduction).

72. Reggio, 2.

73. Michael Ignatieff, *A Just Measure of Pain: The Penitentiary in the Industrial Revolution 1750–1850* (New York: Pantheon Books, 1978), 20.

74. Clive Emsley, Tim Hitchcock and Robert Shoemaker, *The Proceedings of the Old Bailey, Crime Justice and Punishment* (February 28, 2009), http://www.oldbaileyonline.org.uk/static/Punishment.jsp.

75. John Locke, *Concerning Civil Government, Second Essay* (London: Encyclopedia Britannica, Inc., 1952 [1690]), 65. In 1669, Locke had drafted a proposed

constitution for the colony of South Carolina that specified the death penalty for treason and murder and left open the possibility of other capital offenses.

76. William Blackstone, *Commentaries on the Laws of England*. [Four vols. 1765–1769] (Chicago: University of Chicago Press, 1979.), vol. IV, 239.

77. *Id.* at vol. IV, 9.

78. *Id.* at vol. IV, 590.

79. Bernard Schwartz, ed., *The Roots of the Bill of Rights*. [Five vols.] (New York: Chelsea House, 1980.), vol. 2, 385–87.

80. Rory K. Little, "The Federal Death Penalty: History and Some Thoughts About the Department of Justice's Role," *Fordham Urban Law Journal* 26 (March 1999): 347, 363–64. The debate over the dissection provision discussed whether it was cruel to the living not to have the body of a family member for burial. Whether medical schools should be allowed to dissect corpses for study was still a contentious topic in the late eighteenth century, and in England, fights sometimes broke out between the family of the executed criminal and suppliers of bodies to medical schools. For more details, see Clive Emsley, Tim Hitchcock and Robert Shoemaker, *The Proceedings of the Old Bailey, Punishments at the Old Bailey, supra* note 74.

81. Phillip E. Mackey, *Voices Against Death: American Opposition to Capital Punishment, 1787–1975* (Burt Franklin & Co., Inc., 1976), 7–8, as cited by Reggio, 3. See also DPIC.

82. Reggio, 3. See also, R. Bohm, *Deathquest: An Introduction to the Theory and Practice of Capital Punishment in the United States* (Anderson Publishing, 1999); Laura Randa, ed., *Society's Final Solution: A History and Discussion of the Death Penalty* (Lanham, MD: University Press of America, 1997), and Schabas, as cited in DPIC, "History."

83. Dumas Malone, *Jefferson the Virginian* (Boston: Little, Brown and Company, 1948), 269–73.

84. Reggio, 3, DPIC, "History."

85. Reggio, 4, DPIC, "History."

86. Reggio, 4, DPIC, "History."

87. Albert Post, "Early Efforts to Abolish Capital Punishment in Pennsylvania," *The Pennsylvania Magazine of History and Biography* 68 (January 1944): 38, 49–50.

88. Arthur M. Schlesinger, Jr. *The Age of Jackson* (Boston: Little, Brown and Company, 1945), 134–36.

89. Cynthia Nicoletti. "Did Secession Really Die at Appomattox: The Strange Case of U.S. v. Jefferson Davis," *University of Toledo L. Rev.* 41, no. 3(2010): 587–635.

90. Little, Rory K., *supra* at 367–68.

2

Facts, Figures, and Methods of Execution

As 2010 drew to a close, the death penalty in the United States was author-ized in 34 states, the federal government, and the U.S. military.[1] States with the death penalty include Alabama, Arizona, Arkansas, California, Colorado, Connecticut, Delaware, Florida, Georgia, Idaho, Indiana, Kansas, Kentucky, Louisiana, Maryland, Mississippi, Missouri, Montana, Nebraska, Nevada, New Hampshire, North Carolina, Ohio, Oklahoma, Oregon, Pennsylvania, South Carolina, South Dakota, Tennessee, Texas, Utah, Virginia, Washing-ton, and Wyoming. Of these, Kansas, New Hampshire, and the U.S. military have had no executions since 1976. In February 2008, the Nebraska Supreme Court ruled electrocution, the State's sole method of execution, unconstitu-tional. With no alternative method of execution, Nebraska effectively has no death penalty. The District of Columbia and 16 additional states— Alaska, Hawaii, Illinois, Iowa, Maine, Massachusetts, Michigan, Minnesota, New Jersey, New Mexico, New York, North Dakota, Rhode Island, Vermont, West Virginia, and Wisconsin—are without the death penalty. In 2004, the New York Supreme Court ruled that existing death penalty procedures violated the state constitution. When the New York legislature did not enact procedural reforms, the death penalty was effectively eliminated in the state. New Mexico abolished the death penalty in 2009, but the repeal was not retroactive. Two inmates remain on New Mexico's death row with lethal injection protocols still in place. Most recently, Illinois repealed the death penalty in 2011.

Table 2.1
Number of Executions (through April 27, 2011)

Year	Number
1976	0
1977	1
1978	0
1979	2
1980	0
1981	1
1982	2
1983	5
1984	21
1985	18
1986	18
1987	25
1988	11
1989	16
1990	23
1991	14
1992	31
1993	38
1994	31
1995	56
1996	45
1997	74
1998	68
1999	98
2000	85
2001	66
2002	71
2003	65
2004	59
2005	60
2006	53
2007	42

Table 2.1   (Continued)

Year	Number
2008	37
2009	52
2010	46
2011	12

Source: Death Penalty Information Center

Table 2.1 shows that from 1976 through April 27, 2011, 1,246 persons were executed in the United States. Ninety-eight people were executed in 1999, the highest number during this period.[2]

The number of executions in 2008 (37) was the lowest since 1994 (31). The number of executions in 2010 (46) was less than half the number of executions in 1999 (98).

Some racial patterns are of interest. Of those put to death since 1976, 434 were Black (35%), 91 were Hispanic (7%), 697 were White (56%), and 24 were classified as "other" (2%). More than 75 percent of the murder victims in cases resulting in an execution were White, even though nationally, only 50 percent of murder victims were White. The race of the victim in death penalty cases from 1976 through January 19, 2010, was as follows: 76 percent White, 15 percent Black, 6 percent Hispanic, and 3 percent other. Two hundred sixty-five persons have been executed for interracial murders since 1976. Of these cases, 15 involved a White defendant and a Black victim and 250 involved a Black defendant and a White victim.[3] The Death Penalty Information Center cites several recent studies on race. One study found that in 96 percent of states reviewed, there were patterns of either race-of-victim or race-of-defendant discrimination or both.[4] Another study revealed that 98 percent of the chief district attorneys in death-penalty states are White and only 1 percent are Black.[5] A study of the death penalty in North Carolina discovered that the odds of receiving a death sentence rose by 3.5 times for defendants whose victims were White.[6] Another study in California found that those who murdered White victims were three times more likely to be sentenced to death than were those who murdered Blacks and four times more likely to be sentenced to death than were those who murdered Latinos.[7]

As of April 1, 2011, there were 62 women on death rows in the United States. Females comprise 1.9 percent of the total death row population in the country. Twelve women were executed from 1976 through 2010. The most

Table 2.2
Women Executed since 1976

Name	State	Date of Execution
Velma Barfield	North Carolina	November 2, 1984
Karla Faye Tucker	Texas	February 3, 1998
Judy Buenoano	Florida	March 30, 1998
Betty Lou Beets	Texas	February 24, 2000
Christina Riggs	Arkansas	May 2, 2000
Wanda Jean Allen	Oklahoma	January 11, 2001
Marilyn Plantz	Oklahoma	May 1, 2001
Lois Nadean Smith	Oklahoma	December 4, 2001
Lynda Lyon Block	Alabama	May 10, 2002
Aileen Wuornos	Florida	October 9, 2002
Frances Elaine Newton	Texas	September 14, 2005
Teresa Lewis	Virginia	September 23, 2010

Source: Office of the Clark County Prosecuting Attorney

recent was Teresa Wilson Lewis. She was executed in Virginia on September 23, 2010.[8] These 12 women are listed in Table 2.2.[9]

Texas and Oklahoma lead the nation in post–1976 executions of females with three each. As indicated in Table 2.4, Texas has executed the most persons overall since 1976 (466) and Oklahoma ranks third, with 96 executions during this time.

One of the strongest modern objections to capital punishment is that it is possible that an innocent person might be wrongly convicted and executed. Since 1973, more than 138 people have been released from death row with evidence of their innocence. From 1973 through1999, there was an average of 3.1 exonerations per year. From 2000 through 2007, the average rose to five such exonerations per year.[10] Table 2.3 displays exonerations by states since 1973.[11]

From the top 10 states on this exoneration list (including "ties"), the states of Florida, Texas, Oklahoma, North Carolina, Alabama, Georgia, and Ohio are also among the top 10 states in number of executions since 1976. Louisiana ranks 11th and Arizona 13th. That is, states that carry out relatively high numbers of executions have made correspondingly higher numbers of errors that were detected prior to execution. The number of executions by state since 1976 is presented in Table 2.4.[12]

Table 2.3
Death Row Exonerations by State: Number Released since 1973

State	Number Released
Idaho	1
Kentucky	1
Maryland	1
Nebraska	1
Nevada	1
Virginia	1
Washington	1
Indiana	2
South Carolina	2
Tennessee	2
California	3
Massachusetts	3
Mississippi	3
Missouri	3
New Mexico	4
Alabama	5
Georgia	5
Ohio	5
Pennsylvania	6
North Carolina	7
Arizona	8
Louisiana	8
Oklahoma	10
Texas	12
Illinois	20
Florida	23

Source: Death Penalty Information Center

Since 1976, Texas has executed more than four times as many persons as has Virginia, the state with the second most executions during this period. Texas continues to use the death penalty more frequently than other states, with 17 executions in 2010, 24 executions in 2009, 18 executions in 2008,

Table 2.4
Number of Executions by State from 1976 through April 27, 2011

State	Total	2008	2009	2010 (December)
Texas	466	18	24	17
Virginia	108	4	3	3
Oklahoma	96	2	3	3
Florida	69	2	2	1
Missouri	68	0	1	0
Alabama	51	0	6	5
Georgia	49	0	3	2
Ohio	44	2	5	8
North Carolina	43	3	0	0
South Carolina	42	3	2	0
Louisiana	28	0	0	1
Arkansas	27	0	0	0
Arizona	25	0	0	1
Indiana	20	0	1	0
Delaware	14	0	0	0
California	13	0	0	0
Mississippi	13	2	0	3
Illinois	12	0	0	0
Nevada	12	0	0	0
Utah	7	0	0	1
Tennessee	6	0	2	0
Maryland	5	0	0	0
Washington	5	0	0	1
Nebraska	3	0	0	0
Pennsylvania	3	0	0	0
Kentucky	3	1	0	0
Montana	3	0	0	0
Oregon	2	0	0	0
Connecticut	1	0	0	0
Idaho	1	0	0	0
New Mexico	1	0	0	0

Table 2.4   (Continued)

State	Total	2008	2009	2010 (December)
Colorado	1	0	0	0
Wyoming	1	0	0	0
South Dakota	1	0	0	0
U.S. Government	3	0	0	0

Source: Death Penalty Information Center

and 26 in 2007. Of the 1,246 executions conducted in the United States since 1976, 574 (46.1%) took place in two states: Texas and Virginia. Texas actually conducted fewer executions in 2010 (17) than in 2009 (24)— a 29-percent drop.[13] Evidence of errors in capital cases in Texas emerged. A court of inquiry concluded that evidence used to convict Cameron Willingham of arson was unreliable. Willingham was executed in 2004. In another case, new DNA tests revealed that misleading evidence had been presented at the trial of Claude Jones, who was executed in 2000. A strand of hair that had been used to place Jones at the murder scene belonged to the victim, not to Jones.[14] Although these developments do not prove that innocent persons were executed, questionable evidence was used to obtain the convictions.

Some regional patterns are also apparent. Table 2.5 demonstrates some regional patterns. By far, most executions since 1976 have taken place in the South, followed, in descending order of frequency, by the Midwest, the West, and the Northeast.[15]

Consider also the corresponding regional murder rates per 100,000 from 2008 as displayed in Table 2.6.

Table 2.5
Executions by Region from 1976 through April 27, 2011

Region	Number	Percentage
South	1,023	82.1
Midwest	148	11.9
West	71	5.7
Northeast	4	0.3

Source: Death Penalty Information Center

Table 2.6
Murder Rates Per 100,000

Region	Murder Rate
South	6.0
West	4.5
Midwest	4.6
Northeast	3.8
National	5.0

Source: Death Penalty Information Center

As in previous years, the 2009 FBI Uniform Crime Report indicated that the South had the highest murder rate of any region in the country. The South also has had the highest execution rate, accounting for more than 80 percent of all executions carried out since 1976. The Northeast, with the lowest murder rate, has conducted the fewest executions over these years.[16]

As shown in Table 2.7, the number of death sentences per year has declined since the peak year of 1996, when 315 death sentences were handed down. In 2007, 2008, 2009, and 2010, there were 120, 119, 112, and 112, respectively. Since this is between two to three times the number of executions per year, death rows continue to grow, but more slowly.[17]

As displayed in Table 2.8, various methods of execution have been employed in contemporary times, including lethal injection, electrocution, lethal gas, hanging, and firing squads. The vast majority of states, as well as the federal government, provide for execution by lethal injection. The inmate is strapped onto a gurney with ankle and wrist restraints. A cardiac monitor is attached to a printer outside the execution chamber. Most jurisdictions use a combination of three drugs. At the warden's signal, sodium pentothal or sodium thiopental, a barbiturate that renders the inmate unconscious, is administered. If properly administered, the first drug ensures that the person does not feel pain. Next, pancuronium bromide, a muscle relaxant that paralyzes the lungs and diaphragm, is introduced to stop respiration. Finally, potassium chloride is used to cause cardiac arrest. Medical ethics prevent doctors from participating actively in executions, but a doctor is present to certify that the prisoner is dead. The most common problems are collapsing veins or an inability to insert the IV properly.[18]

Twenty jurisdictions provide for alternative methods of execution depending upon the choice of the inmate, the date of execution or sentence, or the possibility of the preferred method being held unconstitutional.[19] Nebraska

Table 2.7
Death Sentences

Year	Number of Death Sentences
1993	287
1994	313
1995	313
1996	315
1997	268
1998	294
1999	277
2000	224
2001	159
2002	166
2003	152
2004	140
2005	139
2006	123
2007	120
2008	119
2009	112
2010	112 (As of April 27, 2011)

Source: Death Penalty Information Center

Table 2.8
Executions from 1976 through April 27, 2011 by Method Used

Number of Executions	Method
1072	Lethal injection
157	Electrocution
11	Gas chamber
3	Hanging
3	Firing squad

Source: Death Penalty Information Center

is the only state that does not have lethal injection as a primary or optional method of execution. Nebraska provided electrocution as the sole method of execution. As noted, when this method was invalidated by the state Supreme Court, Nebraska's death penalty was, in effect, suspended. Since 1976, most executions have been carried out by lethal injection.[20]

In recent years, only three inmates have been executed by firing squads. All occurred in Utah. Gary Gilmore in 1977, John Albert Taylor in 1996, and, most recently, Ronnie Lee Gardner in 2010 were executed in this manner. This method was popular in the military during wartime, but there has only been one such execution since the Civil War: Private Eddie Slovik on January 31, 1945, during World War II. Only three states—Idaho, Oklahoma, and Utah—currently authorize firing squads as a method of execution. All three provide for lethal injection as the primary method. Shooting is used as an alternative contingent upon the choice of the inmate, impracticality of lethal injection, or lethal injection being held unconstitutional.[21]

A traditional firing squad consists of three to six shooters. The inmate is tied to a chair or stake. The shooters aim at the chest because this is an easier target to hit than the head. The officer in charge administers a final shot to the head of the inmate in the event that the initial volley fails to produce death. In Utah,

Execution chamber equipped with chair, restraints, and sandbags after the execution by firing squad of convicted murderer Ronnie Lee Gardner at Utah State Prison on June 17, 2010. (AP/ Wide World Photos)

the offender is placed in a specially designed chair. A pan is placed beneath the chair to catch and conceal blood and other fluids. A head restraint holds the inmate's head and neck in an upright position. The offender is dressed in dark blue clothing with a white cloth circle attached by Velcro to an area over the heart. Sandbags are placed behind the inmate to absorb the bullets and prevent ricochets. Twenty feet in front of the offender is a wall with firing ports for the members of the firing squad. Following the offender's statement, a hood is placed over the inmate's head. The warden leaves and shooters aim their rifles at the white cloth circle on the offender's chest. On the command to fire, the shooters fire simultaneously. One member of the firing squad has a blank charge in his rifle, but no member knows which one has fired the blank charge.[22]

Hanging is the oldest method of execution in the United States. It fell out of favor during the twentieth century following numerous botched attempts. If careful measuring and planning are not done, strangulation or beheading can occur. Electrocution replaced hanging for a time as the most common method. There have been only three executions by hanging since 1977: Westley Dodd (1993) and Charles Campbell (1994), both in the state of Washington, and, most recently, Billy Bailey (1998) in Delaware. Only three states—Delaware, Washington, and New Hampshire—currently authorize hanging as a method of execution. All three provide for lethal injection as the primary method.[23]

An inmate to be hanged is escorted, in restraints, to the gallows area and is placed over a hinged trap door. Following the offender's last statement, a hood is placed over the inmate's head. Restraints are also applied. A determination of the appropriate amount of "drop" is based on the inmate's size and is calculated using a standard military execution chart for hanging. An inmate is weighed the day before the execution and a rehearsal is conducted using sandbags the same weight as the prisoner. A rope of manilla hemp is used. The rope is of at least 3/4" and not more than 1 1/4" in diameter and is approximately 30 feet in length. It is soaked and stretched while drying to eliminate any spring or stiffness. The hangman's knot is tied pursuant to military regulations. The knot is treated with wax, soap, or clear oil to make sure that the rope slides smoothly through the knot. The noose is placed around the offender's neck, with the knot behind his or her left ear, which will cause the neck to snap. The trap door opens, the inmate drops, and, if properly done, death is caused by dislocation of the third and fourth cervical vertebrae.[24]

The gas chamber as an execution method was inspired by the use of toxic gas during World War I. Nevada, in 1924, was the first state to execute an inmate in this way. Lethal gas has been used for execution 31 times. Walter LeGrand was the last inmate to be executed in this fashion. His execution took place in Arizona on March 3, 1999. Only four states—Arizona, California, Missouri, and Wyoming—currently authorize lethal gas as an alternative method of execution. All four use lethal injection as the primary method.[25]

Most jurisdictions with provisions for executions by lethal gas use an airtight steel execution chamber. The inmate is placed in a chair and restrained at the chest, waist, arms, and ankles. The offender wears a mask during the execution. The chair has a metal container beneath the seat. Cyanide pellets are placed in this container. A metal canister under the container is filled with sulfuric acid. Three executioners participate. Each turns one key. When all three keys are turned, the cyanide pellets drop into the sulfuric acid, producing lethal gas. Unconsciousness can occur quickly if the offender takes a deep breath. If the inmate holds his or her breath, death can take considerably longer and the prisoner goes into convulsions. Death is estimated to occur within 6 to 18 minutes. A heart monitor is read in the control room. After the warden pronounces the inmate dead, ammonia is pumped into the execution chamber to neutralize the lethal gas. Exhaust fans remove remaining fumes from the room into two scrubbers. The neutralizing process takes approximately 30 minutes from the time of death.[26]

From 1930 through 1980, electrocution was the most common method of execution in the United States. In addition to previously discussed Nebraska, seven states—Alabama, Arkansas, Florida, Kentucky, Oklahoma, South Carolina, Tennessee, and Virginia—currently provide for electrocution as an as an alternative execution method. Witness accounts of burning and failure to cause death without repeated shocks caused electrocution to be replaced with lethal injection as the most common method of execution. Of countries outside the United States that utilize capital punishment, none provide for execution by electrocution. It is of some interest to note that the Humane Society of the United States and the American Veterinarian Medical Association both reject electrocution as a method of euthanasia for animals. Paul Warner Powell is the most recent person to have been executed in this way. He died in the Virginia electric chair on March 18, 2010.[27]

In his dissent to the Supreme Court's denial of *certiorari* in *Glass v. Louisiana* (1985), Justice William Brennan said that electrocution was comparable to "disemboweling while alive, drawing and quartering, public dissection, burning at the stake, and breaking at the wheel." Brennan noted that prisoners sometimes catch on fire and that witnesses hear a sound "like bacon frying" while the "sickly sweet smell of burning flesh permeates the chamber." The prisoner "almost literally boils" and when the autopsy is performed, the liver is so hot that doctors have reported that it "cannot be touched by the human hand."

Typical electrocution protocols provide for the use of a wooden chair with restraints and connections to an electric current. The chair is made of oak. It is set on a rubber mat and is bolted to a concrete floor. The inmate is placed in the chair. Lap, chest, arm, and forearm restraints are secured. A leg piece is attached to the inmate's right calf and a sponge and electrode are also attached. A metal headpiece includes a leather hood to conceal the offender's face. The metal part of the headgear includes a copper wire mesh screen to which the electrode is attached. A wet sponge is placed between the electrode and the inmate's scalp. The circuit breaker is engaged and an automatic cycle lasting 38 seconds begins. A current of electricity passes through the offender's body. If the inmate is not pronounced dead, the cycle is repeated.[28]

Oklahoma was the first state to adopt lethal injection as an execution method. Texas performed the first lethal injection in 1982 with the execution of Charlie Brooks. The 35 states that prescribe lethal injection as the sole or primary method of execution include Alabama, Arizona, Arkansas, California, Colorado, Connecticut, Delaware, Florida, Georgia, Idaho, Indiana, Kansas, Kentucky, Louisiana, Maryland, Mississippi, Missouri, Montana, Nevada, New Hampshire, New Mexico, New York, North Carolina, Ohio, Oklahoma, Oregon, Pennsylvania, South Carolina, South Dakota, Tennessee, Texas, Utah, Virginia, Washington, and Wyoming. The federal government also uses lethal injection as the primary method. However, the Violent Crime Control Act of 1994 provides that the method to be used is that of the state in which the conviction took place.[29]

Public support for capital punishment peaked in 1994 when 80 percent of those surveyed by Gallup indicated that they favored the death penalty for persons convicted of murder. In May 2006, the Gallup Poll found that overall support of the death penalty was down to 65 percent. The same poll revealed that when respondents were given the alternative sentencing option of life imprisonment with absolutely no possibility of parole, more chose life imprisonment (48%) than the death penalty (47%).[30] Table 2.9 displays Gallup Poll results since 1994.[31]

Venezuela (1853) and Portugal (1867) were the first nations to abolish the death penalty.[32] Today, it has been virtually abolished throughout western Europe and Latin America. Jamaica retains the death penalty but has not executed anyone since 1988; under Jamaican law, a death sentence that is not carried out within five years of sentencing is commuted to life imprisonment.

China currently holds first place in using the death penalty. Although figures on executions are not released to the public, it is estimated that China executes several hundred people per year. China is followed in the number of executions by Iran, Saudi Arabia, Pakistan, and the United States. A broad swath of Asian (Pakistan, Afghanistan, Bangladesh, Japan, Vietnam, Singapore, Indonesia) and Middle Eastern countries (Iraq, Yemen, Kuwait, Syria), and some African nations (Equatorial Guinea, Libya, Sudan, Ethiopia, Botswana) also retain

Table 2.9
Gallup Polls: "Are You in Favor of the Death Penalty for a Person Convicted of Murder?"
(Results Displayed as Percentages)

Date	For	Against	No Opinion
September 6–7, 1994	80	16	4
May 11–14, 1995	77	13	10
February 8–9, 1999	71	22	7
February 14–15, 2000	66	28	6
June 23–25, 2000	66	26	8
August 29–Sept 5, 2000	67	28	5
February 19–21, 2001	67	25	8
May 10–14, 2001	65	27	8
October 11–14, 2001	68	26	6
May 6–9, 2002	72	25	3
October 10–13, 2002	70	25	5
May 5–7, 2003	74	24	2
May 19–21, 2003	70	28	2
October 6–8, 2003	64	32	4
May 2–4, 2004	71	26	3
May 2–5, 2005	74	23	3
October 13–16, 2005	64	30	6
May 2–5, 2006	65	28	7
October 4–7, 2007	69	27	4

Source: Office of the Clark County Prosecuting Attorney

the death penalty. In Eastern Europe, only Belarus has continued to use the death penalty.[33]

Canada abolished the death penalty in 1976. The South African constitutional court prohibited the death penalty as inhumane in 1995, the year after apartheid ended. Between 1989 and 1995, two dozen other countries abolished the death penalty. More than half of all nations have abolished the death penalty. The United Nations General Assembly enacted a formal resolution urging nations to abolish the death penalty.[34] Mexico refuses to extradite criminals to the United States unless there is a commitment that the death penalty will not be sought against them. Predictably, this has resulted in attempts by murderers in Texas to flee to Mexico. Murderers have also fled to Canada from the United States, even appearing on television to explain it was because of Canada's lack of a death penalty, but Canada decides on a case-by-case basis whether it will or will not return to the United States anyone likely to be executed.[35]

NOTES

1. DPIC Document, "Facts About the Death Penalty," http://www.deathpenalty info.org/FactSheet.pdf (April 29, 2011).

2. DPIC, "Facts."

3. DPIC, "Facts."

4. See Prof. David Baldus's report to the ABA, 1998, as cited in DPIC, "Facts." A Baldus study figured prominently in *McCleskey v. Kemp* (1987), discussed elsewhere in this book.

5. Jeffrey Pokorak, *Cornell Law Review*, 1998, as cited in DPIC, "Facts."

6. Jack Borger and Isaac Unah, University of North Carolina, 2001, as cited in DPIC, "Facts."

7. Pierce and Radelet, *Santa Clara Law Review*, 2005, as cited in DPIC, "Facts."

8. NAACP Legal Defense Fund, January 1, 2010, cited in DPIC, "Facts."

9. See Clark County Prosecuting Attorney document "The Death Penalty in the U.S. (1976–2008)," http://www.clarkprosecutor.org/html/death/dpusa.htm (December 31, 2010).

10. Staff Report, House Judiciary Subcommittee on Civil and Constitutional Rights, October 1993, with updates from DPIC, as cited in DPIC, "Facts."

11. DPIC, "Facts."

12. DPIC, "Facts."

13. DPIC, "Facts."

14. DPIC, "The Death Penalty in 2010: Year End Report," December 2010.

15. DPIC, "Facts." Federal executions are listed in the region in which the crime was committed.

16. DPIC, "Facts."

17. Bureau of Justice Statistics, "Capital Punishment 2006," as cited in DPIC, "Facts." The 2009 figure is based on DPIC research.

18. See Clark County Prosecuting Attorney document, "Methods of Execution," http://www.clarkprosecutor.org/html/death/methods.htm (December 31, 2010). In *Baze and Bowling v. Rees*, 553 U.S. 35 (2008), the U.S. Supreme Court rejected the claim of two Kentucky inmates that the state's lethal injection process constituted cruel and unusual punishment. The case is discussed elsewhere in this book.

Some material regarding methods of execution was expanded upon in Melusky, "From Burning at the Stake to Lethal Injection: Evolving Standards of Decency and Methods of Execution," a paper delivered at a meeting of the National Science Association, Las Vegas, NV (April 17–19, 2011).

19. Clark County Prosecuting Attorney document, "Methods of Execution."

20. DPIC, "Facts."

21. Clark County Prosecuting Attorney documents, "Methods of Execution" and "U.S. Executions since 1976."

22. Clark County Prosecuting Attorney document, "Methods of Execution."

23. Clark County Prosecuting Attorney documents, "Methods of Execution" and "U.S. Executions since 1976."

24. Clark County Prosecuting Attorney document, "Methods of Execution."

25. Clark County Prosecuting Attorney documents, "Methods of Execution" and "U.S. Executions since 1976."

26. Clark County Prosecuting Attorney document, "Methods of Execution."

27. Clark County Prosecuting Attorney documents, "Methods of Execution" and "U.S. Executions since 1976."

28. Clark County Prosecuting Attorney document, "Methods of Execution."

29. Clark County Prosecuting Attorney document, "Methods of Execution." As discussed previously, in 2004, the New York Supreme Court invalidated existing death penalty procedures. The state legislature did not enact revisions, effectively suspending the death penalty in New York.

30. DPIC, "Facts." Five percent of those surveyed expressed no opinion. See also Clark County Prosecuting Attorney document, "Public Opinion Polls," http://www.clarkprosecutor.org/html/death/opinion.htm (December 31, 2010).

31. Adapted from Clark County Prosecuting Attorney document, "Public Opinion Polls."

32. "Arguments For and Against Capital Punishment," http://www.capital punishmentuk.org/thoughts.html (December 31, 2010).

33. Quintin Chatman, ed., "Death Penalty Roundtable." *The Champion* 32 (July 2008): 14–21.

34. Hugo Adam Bedau, "The Case Against The Death Penalty," The American Civil Liberties Freedom Network, http://www.aclu.org/capital/general/10441pub 19971231.html (13 March 2009).

35. See *Beard v. Kindler*, 558 U.S. (2009). In 1982, Joseph Kindler murdered a codefendant who was about to testify against Kindler in a Pennsylvania burglary trial. After a jury recommended Kindler receive the death penalty, he escaped and fled to Canada, where he fought extradition, escaped from Canadian prison, then fought extradition again. Returned to Pennsylvania in 1991 for the formality of hearing his sentence pronounced by the court, Kindler has litigated challenges to his death sentence for the last 19 years. A federal appeals court overturned Kindler's sentence because it believed the jury instruction to be erroneous, but the Supreme Court vacated that decision and told the lower court to consider whether Kindler had forfeited his right to have his appeal heard by fleeing from justice.

3

The United States Constitution and Capital Punishment

The capital punishment debate in the United States must be considered against a constitutional backdrop because it has evolved from a political debate over liberty versus authority into a legal debate over how decisions are made in a deliberately fragmented government. The United States Constitution provides a basic framework for the American political system. It establishes structures and rules and prescribes how public officials will be selected. It delegates powers to governmental institutions. It also places limits on governmental powers by specifying that individuals possess certain rights that may not be infringed.

The Constitution was written in 1787. No constitution in the world has lasted as long as that of the United States. Nearly two-thirds of the world's 160 national constitutions have been written or revised since 1970. Only 14 predate World War II. The average nation has had two constitutions since 1945.[1] The United States Constitution has proven to be extremely durable.

The original Constitution contained just 4,223 words. That word count would cover approximately 17 double-spaced pages using any standard word-processing program. The first 10 amendments (originally called "articles"), known as the Bill of Rights, were drafted almost immediately and were ratified in 1791. But only 17 amendments have been added since that time. Two of these amendments—the 18th, establishing, and the 21st, repealing, Prohibition respectively—cancel each other. How has such a short Constitution remained viable for so long?

The secret to the Constitution's durability is its language. Many provisions were written in rather general, open-ended fashion. For example, the Constitution grants Congress the power to make laws "necessary and proper" to execute its enumerated powers. It guarantees the right to a "speedy trial" by an "impartial jury." It prohibits "unreasonable searches and seizures." It requires that arrest and search warrants be accompanied by "probable cause." What do these and other constitutional phrases mean? The framers did not specify.

The use of such open-ended language can be traced, in part, to the framers' inability to resolve certain disputes in more concrete fashion. To cite just one example, the framers were unable to reach an acceptable compromise concerning voting rights. They finally decided to let each state set its own suffrage requirements. Wide variations resulted. However, in other places, the Constitution's sometimes-ambiguous language can also be credited to the framers' foresight and ingenuity. They were not drafting a mere traffic code that could be revised easily, conveniently, and frequently. The relatively open language of the Constitution permits it to evolve with changing times. The framers laid down a series of general concepts and fundamental principles, but they left the precise meaning of their words to future generations. Such constitutional flexibility is the key to the document's continuing relevance and viability, making it a growing, changing, "living Constitution."[2] The use of that phrase is a red flag to some because the Supreme Court members most notably associated with it in the 1970s and 1980s, Justices William Brennan and Thurgood Marshall, used it to mean that the Constitution mandated a particular set of political choices, including the abolition of the death penalty.[3] Nevertheless, the term accurately describes the point that without the need of revolution or amendment, the document written to set up the federal government of a strip of former English colonies along the Atlantic coast in the days of sailing ships has been adequate to frame the government of an administrative and bureaucratic state with global commitments.

An imprecise constitution requires interpretation. From the beginning, courts have been asked to interpret the Constitution and to apply it to contemporary matters. The interpretive discretion of judges is considerable, but it is not unlimited. Judges are expected to rely upon relevant precedents, the actual text of the provision in question, legislative history, and the assumed intent of the framers. Even the most activist judges do not feel free to substitute what they consider to be wise policy for the decisions made by the elected representatives of the people. They are not free to write their own policy preferences into the law. But while judicial discretion is limited, judging is not a purely mechanical process.

Consider the term "intent of the framers."[4] It can be difficult to determine what the framers really intended. They sometimes disagreed. Records are incomplete. For that matter, who should be included when consulting these "framers" if we are to follow their intent? Seventy-four delegates were originally selected to attend the Constitutional Convention. Nineteen refused or were unable to attend. Fifty-five delegates attended. Of these, 13 left early. Four of these 13—Luther Martin and John Mercer of Maryland and John Lansing and Robert Yates of New York—left in protest. Certainly, the views of the 39 delegates who participated in the 1787 Constitutional Convention in Philadelphia and who voted to approve the document are relevant. But what about three delegates—Elbridge Gerry of Massachusetts and George Mason and Edmund Randolph of Virginia—who participated in the debates, who helped to shape the constitutional text, but who refused to sign on the final day? Do their views matter to us today? Should their views be taken into account? It is also important to recall that the Constitution did not take effect until it was ratified by nine states. State-level ratification conventions were held to make these decisions. What about the views expressed by delegates who participated in these state ratification conventions? Do their intentions count? Furthermore, even if we could agree on whose views are relevant and even if we could ascertain the framers' intentions, should judges ignore more than two centuries of legal developments since the framers' time?

If the Constitution were more explicit, fewer disputes about its meaning would arise and it would not make much difference who the judges were. But the document would require constant revision to account for technological and social changes.

The Eighth Amendment prohibits "excessive bail" and "excessive fines." What is "excessive"? The framers wisely did not specify a dollar amount here, for if they had, periodic constitutional amendments would be necessary to adjust for changes in the cost of living—"constitutional cost of living adjustments" as it were. In addition, wealth is relative. What is excessive for one person may be a trifling amount or pocket change for another.

The Eighth Amendment also prohibits "cruel and unusual punishments." What does this phrase mean? Does it mean the same thing now as it did during the framers' times? Did it mean the same thing when the framers considered it in 1791 as it did when Parliament considered the phrase in the English Bill of Rights in 1689? Does the phrase apply to anything other than execution methods? Reflect upon history's drowning pits, crucifixions, pressing boards, and the like. Today, most would reject torture, mutilation, and boiling as unacceptable forms of punishment. Most would agree that burning at the stake, drawing and quartering, or breaking someone on the wheel are cruel and unusual punishments, but that was not always the case. The guillotine was welcomed as a progressive reform when it was introduced in the eighteenth century. Previously, an inept or drunken executioner might have required several blows to sever a head. An improperly fashioned noose could leave the condemned person to suffocate slowly. As discussed previously, if the drop is too short, slow death by strangulation results. If the drop is too long, the head may be torn from the body. The nineteenth century's technological solution to botched hangings was the electric chair. Electric chairs have malfunctioned with gruesome results. Witnesses have reported smoke rising from the head and the smell of burning flesh. It is uncertain how long the electrocuted individual remains conscious. In the twentieth century, some states moved to use of the gas chamber as a more humane method for performing executions. In the twenty-first century, most states and the federal government have moved to lethal injections, and the debate over cruelty continues as a question of whether one drug or a combination of drugs is most effective.

There is no doubt that some methods are more painful than others. Some opponents of capital punishment, however, argue that the notion of any "humane execution" is a contradiction in terms. Such arguments hold that capital punishment is barbaric. It is offensive to prevailing standards of decency. Its legitimacy does not turn on *how* it is applied. Capital punishment is *absolutely* prohibited by the Eighth Amendment. It is *always* cruel and unusual punishment. Period. In response, it can be argued that the framers of the Constitution unquestionably did not intend to ban capital punishment. They revealed their acceptance of capital punishment in the text of the Fifth Amendment, which provides that persons shall not be deprived of "life, liberty, or property without due process of law." *Life*, liberty, or property. Persons *can* be deprived of their lives provided that they receive due process of law. Here, their intent seems clear.

The question that comes immediately to mind, however, is: What is "due process of law"? Whatever it is, if you receive it, you can be deprived of your property, your liberty, and even your life! A complete answer is beyond the scope of this volume. Suffice it to say at present that due process involves the belief that all persons are entitled to fundamentally fair treatment. Coercing a defendant into confessing to a crime, denying the defendant the right to counsel, and trying the defendant before a biased jury would be unfair. Inconsistent or racially biased sentencing is unfair. For these reasons, courts have used the Due Process Clause of the Fifth and Fourteenth Amendments to review how capital cases are brought to court and tried and how sentences are determined.

Moreover, the Supreme Court has held that the concept of cruel and unusual punishment is not restricted to capital cases. Noncapital punishments can be cruel and unusual if they are arbitrary or excessive. A sentence disproportionate to the crime may be considered cruel and unusual. But constitutionally disproportionate punishment is a rare bird: the Supreme Court in *Ewing v. California* (2003) held that under a mandatory sentencing system, a three-time offender might be sentenced to life imprisonment (with opportunity for parole after 25 years) for shoplifting three golf clubs. Lesser sentences can catch the public eye. In 1994, Michael Fay, an American citizen who committed an offense in Singapore, was sentenced to be beaten with a cane. The event took place outside United States jurisdiction and many Americans, unaware that until 1839, federal law had provided for flogging, too, were outraged and debated whether such forms of punishment are acceptable. What about the so-called chemical castration of sex offenders? So far the Supreme Court has avoided giving an opinion on the subject.

Prison conditions also have given rise to Eighth Amendment claims. Supreme Court Justice Clarence Thomas and some academics have pointed out the difficulties of using the Eighth Amendment as a source of law to regulate prison conditions, since in most cases those conditions are not themselves intended as punishment. Nevertheless, the body of law regulating prison medical care, discipline, and uses of force has been extensively developed by judges in the last 40 years. Prison litigation has taken an increasing share of the federal courts' time and resources, paradoxically just as states and cities began spending unprecedented amounts of money to build modern prisons and jails: in the early 1970s, only about 2,000 lawsuits were filed by prisoners in state and county prisons, but by the 1990s, nearly 40,000 were being filed annually, even though modern prisons were vastly improved in almost every respect. Congress made one major effort to change the law in this area in 1996 by enacting the Prison Litigation Reform Act. The Act abolished free filing of prisoner complaints: inmates are now required to pay the same filing fee that all litigants do (currently $350) even if they have to pay it in installments, and after three meritless complaints, a prisoner has to pay the full fee at the outset of the case. The Act also significantly reduces the power of federal judges to release prisoners on the grounds of overcrowding or to issue orders supervising the management of state and local prisons. Both had been the sources of great political friction, particularly in the 1980s. After 1996, prison lawsuits in federal court dropped markedly at first but have steadily increased in recent years and are now approaching 50,000 per year.

Finally, neglect of mitigating circumstances and/or exaggeration of aggravating circumstances can produce constitutional objections. When determining whether punishment is cruel or unusual, most recent court decisions have been concerned with whether the punishment fits the crime or whether it is the one intended by the legislature.[5]

But let us dig a little deeper for the constitutional record of the death penalty in the United States. To begin as close to the beginning as possible, in 1775, the year before the Declaration of Independence, the Second Continental Congress met to coordinate the colonies' action against the British. A committee chaired by Pennsylvania's John Dickinson was appointed to draft the Articles of Confederation in 1778, and the Articles set up a loose central government with power over the conduct of wars and foreign policy. After all the colonies had ratified them, the Articles took effect in March 1781 with the cessation of military action in the Revolutionary War. The Articles provided for a Congress but no president or other form of executive officer and no judiciary. The Articles of Confederation made no attempt to establish any criminal laws for the nation or to limit the penalties provided in any state's laws and provided, to the contrary, that any power not "expressly delegated" to the United States was retained by each state.

The Articles proved unsatisfactory to unite the newly independent states in their commercial dealings with one another or with England or to establish an effective means to retire the debts incurred by Congress in financing the Revolutionary War. Attempts to amend the Articles to allow Congress to levy taxes or to strengthen the central government's power to execute the laws foundered on rivalry between different sections of the country and on the requirement that any amendment to the Articles be unanimously approved. In September 1786, delegates from five states attended a conference in Annapolis, Maryland, to discuss interstate commercial problems. At about the same time, armed resistance to property foreclosures broke out in western Massachusetts. Led by Revolutionary War veteran Daniel Shays, the rebellion was sparked by complaints that the state was trying to retire its war debt on the backs of the farmers, and the unrest caused courthouses to close and public officials to flee. The confluence of crises caused some observers to fear that the new country was slipping into anarchy.

Shays' Rebellion was quelled by early 1787, at about the same time the Articles of Confederation Congress approved a follow-up to the Annapolis convention for the purpose of proposing amendments to the Articles of Confederation "to render the constitution of the Federal Government adequate to the exigencies of the Union." From May to September 1787, critics of the Articles of Confederation and proponents of a stronger national government met in Philadelphia. Going far beyond simple amendment, the delegates spent the summer of 1787 debating the fundamental reorganization of national government and its powers and, by September 1787, had drafted what became the Constitution.

Shays' Rebellion had, in a small way, contributed to the drafting of the Constitution, but issues of crime and punishment had little to do with the widespread dissatisfaction with the Articles of Confederation or, for that matter, the Revolutionary War. Taxation without representation and

The U.S. Constitution is signed at the Constitutional Convention of 1787 in Philadelphia. After widespread dissatisfaction concerning the Articles of the Confederation, supporters of a stronger national government came together to draft and sign the Constitution of the United States. (Library of Congress)

interference with colonial self-government had been the chief complaints that motivated the signing of the Declaration of Independence. It certainly was not dissatisfaction with the harshness of English criminal law: in fact, the only two abuses of English criminal law by King George III and his ministers that were included in the list of grievances in the Declaration of Independence in 1776 were the deprivation of the right to a jury trial and the right to be tried in the place where the crime was committed and not transported "beyond Seas." These grievances mostly related to the attempts by British customs officials to collect taxes and customs duties by steering trials to admiralty courts in England and the West Indies, which sat without juries and therefore contained no friendly faces for American smugglers.[6]

In 1787, 11 years after the Declaration of Independence and with the danger of being taken to London for an admiralty court trial long past, specific protections against the two grievances listed in the Declaration of Independence were written into Article III, Section 2, Clause 3 of the new Constitution. A guarantee against cruel and unusual punishment was not included. In fact, James Madison's notes of the proceedings of the Constitutional Convention in the Summer of 1787 reflect little debate on the subject of crimes other than treason. The principal controversy in the drafting of the

Constitution was over how to apportion representation in Congress. The few provisions that dealt with criminal law mostly affected procedure or the definition of treason, not the severity of penalties. Congress had the power to impeach the President and other officers, but there would be no repeat of Parliament's execution of Charles I: Article I, Section 3 limited the punishment for impeachment to removal from office. An impeached official was still subject to appropriate prosecution in a court of law, however. Prohibitions against any "bills of attainder" and "ex post facto Law" in Article I, Section 9 were based on the same principle as Article I, Section 3: Congress had no power to condemn without a trial or make retroactive criminal laws. These prohibitions did not, however, regulate what punishments could be imposed after trial. As for treason, Article III, Section 3 limited Congress's power to punish the family of a traitor but declared without qualification that "Congress shall have the power to declare the Punishment of Treason." Article I, Section 8 likewise gave Congress the power to define "and punish" piracy and other felonies on the high seas and offenses against the law of nations. Since the traditional penalty for both piracy and treason was death, we can presume that everyone understood that the new federal government could impose the death penalty.

As you can see, constitutional provisions were written in rather general, open-ended terms, in some cases because the framers so thoroughly understood the accepted meaning of the terms that they needed no elaboration and in some cases because the framers deliberately left certain disputes unresolved until another day. The silence of the Constitution about cruel and unusual punishments is for the former reason, not the latter. It is *probable* that the framers would have said that the Constitution did not authorize cruel or unusual punishments even for pirates and traitors. It is *certain* that the framers did not deliberately omit more extensive discussion of crime and punishment in the document because there was controversy over the subject and they needed to defer it to another day.[7] Because the Constitution created a federal system, they understood that state law would govern almost all crime and punishment.

After the signing of the Declaration of Independence, and in some cases before it, the States had taken care to declare that although they were free of English sovereignty, they would retain the better parts of England's civil and criminal law. Eleven states drafted new constitutions between 1776 and 1778. In most cases, the major change was the weakening or even elimination of the power of the governor and the transfer of power to the legislature. What tinkering was done with existing laws was to express a commitment to the liberties of Englishmen the colonists had believed were under attack.

One significant example was Virginia's Declaration of Rights, modeled on the English Declaration of Rights of 1688, drafted for the Virginia Colonial Convention by George Mason after the royal governor dissolved Virginia's House of Burgesses. The Declaration included the provision "That excessive bail ought not to be required nor excessive fines imposed, nor cruel and unusual punishments inflicted." Whether copying English law directly or by way of George Mason, virtually identical prohibitions soon appeared in the 1776 Declarations of Rights enacted by Delaware, Maryland, and North Carolina and in subsequent versions of state constitutions or Bills of Rights enacted in 1783 in New Hampshire, in 1787 in New York, and in 1790 in South Carolina and Pennsylvania.[8]

To George Mason and his contemporaries, "cruel and unusual punishments" did not mean the death penalty. As an example, Thomas Jefferson was part of the committee charged with declaring what criminal law Virginia would follow after independence. In 1779, he drafted "A Bill for Proportioning Crimes and Punishments."[9] The bill is notable both for its retention of capital punishment and for Jefferson's comments on capital punishment. Jefferson prefaced the bill with the statement that the reformation of offenders was one of the objects of law and was not "effected at all by capital punishments, which exterminate instead of reforming, and should be the last melancholy resource against those whose existence is become inconsistent with the safety of their fellow citizens." Following Beccaria, whom Jefferson cited throughout his private footnotes, Jefferson proposed to substitute labor on public works for the death penalty in manslaughter, counterfeiting, arson, robbery, burglary, and theft cases so that the criminals "might be rendered useful in various labors for the public, and would be living and long-continued spectacles to deter others from committing the like offences." Jefferson's code nevertheless prescribed death by hanging for murder and treason, death by poison for murder by poisoning, castration for rape, and ducking and flogging "at the discretion of a jury, not to exceed fifteen stripes," for fortunetelling.

AMENDING THE CONSTITUTION

The lack of an explicit prohibition in the Constitution against the infliction of cruel and unusual punishments, whatever that meant, was nevertheless one of the many perceived flaws that the Antifederalists, as those opposed to the new stronger central government came to be called, stressed in their efforts to block ratification of the Constitution or to call for a second Constitutional Convention. In the 1788 ratifying convention in Virginia, delegate Patrick Henry (who had refused to go to Philadelphia because "he smelled a rat") objected with his usual rhetorical vehemence to the lack of a provision banning cruel and unusual punishments:

What has distinguished our ancestors?—That they would not admit of tortures, or cruel and barbarous punishment. But Congress may introduce the practice of the civil law, in preference to that of the common law. They may introduce the practice of France, Spain, and Germany—of torturing, to extort a confession of the crime. They will say that they might as well draw examples from those countries as from Great Britain, and they will tell you that there is such a necessity of strengthening the arm of government, that they must have a criminal equity, and extort confession by torture, in order to punish with still more relentless severity. We are then lost and undone.[10]

A similar objection was made by Abraham Holmes in the Massachusetts ratifying convention:

They are nowhere restrained from inventing the most cruel and unheard-of punishments and annexing them to crimes; and there is no constitutional check on them, but that *racks* and *gibbets* may be amongst the most mild instruments of their discipline.[11]

The remarks by Henry and Holmes appear to be less concerned with punishment after conviction and more to be concerned with the possibility that the federal government might create specialized prerogative courts like the ones the Tudor and Stuart kings had created in England, and worse, that they would be based on the Roman civil law model and adopt rules of procedure used on the Continent. Opponents of ratification professed to fear that this would permit the use by federal judges of torture as an inquisitorial device, even as France and other European countries were on the verge of abolishing the practice. Whether the objections addressed genuine fears or not, these and similar criticisms had great rhetorical effect. Antifederalists throughout the United States, and some Federalists as well, felt that protection against cruel and unusual punishments and the other keystones of English liberty spelled out in the English Bill of Rights also should be expressly set out in the Constitution.

James Madison protested that imitating the English experience in this respect was unnecessary, even counterproductive, because the contemporary European theory was that charters were grants of rights by the king to the people. To the contrary, Madison argued, the Constitution was a charter of powers granted by the people to the government.

New York was both geographically and politically central to the contest over ratification. Madison, with Alexander Hamilton and John Jay of New York, wrote a series of 85 essays in support of ratification known as *The Federalist Papers* that were published in New York City newspapers between

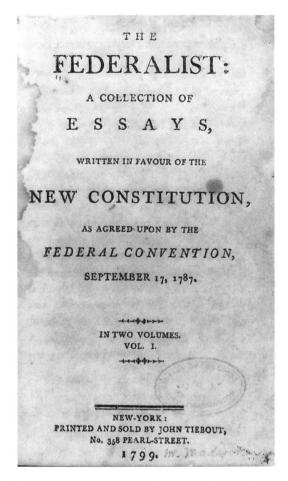

Title page of *The Federalist*, published in 1799. (Library of Congress)

October 1787 and May 1788.[12] In *Federalist*, No. 84, Hamilton argued that a Bill of Rights was inconsistent with the concept that the people were sovereign. Because no power to impose cruel and unusual punishments was ever delegated to the new national government, Hamilton argued, none existed. As such, a written Bill of Rights was unnecessary. Worse, argued Hamilton, any attempt to list what governmental abuses were prohibited might invite "men disposed to usurp" power to act on the policy that anything not specifically prohibited was permitted. That is, a written Bill of Rights was dangerous if some important right might inadvertently be omitted.

New Hampshire became the ninth state to ratify the Constitution on June 21, 1788, making the new form of government legally valid. The indispensable ratification by Virginia took place four days later and that of New York in the following month. Both Virginia and New York's ratification statements called for an explicit ban on cruel and unusual punishment. Massachusetts, South Carolina, and New Hampshire had ratified the Constitution with proposed amendments, and so did North Carolina and Rhode Island when they eventually ratified in November 1789 and May 1790, respectively. To satisfy these demands, to forestall attempts to call a second Constitutional Convention, and to fulfill the campaign promise he made while campaigning in Virginia in the election of 1789 for a seat in the House of Representatives, James Madison introduced proposed amendments to the Constitution in the fall of 1789. Madison used George Mason's language from the Virginia Declaration of Rights banning cruel and unusual punishment as the model for one of the proposed amendments submitted for ratification by the states in 1789. By December 15, 1791, 10 amendments had been ratified by the necessary three-fourths of the states,[13] and the Eighth Amendment was in effect. There had been little recorded debate on the subject in the First Congress, and what little there had been featured opposition to the amendment. Samuel Livermore of New Hampshire told his fellow representatives:

The clause seems to express a great deal of humanity, on which account I have no objection to it; but, as it seems to have no meaning in it, I do not think it necessary. What is meant by the terms "excessive bail?" Who are to be the judges? What is understood by "excessive fines?" It lays with the court to determine. No cruel and unusual punishment is to be inflicted; it is sometimes necessary to hang a man, villains often deserve whipping, and perhaps having their ears cut off; but are we, in future, to be prevented from inflicting these punishments because they are cruel? If a more lenient mode of correcting vice and deterring others from the commission of it could be invented, it would be very prudent in the legislature to adopt it; but until we have some security that this will be done, we ought not to be restrained from making necessary laws by any declaration of this kind.[14]

Despite Livermore's warnings against being soft on crime, the notes of the debate indicate that the amendment "was agreed to by a considerable majority."[15]

The Eighth Amendment was not drafted to give judges a way to restrain bloodthirsty legislators. To the contrary, the framers had faith in the legislature. Most were legislators. More of them feared judges, and federal judges in particular, as enemies of liberty.[16] Modern slogans about three equal branches of government notwithstanding, judicial weakness and dependence on the other two branches, not equality, was the way the framers meant things to be.[17] Hamilton explained in *Federalist*, No. 78, that the federal judiciary was designed to be the least dangerous branch, exercising judgment but not will, controlling neither the legislative-branch purse nor the executive-branch sword. He further attempted to allay fears of a federal judiciary in *Federalist*, No. 80, by claiming that danger of "judiciary encroachments on the legislative authority . . . is in reality a phantom." Hamilton had real fears to allay because down through the seventeenth century, judges appointed by the king and subservient to the Crown had been some of Parliament's most determined foes. Parliament's supremacy over the king had been accomplished, in fact, with the beheading of King Charles I in 1649 and announced in law with the acceptance of the Bill of Rights in 1689 and Act of Settlement in 1701 by William and Mary. In the latter act, Parliament took care to provide that judges would hold office "during good behavior" instead of at the pleasure of the king but were removable by Parliament. By confirming that judges were secure in their offices from the king, Parliament created the possibility of something new in history, a judiciary as an independent branch of government. At the end of the eighteenth century, the framers' imitation of their example made possible the American experiment of judges using a written Constitution as the means of protecting individual rights from government intrusion.

By granting the crown to William and Mary only under the condition of accepting Parliament's legislation, Parliament had plainly declared itself the "senior partner" in English government. The founders of this country were determined partisans of that tradition of legislative supremacy. The United States first constitution, the Articles of Confederation, for all practical purposes was only a legislature with no executive or judicial branches. Even when that system proved inadequate and they sought a new written Constitution, they looked almost exclusively to England's unwritten constitution as their model. In some respects, they misinterpreted what they saw. Separation of powers, for instance, though highly praised by Montesquieu, was an effect of Parliament's freedom from royal control, not a cause of that freedom. After all, modern bureaucracies routinely combine law making, law enforcement, and adjudication within their agencies, yet few people fear tyranny will result from this.

In other respects, the Americans were behind the times in what they saw. Although religious dissenters and those with other needs to get out of town quickly came to America throughout the seventeenth century, after the Glorious Revolution, there was no reason for the upper-class Whigs to flee the Crown: in the eighteenth century, they ran England. The traffic went in the other direction, as many established families in Virginia and Massachusetts sent their sons back to England for education and to catch up on the latest fashions.[18] For the most part, political fashions were likewise produced in England and consumed in America. The preeminent example is Blackstone's *Commentaries*: published just before independence, it sold, according to

Edmund Burke, almost as many copies in the colonies as in England.[19] In addition to copies brought back by Americans educated at the Inns of Court in London, prepublication sales of the 1771 American edition of the *Commentaries* reached 1,500.[20]

Some of the ideas the colonies and, later, the newly independent United States imported were just a little out of date. For example, the Second Amendment's guarantee of the right to bear arms was a relic of the fear in the 1600s that the King, whether James I, Charles I, Charles II, or James II might attempt to create a standing army and become an absolute monarch. The Third Amendment's ban on the peacetime quartering of troops on private property was similarly a proposed solution to a past political controversy that no one expected to recur in America.[21] Other provisions of the first eight amendments contain similar anachronistic solutions to crises from English history, not to contemporary American controversies.

This is true of the Eighth Amendment, too. The language of the prohibition against "cruel or unusual punishments" in the Northwest Ordinance and the almost identical prohibition against "Cruel and Unusual Punishments" in the Eighth Amendment was a comfortable phrase well-rooted in English history. But for that very reason, the prohibition was, like some of the other amendments, more rhetorical reassurance against the Bloody Assizes than a response to the tide of cruel executions after Shays' Rebellion, executions that never took place. There was no attempt to define what practices were banned by the Eighth Amendment, because America was widely noted for the leniency of its criminal penalties.[22] The first federal crime bill passed in 1790 contained a mandatory death penalty by hanging for treason, murder, piracy and other offenses on the high seas, and counterfeiting. There was some controversy in the First Congress over the provision directing that an executed defendant's body should be delivered to medical schools for use in training doctors, but none over the death penalty itself.[23]

The common law—law made by judges on a case-by-case basis—had evolved in England over centuries in which the king was looked upon as the source of justice. His appointees, the judges, served as "lions under the throne," the king's representatives responsible for defining crimes and determining their punishment. In England, that judicial lawmaking role lingered for more than a century after Parliament had displaced the King as the country's maker of laws. In the United States, from the start, there was no Crown, and under the Constitution, it was clear that Congress made the law. The President was no elected king, and his duty was to faithfully execute—not make—the law. But even in this country, the concept of crime as something defined by statute and with punishment fixed by the legislature was something novel in the eighteenth century and still developing in the nineteenth.

Through the nineteenth century, in state after state, judges steadily withdrew (or were evicted by legislatures) from their historic role of defining crimes and punishments until, in time, their role was limited to what it is now, trying individual cases and imposing penalties set by the legislature. In the federal judiciary, this shift in the theory of crime and punishment from judge-defined crimes to legislature-defined crimes was announced early, during John Marshall's career as the fourth Chief Justice of the Supreme Court.

On May 7, 1806, the *Connecticut Courant* accused President Jefferson and the Congress of having secretly voted a bribe of $2 million dollars to Napoleon Bonaparte "for leave to make a treaty with Spain." The judges of the lower federal courts were divided over the question of whether they had jurisdiction, like their counterparts in England, to try the defendants for criminal libel despite the absence of a statute. The Supreme Court[24] had already, in *Marbury v. Madison* (1803) and *Fletcher v. Peck* (1810), claimed the power of judicial review, that is, its power to *interpret* the Constitution "to say what the law is," and whether federal or state statutes were constitutionally valid. However, the Court now made it clear, in *United States v. Hudson and Goodwin* (1812), that it was the job of the legislature and not the judiciary to decide what the law would be in the first place:

Although this question is brought up now for the first time to be decided by this Court, we consider it as having been long since settled in public opinion.

* * *

The only ground on which it has ever been contended that this jurisdiction could be maintained is, that, upon the formation of any political body, an implied power to preserve its own existence and promote the end and object of its creation, necessarily results to it.

* * *

But . . . it would not follow that the Courts of that Government are vested with jurisdiction over any particular act done by an individual in supposed violation of the peace and dignity of the sovereign power. The legislative authority of the Union must first make an act a crime, affix a punishment to it, and declare the Court that shall have jurisdiction of the offence.

If the Supreme Court had not withdrawn from the federal judiciary the power to write its own criminal code, the Supreme Court and the lower federal courts might have been forced to engage in the kind of internal debate over the permissible scope of criminal sanctions that it reached out to undertake in the twentieth century. But Marshall expressed the unanimous opinion of the Court that it was the job of "the legislative authority" to "affix a punishment" to a crime. Because the Court and Congress did not noticeably disagree about what punishments were cruel and unusual, this left the Eighth Amendment without much use for a century.

Supreme Court Justice Joseph Story, who, like Chief Justice Marshall, served for more than three decades on the court and who also was one of Harvard Law School's first professors, published *Commentaries on the Constitution*, perhaps the most influential legal treatise in America since Blackstone's *Commentaries*. Story's *Commentaries* went through several editions as a guide to the Constitution for nineteenth-century lawyers. Writing in 1833, Story dismissed the Eighth Amendment as of historical interest only:

This is an exact transcript of a clause in the bill of rights, framed at the revolution of 1688. The provision would seem to be wholly unnecessary in a free government, since it is scarcely possible, that any department of such a government should authorize, or justify such atrocious conduct. It was, however, adopted as an admonition to all departments of the national government, to warn them against such violent proceedings, as had taken place in England in the arbitrary reigns of some of the Stuarts.[25]

Story reflected the thinking of the time in three respects. First, the Eighth Amendment was an admonition to all departments of the national government, but not to the states. Second, it was scarcely possible that Congress would authorize or the judiciary justify "cruel punishments." In other words, the cruel and unusual punishments clause was proper in the English Bill of Rights because in 1688, judges were still dangerous tools of the Crown who had considerable power to control the substance of the criminal law. In the United States, by contrast, the Constitution already restrained the power of judges to be cruel because it gave Congress the power to create or abolish the lower federal courts and to prescribe their jurisdiction, powers Congress had not been shy about using. Further, Congress hardly needed the Bill of Rights to tell itself not to be cruel because the legislature, in the view of Story and his age, was the very guardian of the people's liberties. Third, that the death penalty was not cruel was so well understood that Story need not even mention it. Compared to the loud and growing debate over slavery, capital punishment rated hardly a whisper.

In the generation after Story, Justice Thomas Cooley of the Michigan Supreme Court published, in 1868, *A Treatise on the Constitutional Limitations Which Rest Upon the Legislative Power of the States of the American Union*.[26] Like Story, Cooley believed that the Cruel and Unusual Punishment Clauses in state constitutions that paralleled the Eighth Amendment in the federal Constitution restrained a legislature's power to declare punishments by statute. He could ignore the other "departments" mentioned by Story, because by this time judges had the power to pronounce sentence or to choose a punishment within a range fixed by the legislature but retained almost no power to declare criminal punishments generally. Cooley's view is worth noting:

It is certainly difficult to determine precisely what is meant by 'cruel and unusual punishment.' Probably any punishment declared by statute for an offense which was punishable in the same way at the common law could not be regarded as cruel or unusual, in the constitutional sense. And probably any new statutory offense may be punished to the extent and in the mode permitted by the common law for offenses of similar nature. But those punishments which in any state had become obsolete before its existing constitution was adopted, we think may well be forbidden by it as cruel and unusual.

Cooley's treatise added an important new observation: the concept of cruelty could *evolve*. The United States had been born into an age that already believed in the idea of progress, but this was the era of Darwin's *Origin of Species* (1859), and Cooley perhaps took something new from his times. If the death penalty had become obsolete and was out of use, as was the case in Michigan, then perhaps Cooley was suggesting that it was unusual and therefore beyond the power of the legislature to revive. Punishments could, in other words, go extinct.

Although the death penalty was commented on by thinkers like Cooley and fiercely debated in state legislatures, the Supreme Court in the nineteenth century never entered the debate over what criminal penalties the states could impose or, with few exceptions, what procedures the states could use to impose them. As Cooley noted, there were already prohibitions against cruel and unusual punishment in most state constitutions. Second, the nineteenth century generally was a time when death penalty laws were being increasingly limited. Third, there was no legal basis for the Supreme Court to apply the Eighth Amendment to most death penalty cases because those cases took place in state courts under state law. The Supreme Court could not declare that cruel and unusual punishment meant the same thing in Vermont as in Georgia, for instance, because until well after the ratification of the Fourteenth Amendment in 1868, the Eighth Amendment, like the rest of the Bill of Rights, was a set of limits that applied only to the powers of the federal government. The Supreme Court, again in an opinion written by Chief Justice Marshall, had expressly held that to be so in *Barron v. Baltimore* (1833). Barron owned a wharf in the Baltimore harbor that became useless as a result of municipal improvements to the harbor that caused silt to accumulate and prevented large ships from docking. Barron sued, claiming that the City of Baltimore had taken his property without just compensation, something the federal government would be prohibited from doing by the Fifth Amendment. Barron contended that the amendment should protect him from state and local government action as well. Chief Justice Marshall held for a unanimous court that the Fifth Amendment's limitations were "naturally, and, we think, necessarily applicable" only to the federal government, and that if the framers of the amendments had "intended them to be limitations on the powers of the State governments they would have imitated the framers of the original Constitution, and expressed that intention."

In 1868, in the wake of the Civil War, "that intention" of subjecting the states to the Constitution was expressed in the Fourteenth Amendment. Section 1 of the amendment, after reversing the *Dred Scott* decision by providing that "all" persons including African-Americans were citizens of the United States, placed a new limitation directly on the states:

No State shall make or enforce any law which shall abridge the privileges and immunities of citizens of the United States, nor shall any State deprive any person of life, liberty, or property without due process of law; nor deny to any person within its jurisdiction the equal protection of the laws.

Like the Fifth Amendment, the Fourteenth clearly contemplated that a state could deprive a person of life as long as it provided due process, but what process was due? Unfortunately, the sponsors of the Fourteenth Amendment had been no more specific than in the Fifth Amendment, and each ratifying state had a different set of criminal penalties and procedures.[27]

The Supreme Court began to fill in the blanks in the meaning of due process in the succeeding decades. That counsel for criminal defendants would seek to use this process of interpreting the Fourteenth Amendment and that this interpretive process would ultimately have an impact on the death penalty can be first seen in *Hurtado v. California* (1884). Hurtado was sentenced to death for murder. In California, a prosecution for murder started by the filing of a simple complaint, called an "information," by the prosecutor. The Fifth Amendment, by contrast, required the federal government in capital cases to use the centuries-older practice of a grand jury hearing the prosecutor's evidence and returning an indictment. Hurtado argued that the Fourteenth Amendment's requirement of due process meant that California must now use the indictment procedure, too, and because California had not, he was at least entitled to a new trial. Justice Stanley Matthews's majority opinion upheld the conviction. In a foreshadowing of the debates of the twentieth century over the meaning of "cruel and unusual," the majority opinion by Matthews and the dissent by the first Justice John Marshall Harlan looked to the history of English criminal procedure since the *Magna Carta* and drew quite different conclusions. The majority observed that "due process" historically excluded bills of attainder, bills of pains and penalties, acts of confiscation, acts reversing judgments or directly transferring one man's estate to another, "and other similar special, partial, and arbitrary exertions of power under the form of legislation." There was nothing in the use of an information instead of an indictment, the majority held, that resembled these practices. After declaring that there was nothing in the concept of due process that prohibited either changes in laws or differences in procedure in different jurisdictions, Matthews and the majority held:

It follows that any legal proceeding enforced by public authority, whether sanctioned by age and custom or newly devised in the discretion of the legislative power in furtherance of the public good, which regards these principles of liberty and justice, must be held to be due process of law.

In dissent, Justice John Marshall Harlan, most famous today for his historic dissent in *Plessy v. Ferguson* (1896), drew the opposite conclusion from the same history:

If particular proceedings, conducted under the authority of the general government, and involving life, are prohibited because not constituting that due process of law required by the fifth amendment of the constitution of the United States, similar proceedings, conducted under the authority of a state, must be deemed illegal, as not being due process of law within the meaning of the fourteenth amendment. The words "due process of law," in the latter amendment, must receive the same interpretation they had at the common law from which they were derived and which was given to them at the formation of the general government.

The boundaries of the debate were marked out. Either due process meant exactly what it meant from the beginning and meant the same thing everywhere, or due process was flexible, could evolve, and could mean different things in different places at the discretion of the legislature. Notice, however, that it was the *proponents* of executing Hurtado who were the ones advocating a flexible living interpretation of due process. The justices insisting that good jurisprudence required adherence to the original meaning of the constitutional text were the ones arguing *against* executing Hurtado. A century later, the arguments would stay the same, but the sides making the arguments would switch: death penalty advocates now argue that the Bill of Rights permitted capital punishment in 1791 and opponents are free to amend it, but not to ignore it, while death penalty opponents deride the view that the meaning of the Bill of Rights was fixed in 1791 as tantamount to saying that the Bill of Rights has an expiration date.

That the concept of a flexible "living constitution" could help criminal defendants as well as hurt them was seen in the very year after *Hurtado.* In

Ex parte Wilson (1885), the Supreme Court came close to adopting Judge Cooley's suggestion that punishments could be constitutional in one age but unconstitutional in the next. Wilson was sentenced to 15 years at hard labor for counterfeiting government bonds. Like Hurtado, Wilson had been charged by information and not in an indictment returned by a grand jury. Unlike Hurtado, Wilson was being prosecuted in federal court, so the Fifth Amendment undoubtedly required a grand jury indictment so long as Wilson's crime was capital or "infamous." Responding to the prosecution's argument that Wilson's crime was not infamous because Congress had not declared punishment at hard labor to be infamous, the Court unanimously held:

What punishments shall be considered as infamous may be affected by the changes of public opinion from one age to another. In former times, being put in the stocks was not considered as necessarily infamous. And by the first judiciary act of the United States, whipping was classed with moderate fines and short terms of imprisonment in limiting the criminal jurisdiction of the district courts to cases 'where no other punishment than whipping, not exceeding thirty stripes, a fine not exceeding one hundred dollars, or a term of imprisonment not exceeding six months, is to be inflicted.' Act September 24, 1789, c. 20, § 9, (1 St. 77.) But at the present day either stocks or whipping might be thought an infamous punishment.

By declaring that a particular punishment was severe enough to require an indictment under the Fifth Amendment, the Court was still a large step from declaring that a punishment was cruel and unusual and thus banned by the Eighth Amendment. But it was an important indicator that the Supreme Court thought the trend of the times was toward ever more lenient penalties, so that what was once commonplace was now infamous.

But capital punishment was still not in any case believed to be cruel or unusual by the Supreme Court, as the Court showed in a case from the Utah Territory, *Wilkerson v. Utah* (1878). Wilkerson was a convicted murderer who appealed from the judgment of the territorial court, where the Eighth Amendment applied, that he be executed by a firing squad. Wilkerson argued that he should not be shot, although he apparently conceded that he could be hanged. An earlier statute providing that he could be beheaded had been repealed. Justice Clifford delivered the unanimous opinion of the Court affirming the sentence:

Cruel and unusual punishments are forbidden by the Constitution, but the authorities referred to are quite sufficient to show that the punishment of shooting as a mode of executing the death penalty for the crime of murder in the first degree is not included in that category, within the meaning of the eighth amendment. Soldiers convicted of desertion or other capital military offences are in the great majority of cases sentenced to be shot, and the ceremony for such occasions is given in great fulness by the writers upon the subject of courts-martial.

* * *

Where the conviction is in the civil tribunals, the rule of the common law was that the sentence or judgment must be pronounced or rendered by the court in which the prisoner was tried or finally condemned, and the rule was universal that it must be such as is annexed to the crime by law. Of these, says Blackstone, some are capital, which extend to the life of the offender, and consist generally in being hanged by the neck till dead.

* * *

Such is the general statement of that commentator, but he admits that in very atrocious crimes other circumstances of terror, pain, or disgrace were sometimes superadded. Cases mentioned by the author are, where the prisoner was drawn or dragged to the place of execution, in treason; or where he was embowelled alive, beheaded, and quartered, in high treason. Mention is also made of public dissection in murder, and burning alive in treason committed by a female. History confirms the truth of these atrocities, but the commentator states that the humanity of the nation by tacit consent allowed the mitigation of such parts of those judgments as savored of torture or cruelty, and he states that they were seldom strictly carried into effect.

* * *

Difficulty would attend the effort to define with exactness the extent of the constitutional provision which provides that cruel and unusual punishments shall not be inflicted; but it is safe to affirm that punishments of torture, such as those mentioned by the commentator referred to, and all others in the same line of unnecessary cruelty, are forbidden by that emendment to the Constitution.

* * *

Had the statute prescribed the mode of executing the sentence, it would have been the duty of the court to follow it, unless the punishment to be inflicted was cruel and unusual, within the meaning of the eighth amendment to the Constitution, which is not pretended by the counsel of the prisoner. Statutory directions being given that the prisoner when duly convicted shall suffer death, without any statutory regulation specifically pointing out the mode of executing the command of the law, it must be that the duty is devolved upon the court authorized to pass the sentence to determine the mode of execution and to impose the sentence prescribed.

As *Wilkerson* shows, the Eighth Amendment was assumed by the Court to preclude only tortures such as drawing and quartering, public dissection, and burning alive, which counsel for Wilkerson "could not pretend" resembled death by firing squad.

Twelve years later, in 1890, burning alive came to the Supreme Court in a form not anticipated by Justice Clifford. *In re Kemmler* (1890) was a challenge to New York's adoption of electrocution as its modern method for capital punishment. William Kemmler was the first man condemned to die in the electric chair at Auburn State Prison, which had been the state's model progressive reformatory. Accepting completely the determination made by New York's highest court that electrocution was a humane way to die, Chief Justice Fuller spoke for a unanimous Supreme Court. He avoided any reexamination of the New York courts' determination, after an evidentiary hearing, that electrocution was humane:

It appears that the first step which led to the enactment of the law was a statement contained in the annual message of the governor of the state of New York, transmitted to the legislature January 6, 1885, as follows: "The present mode of executing criminals by hanging has come down to us from the dark ages, and it may well be questioned whether the science of the present day cannot provide a means for taking the life of such as are condemned to die in a less barbarous manner. I commend this suggestion to the consideration of the legislature." The legislature accordingly appointed a commission to investigate and report "the most humane and practical method known to modern science of carrying into effect the sentence of death in capital cases." This commission reported in favor of execution by electricity.

* * *

It is not contended, as it could not be, that the eighth amendment was intended to apply to the states, but it is urged that the provision of the fourteenth amendment, which forbids a state to make or enforce any law which shall abridge the privileges or immunities of citizens of the United States, is a prohibition on the state from the imposition of cruel and unusual punishments, and that such punishments are also prohibited by inclusion in the term "due process of law."

* * *

So that, if the punishment prescribed for an offense against the laws of the state were manifestly cruel and unusual as burning at the stake, crucifixion, breaking on the wheel, or the like, it would be the duty of the courts to adjudge such penalties to be within the constitutional prohibition. And we think this equally true of the eighth amendment, in its application to congress.

* * *

The enactment of this statute was, in itself, within the legitimate sphere of the legislative power of the state, and in the observance of those general rules prescribed by our systems of jurisprudence; and the legislature of the state of New York determined that it did not inflict cruel and unusual punishment, and its courts have sustained that determination. We cannot perceive that the state has thereby abridged the privileges or immunities of the petitioner, or deprived him of due process of law.

Despite the confidence of the Supreme Court in the accuracy of New York's determination that electrocution was humane, the execution of Kemmler was

Ethel (left) and Julius Rosenberg ride to separate prisons following their espionage convictions on March 29, 1951. The Rosenbergs were sentenced to death by electrocution. (Library of Congress)

protracted and gruesome, so disturbing that the next five electrocutions were closed to witnesses.[28] The electric chair was moved to Sing Sing Prison in 1891, where it remained for the next 72 years and 614 executions,[29] most famously those of Julius and Ethel Rosenberg in 1953.

In 1892, the Supreme Court heard the appeal of John O'Neil, a New Yorker who sold alcoholic beverages, some of which were to be delivered to Vermont, a dry state. Jurors in Vermont convicted O'Neil of 307 counts of selling intoxicating liquors without a license, one count for each bottle. He was sentenced to pay a fine of $6,140 ($20 dollars a bottle) plus costs. To ensure the payment of this sum, it was ordered that if O'Neil did not pay the fine promptly, he would be confined at hard labor in the house of correction for more than 54 years. In *O'Neil v. Vermont* (1892), the Supreme Court dismissed the challenge to the conviction on procedural grounds, holding that the issue of cruel and unusual punishment had not been properly raised, and besides, the Eighth Amendment did not apply to the states. Justice Field's dissent from the dismissal argued that the punishment was both unusual and cruel:

That designation, it is true, is usually applied to punishments which inflict torture, such as the rack, the thumb-screw, the iron boot, the stretching of limbs, and the like, which are attended with acute pain and suffering. Such punishments were at one time inflicted in England, but they were rendered impossible by the declaration of rights, adopted by parliament on the successful termination of the revolution of 1688, and subsequently confirmed in the bill of rights. It was there declared that excessive bail ought not to be required, nor excessive fines imposed, nor cruel and unusual punishments inflicted. From that period this doctrine has been the established law of England, intended as a perpetual security against the oppression of the subject from any of those causes.

* * *

The inhibition is directed, not only against punishments of the character mentioned, but against all punishments which by their excessive length or severity are greatly disproportioned to the offenses charged. The whole inhibition is against that which is excessive either in the bail required, or fine imposed, or punishment inflicted.

* * *

The state may, indeed, make the drinking of one drop of liquor an offense to be punished by imprisonment, but it would be an unheard-of cruelty if it should count the drops in a single glass, and make thereby a thousand offenses, and thus extend the punishment for drinking the single glass of liquor to an imprisonment of almost indefinite duration. The state has the power to inflict personal chastisement, by directing whipping for petty offenses,—repulsive as such mode of punishment is,—and should it, for each offense, inflict 20 stripes, it might not be considered, as applied to a single offense, a severe punishment, but yet, if there had been 307 offenses committed, the number of which the defendant was convicted in this case, and 6,140 stripes were to be inflicted for these accumulated offenses, the judgment of mankind would be that the punishment was not only an unusual, but a cruel, one, and a cry of horror would rise from every civilized and Christian community of the country against it. It does not alter its character as cruel and unusual that for each distinct offense there is a small punishment, if, when they are brought together, and one punishment for the whole is inflicted, it becomes one of excessive severity.

Although Justice Field's denunciation of Vermont's laws was, after all, a dissent, he was probably not alone on the Court in his dismay at the unusually severe penalty imposed in a relatively new approach to the perceived dangers of drinking, and one wonders how the law might have developed if O'Neil's attorney had properly raised the issue of cruel and unusual punishment.[30] The Supreme Court was hardly a hanging court. In *Winston v. United States* (1899), the Court reversed three murder convictions in the District of Columbia in which the trial judges had instructed juries that they should avoid the death sentence only if the defendants had demonstrated some good reason for a lesser penalty. The justices held that Congress's abolition in 1897 of the mandatory death penalty for federal crimes gave the jury unfettered discretion to order the imposition of a life sentence rather than the death penalty. The Supreme Court also did not hesitate in this era to strike down other criminal punishments imposed by federal laws that it believed were unauthorized by the Constitution. In 1896, the Court unanimously overturned a sentence of 60 days' hard labor imposed on illegal aliens by an immigration official. In *Wong Wing v. United States* (1896), the Court held that while Congress could order Chinese immigrants deported and even confine them while awaiting removal, it had no authority to give an immigration official the power to sentence them to hard labor: that was a criminal punishment and therefore required a trial in a court. But *Winston* and *Wong Wing* were federal cases. As *Kemmler* showed, the attitude of the Supreme Court toward state law that imposed the death penalty for crimes that had always been felonies remained the traditional hands-off one.[31] And almost all the death penalty cases were brought in state courts under state law.

A NEW DIRECTION?

In 1910, the Supreme Court overturned a criminal sentence for the first time on the ground that it was cruel and unusual punishment. Paul Weems, a disbursing officer of the government installed in the Philippines by the United States after the Spanish American War, was convicted of falsifying public documents to enrich himself by about 600 pesos. Under the law in force in the Philippines, which had been adopted from the Spanish penal code, Weems was sentenced to not less than 12 years of *cadena temporal*, that is, hard labor while fettered in chains from the wrists to the ankles. Weems was forbidden visitors while in prison, and after release, the law required Weems to register his address with the authorities for the rest of his life and to submit to searches at any time.

Justice Joseph McKenna[32] wrote for the majority that Weems' punishment violated the Eighth Amendment, which Congress had made part of Philippine law by statute. After review of the debates in the First Congress over the Eighth

Amendment and the commentaries by Story and Cooley, McKenna had to concede that the Eighth Amendment gave the judiciary no authority to rewrite a legislature's code of crimes and punishments. Nevertheless, McKenna claimed that *Wilkerson, Kemmler,* and *O'Neil,* taken together, stood for the principle that the "cruel and unusual punishment" banned by the Eighth Amendment included not only physical torture, "but . . . all punishments which, by their excessive length or severity, are greatly disproportioned to the offenses charged." In the Court's most important contribution from this era to the death penalty decisions that would be handed down 50 years later, McKenna offered this principle of constitutional interpretation:

The clause of the Constitution in the opinion of learned commentators may be therefore progressive, and is not fastened to the obsolete but may acquire meaning as public opinion becomes enlightened by a humane justice.

With just a slight hint that the features of Weems's punishments—chains, isolation, and registration with the authorities—smacked of the Spanish Inquisition, the Court held that the severity of Weems's punishment, especially when compared to federal law, made it cruel and unusual. It is ironic that the condition of perpetual registration imposed on Weems that the Court appeared to single out as peculiarly severe is one routinely imposed today.

But the decision in *Weems* drew little interest and less imitation. A short, unsigned student note in the *Harvard Law Review* commented that the decision approved "the extension of [the Eighth Amendment's] scope to keep pace with the increasing enlightenment of public opinion." The comment from the academy never discussed the penalties actually imposed on Weems or the Court's reasoning, confining itself to the observation that the "ordinary death penalty" was "universally permitted" by the Eighth Amendment and that "a new and humane method of inflicting the old punishment of death," such as electrocution, or the punishment of death imposed for a new crime like attempted train robbery, was neither unusual or cruel.[33] Well into the middle of the twentieth century, courts cited *Weems* only to dismiss it, as they upheld punishments, from flogging with a cat-of-nine tails to surgical sterilization, against arguments that the Cruel and Unusual Punishments Clause forbade them.[34]

The relatively minor changes pronounced by the Supreme Court in crime and punishment did not mean the nation as a whole was not changing or that the Supreme Court's role in it was not changing significantly in ways that would eventually affect its decisions about capital punishment. The final decade of the nineteenth century had seen the United States involved in a war with Spain that temporarily gained what some hoped and others feared would be an overseas empire. The new century would also see the adoption of a more activist approach to government regulation of the domestic economy. More importantly, for the most part, Americans abandoned their original understanding of the purpose of government as securing life, liberty, and the pursuit of happiness but otherwise doing nothing to affect whether individuals would sink or swim in favor of a much more interventionist role for government. The invention of and proliferation of regulatory commissions like the Interstate Commerce Commission and the Federal Trade Commission and the delegation of the increasingly complex work of governing to appointed professionals to administer the tariff laws and new legislation like the Pure Food and Drug Act was not just inevitable but welcomed across the political spectrum.

This new confidence in progressive and professional government extended to criminal law as well. Notable public figures like John Dewey called for "Scientific Penology" and renewed interest in rehabilitation as a goal of the criminal justice system. In the last quarter of the nineteenth century, states began to experiment with innovations such as an indeterminate sentence accompanied by the possibility of parole and the use of separate courts for juvenile offenders. In 1891, the federal government finally began building its own prison system instead of housing federal prisoners in state prisons or city jails when Congress authorized the building of federal penitentiaries at Atlanta, Georgia, Leavenworth, Kansas, and McNeil Island, Washington. In the same year, Congress passed the Evarts Act (named after New York senator William Evarts, who had been part of the prosecution team against Jefferson Davis and who had defended President Andrew Johnson after his impeachment), which attempted to take some of the pressure off the increasingly busy Supreme Court by creating the modern three-tiered structure of federal courts. District court judges heard most federal criminal trials. The innovation was the creation of the new Courts of Appeals, which reviewed cases within a multistate region known as a "circuit." Final review remained in the Supreme Court. To understand how important the creation of the Courts of Appeal was to criminal cases, consider that the Supreme Court held in *McKane v. Durston* (1894), and has never overruled its holding, that the Constitution's Due Process Clauses do not *require* any appeal from a criminal conviction. In fact, federal criminal trials had, until 1891, been held for almost 100 years without a right to an appeal in most cases, even from a death sentence. Being able to obtain a second look at your federal criminal conviction from someone other than the judge who tried you was a significant procedural protection.

The next major innovation came in 1925, when Chief Justice William Howard Taft (who had been president from 1909 to 1913) persuaded Congress to enact the Judiciary Act of 1925. The "Judges Bill" reduced the types of cases that the Supreme Court was *required* to hear and provided that the Court could, instead, choose to review the decision of a lower court by issuing a writ of *certiorari*. If the Supreme Court wished to deny *certiorari*, the Court could let the decision of the Courts of Appeal stand without comment. What the nation at large noticed was that the Supreme Court could now shape the law by picking and choosing which cases it wished to review. The Supreme Court no longer even attempted to sit merely to correct the errors of lower courts but rather to make broad statements about constitutional law and national policy. What criminal defendants, their attorneys, and prosecutors noticed was that these changes made the Courts of Appeal the court of last resort for most litigants. To illustrate, the Supreme Court, in recent years, has received between eight and nine thousand petitions for writs of *certiorari* annually and has decided between 70 and 80 cases each year. That includes the cases the Supreme Court is still legally obligated to hear. It is under no pressure but its own to decide any more cases, and even in its most prolific era decided only about 150 cases each year. A year with five death penalty decisions is a big year for the Court. Meanwhile, the Courts of Appeal receive between 10,000 and 15,000 federal criminal appeals each year, and another five to six thousand appeals from decisions on *habeas corpus* petitions attacking state court convictions. Approximately 200 of those appeals involve death sentences. The Courts of Appeal eventually must decide them all. As a result, only a small percentage of death penalty decisions end in any place other than the Courts of Appeal, courts that few Americans other than lawyers even know exist.

As an illustration, consider two garden-variety death penalty cases decided about a year apart by the same three judges on one Court of Appeals, the Fourth Circuit, which is composed of Maryland, West Virginia, Virginia, North Carolina, and South Carolina. It is typically regarded as a conservative court in a conservative part of the country. In the first case, *Branker v. Gray* (2008), William Gray murdered his wife in 1992 during a bitter divorce, shooting her in the head after tackling her in front of a jogger who heard the victim say, "If you leave he'll kill me." Gray, a prosperous dentist who had his divorce lawyer present during police questioning, washed the gunshot residue off his hands in front of his lawyer; he later refused to take the advice of his attorney and hire a psychiatrist. After being convicted and sentenced to death, Gray appealed with new lawyers to the North Carolina Supreme Court, which affirmed his sentence in 1997. The United States Supreme Court denied *certiorari* a year later. With more new lawyers, Gray filed what is called a collateral attack on his conviction. If a direct appeal is the legal means of claiming that something went wrong at trial, a collateral attack can be described as the legal means of claiming that something went wrong that never got into the trial.

For example, Gray claimed that his trial attorney was ineffective for failing to present evidence of his poor psychiatric condition to stave off the death penalty and therefore violated the Sixth Amendment's guarantee of the assistance of counsel. The trial court rejected this claim in 2000, and the North Carolina Supreme Court again denied relief. In 2002, Gray filed a petition for a writ of *habeas corpus* in federal court, which a federal district judge denied. Gray appealed to a three-judge panel of the Fourth Circuit, which split 2–1 in deciding that Gray was guilty of murder but that Gray's death penalty was invalid because his attorney had indeed violated the Sixth Amendment by failing to present psychiatric testimony that Gray was mentally ill. The dissenting judge pointed out that the majority relied for its decision on a single psychiatric evaluation six years after the murder and disregarded seven eyewitnesses to Gray's actual state of mind at the time of the murder. The United States Supreme Court denied review.

About a year later, the same three judges split 2–1 in *Winston v. Kelly* (2010), with the same judge writing the majority opinion but with the dissent this time complaining the evidence should prevent a death sentence. Leon Winston and another man broke into a Virginia home in 2002 and shot a husband and wife in front of their nine-year-old daughter, who gave conflicting evidence about who pulled the trigger. Virginia law holds that mere accomplices of the triggerman cannot receive the death penalty. Winston was convicted and sentenced to death, and the Virginia Supreme Court affirmed in 2004. After the United States Supreme Court denied *certiorari*, Winston pursued a collateral attack based on his counsel's failure to present evidence that Winston has an I.Q. of 66 and has other mental problems that the Supreme Court in *Atkins v. Virginia* (2002) held are mitigating factors that would prevent a death sentence. Virginia's courts denied relief in 2007, and Winston filed a *habeas corpus* petition in federal district court, which issued partial relief in proceedings in 2008 and 2009. In 2010, the Fourth Circuit panel held that the finding that Winston's trial counsel was not ineffective was a reasonable one, although it did send the matter back for further hearing before the district court. The dissent complained that the admitted evidence of Winston's retardation and manipulability made further proceedings, after which Winston could still get the death penalty, a defiance of the Supreme Court precedent. A few months later, the Supreme Court denied both Winston and the Commonwealth of Virginia's petitions for *certiorari*. The matter remains before the district court considering the *habeas corpus* petition.

Clearly a *habeas corpus* petition is a key part of the death penalty process: Gray may live and Winston may die as a result of it. Everyone has heard that *habeas corpus* is Latin for "you have a body," but what is it? In part, the meaning of *habeas corpus* is as obscure as its Latin origin, but under English law, a writ of *habeas corpus* was originally a command by one court to another court or to a warden to show some reason why a prisoner was being held. In other words, it was a means the king's judges used to make sure that a prisoner was not being held without trial, especially without a trial that could bring money to the royal treasury. By the end of the seventeenth century, this had evolved into a remedy even against the king and was seen by Parliament as a way to prevent arbitrary pretrial detention. In America, the issue was preserved in the Constitution's prohibition against suspension of the writ of *habeas corpus* "except when in Cases of Rebellion or Invasion when the public Safety may require it." In other words, lengthy detention without trial was forbidden.

All first, federal courts could only issue writs to federal prisoners. After the Civil War, Congress amended the *habeas corpus* statute to prohibit detention anywhere in violation of the Constitution or federal law, in part to allow federal judges to release persons taking part in Reconstruction from being put in jail by southern judges. But *habeas corpus* still only examined whether the pretrial detention was legal, that is, whether the state court had jurisdiction over the defendant at all. After trial, a defendant had an appeal, if state or federal law allowed it, and *habeas corpus* had nothing to do with the matter. This led to some obvious injustices, as in *Frank v. Mangum* (1915). Leo Frank was a Jew charged in Georgia with the murder of teenage Mary Phagan. The public sentiment against Frank was manifest, and to avoid being lynched, Frank was not even in the courtroom when the verdict was read. Frank appealed from the denial of his petition for *habeas corpus*, but the Supreme Court stated that no matter how serious, "mere errors in point of law" were to be corrected by an appeal in the state court and were not reviewable in a federal *habeas corpus* petition. Four months later, a lynch mob kidnaped Frank and hanged him, cutting off any review that might have taken place in state court.

Eight years later, the Supreme Court reversed course in *Moore v. Dempsey* (1923) and granted a writ of *habeas corpus* for defendants sentenced to death in Arkansas. Like Frank, they challenged their sentences on the grounds that their trial had been dominated by threats of mob violence and that they had not been afforded due process. The defendants were Black men charged with the murder of a White deputy sheriff, and even though they had been given a trial (which lasted 45 minutes, during which their appointed counsel called no witnesses), their convictions (after 5 minutes of deliberations) were obtained with the pressure of a lynch mob standing literally right outside the courthouse. The Supreme Court issued a writ of *habeas corpus*, reasoning that the defendants were entitled to a hearing to prove their claims, because

Leo Frank's petition for *habeas corpus* was denied by the Supreme Court. Shortly afterward, he was kidnaped from jail and lynched in Marietta, Georgia, on August 17, 1915. (Library of Congress)

the threat of mob violence deprived the defendants of due process of law and that a court so influenced had no genuine claim to jurisdiction. This expansion of the writ of *habeas corpus* provoked a furious dissent from Justice McReynolds, who warned that "the delays incident to enforcement of our criminal laws have become a national scandal and give serious alarm to those who observe."

Habeas corpus was still a rare federal remedy for total breakdowns in the state courts, and hardly a federal get-out-of-jail-free card. For instance, in *Johnson v. Dye* (1949), the Third Circuit Court of Appeals granted the *habeas corpus* petition of a Black inmate who escaped from a Georgia chain gang on the grounds that the frequent beatings and other mistreatment inflicted cruel and unusual punishment on the escaped prisoner. The Supreme Court reversed in a one-sentence order.

But if a "deprivation of due process" that would justify the writ of *habeas corpus* could take place outside the courtroom and after trial, it was a short step to finding that an error in the courtroom during trial that the state court failed to correct also violated the Due Process Clause, and by the 1950s, state court judges were complaining that federal courts were, in essence, using *habeas corpus* petitions as a second round of appeals to second-guess their verdicts.

In *Fay v. Noia* (1963), Justice William Brennan, an ardent foe of capital punishment, took an even more extreme step. Charles Noia was serving a life sentence imposed in 1942 for murder during an armed robbery. Two of his codefendants appealed on the grounds that their confessions had been coerced, and after they were successful, Noia tried that claim, too. Noia was unsuccessful in the state courts of New York because he never appealed on that ground in the state court when it was time to do so. The United States Supreme Court held that so long as Noia had not "deliberately bypassed" the issue in state court, he could challenge his conviction on that ground in a federal *habeas corpus* action. Noia was released because the state could not successfully try him 20 years after the fact.

This expansion of federal *habeas corpus* petitions opened not just one new avenue of relief to a death row inmate, it opened hundreds. Even a sympathetic Supreme Court could directly decide only a few cases each year, but any one of several hundred federal judges could grant a writ of *habeas corpus*. As a result, in direct appeals, the Supreme Court shaped the criminal law for the future, while in *habeas corpus,* district judges overturned convictions that had already been obtained. This was a great source of friction between state courts and federal courts. Even more galling, because *habeas corpus* had begun as a remedy for pretrial detention and never applied to trial errors at all, Congress had never limited when or how many times a petition for a writ of *habeas corpus* could be filed. With no statute of limitations, a death row inmate could be sure his execution would be stayed indefinitely even before *Fay v. Noia* because, after all his state court appeals were finished and the governor decided to issue a warrant for his execution, the inmate could file a *habeas corpus* petition before a federal district judge, followed by an appeal to the federal appellate court for that circuit, followed by a petition for *certiorari* to the Supreme Court. This could and did add years to the average time a sentenced inmate could spend before risking execution, especially since an inmate could file *habeas corpus* petitions as long as a judge would hear them.

The evolution can be illustrated with three cases in which executions were eventually carried out, one from 1942, one from 1953, and one from 1960. During World War II, Richard Quirin and several other German saboteurs were sentenced to death by a military tribunal appointed by President Franklin Roosevelt. Quirin and the others sought writs of *habeas corpus* on the grounds that they should only be tried in civilian courts. The Supreme Court met on July 29, 1942, and rejected that argument the next day. Quirin and the others were executed the day after that. The Court's explanation of its decision was filed in October 1942.

In 1951, Julius and Ethel Rosenberg were sentenced to death in the electric chair at Sing Sing for espionage in wartime. Their counsel presented a petition for a writ of *habeas corpus* on the eve of the executions in June 1953. The Court initially granted a stay but, after a special session, vacated the stay and the sentence was carried out. The Court's explanation was filed a month later, in July 1953.

Caryl Chessman was executed by the State of California in 1960 after a 12-year stay on death row, during which Chessman wrote books asserting his innocence and attacking capital punishment. The Supreme Court granted him a writ of *habeas corpus* in 1957 to review his claim that the record of his trial was improperly assembled after the court reporter died before finishing the transcript, but it ultimately rejected his claims. The governor received clemency petitions from more than 10 million persons, some totally opposed to the death penalty, other opposing the execution because Chessman's death penalty was not for murder but for sexual assaults and two kidnapings he committed after tricking his victims into stopping by pretending to be a police officer by flashing a red light from his automobile. Justice William Douglas, one of the more liberal members of the court, surprisingly dissented with a complaint that could have come from the dissent in *Moore v. Dempsey*:

We meddle mischievously with the law when we issue the writ today. We do not act to remedy any injustice . . . we seize upon a technicality to undo what has been repeatedly sustained both by the California Supreme Court and by this Court.

But back at the turn of the twentieth century, no one would have foreseen that the Supreme Court would even consider these issues. The great controversies of the day were how much the federal government or state governments could intervene in the economy and how far those legislatures could delegate that power to intervene to unelected officials in regulatory agencies.

From the point of view of a corporation challenging state and city regulation of the economy, *Barron v. Baltimore*'s holding that the Bill of Rights did not apply to anyone but the federal government was an obstacle to getting a favorable decision from a federal court, and in the late nineteenth century, business saw federal courts as friendlier places than many state courts and legislatures. To invoke the assistance of federal courts businesses turned to the same provision used by the murderers in *Hurtado v. California* and in *Kemmler*: the undefined Due Process Clause of the Fourteenth Amendment. The Supreme Court first recognized that due process of law meant more than simply procedures followed in court in *Missouri Pacific Railway v. Nebraska* (1896) and *Chicago Burlington & Quincy Railroad Co. v. Chicago* (1897), when the justices announced that states and municipalities could not take a railroad's property unless it was for public use and the railroad received just compensation. Even though the Fifth Amendment did not apply to the states, the Court sidestepped *Barron v. Baltimore* by observing that the Fifth Amendment's requirements were fundamental principles of "due process of law" and therefore, under the Fourteenth Amendment, were now binding on states and municipalities as well as the federal government.

Notice that this living-constitution approach to the Due Process Clause was taken by what today we would call the conservative justices. The liberal justices, who generally were more sympathetic to legislation regulating the economy, complained that the conservative justices were legislating their own values through the Fourteenth Amendment and, in a mirror image of the Supreme Court of the current day, urged judicial restraint. But businesses were not the only ones to react to the Court's rulings: creative lawyers and their clients of all types began raising the arguments that if the Fifth Amendment's protection against taking without just compensation was protected by the Due Process Clause, other provisions of the Bill of Rights were also enforceable against interference by states and localities. This process, called "incorporation" of the Bill of Rights into the Due Process Clause, proceeded by fits and starts. By the late 1920s, the Court had accepted the claim that the First Amendment's freedom of speech was part of "due process of law." The next decade saw the Court receptive to claims that freedom of the press, free exercise of religion, and freedom of assembly were so fundamental that they, too, were part of due process.

Incorporation of the Bill of Rights was a description after the fact of what the Court had done, not a political program by the justices either of liberal or conservative persuasion. What the justices thought they were doing was deciding individual cases as they came to the Court in a manner consistent with the Constitution. As a result of the shifting majorities of the Court over both questions of substance—can government take this action or not?—and the nature of the judicial role—should the Court be deferential to the other branches? should it announce a broad or narrow principle of law?—incorporation proceeded in uneven fashion. One might think that after *Weems,* it would be a short step to incorporate the Eighth Amendment's prohibition of cruel and unusual punishment into the concept of due process, but only five years after *Weems,* the Court decided in *Collins v. Johnston* (1915) that a 14-year sentence for perjury was not excessive punishment prohibited by the Due Process Clause. The Court observed to the contrary that:

to establish appropriate penalties for the commission of crime . . . are functions peculiarly belonging to the several States.

The Court could not agree on a general rule telling the states what functions peculiarly belonged to them and which were regulated by the Due Process

Clause and therefore had to be uniform throughout the country. The Supreme Court had already held in *Hurtado* that the Fifth Amendment's guarantee of indictment by grand jury was not part of due process and affirmed Hurtado's death sentence. In 1900, the Court decided in *Maxwell v. Dow* that due process did not require Utah to provide a 12-man jury (eight was enough in a non-capital case), and in 1908, *Twining v. New Jersey* held that the right against self-incrimination, though important, did not protect two criminal defendants from a state court judge calling to the jury's attention that they had not taken the stand to deny evidence that they were guilty of fraud.

In *Powell v. Alabama* (1932), the court finally incorporated the Sixth Amendment's guarantee of the assistance of counsel, on the basis that the effective assistance of counsel was "at the base of all our civil and political institutions." As in *Moore v. Dempsey*, the defendants in *Powell* were Black and sentenced to death after a conviction in a racially inflammatory trial. The defendant "Scottsboro Boys" were teenagers accused of the rape of two White women on a train after a scuffle between rival Black and White groups of hoboes. Although the defendants had not been lynched, had been represented by counsel, and had received a trial that was not dominated by the threat of mob violence, the Court stated that the fact that defense counsel only appeared for his clients on the morning of trial and had undertaken no preparation or investigation meant that the defendants had not really received representation. *Powell v. Alabama* illustrates the beginning of a trend that would accelerate in the 1950s, of the Supreme Court using the Constitution in an attempt to prescribe uniform minimum standards in criminal cases.

The Supreme Court was long didvided about where those minimum standards could be found. In 1937, in *Palko v. Connecticut*, the Court rejected the claim that the Fifth Amendment's double jeopardy clause was part of the due process of law. Connecticut sought a capital murder conviction against Frank Palko for the killing of his wife but had only convicted him of second-degree murder. Pursuant to state law, the prosecution had successfully appealed Frank Palko's second-degree murder conviction and life sentence on the grounds that the trial judge had made a mistake. On retrial, Palko had been convicted of first-degree murder and sentenced to death. Speaking for the Court, Justice Benjamin Cardozo explained that the State's appeal did not offend due process:

What the answer would have to be if the state were permitted after a trial free from error to try the accused over again or to bring another case against him, we have no occasion to consider. We deal with the statute before us and no other. The state is not attempting to wear the accused out by a multitude of cases with accumulated

The "Scottsboro Boys," nine African American youths, pictured here with civil rights activist Juanita Jackson Mitchell in 1937, were imprisoned in Scottsboro, Alabama, after being falsely accused of raping two white women in a freight car. The boys' convictions were overturned in *Powell v. Alabama* (1932), when the U.S. Supreme Court declared that the defendants, who had not been given adequate time to prepare a defense, were denied due process. (Library of Congress)

trials. It asks no more than this, that the case against him shall go on until there shall be a trial free from the corrosion of substantial legal error. . . . This is not cruelty at all, nor even vexation in any immoderate degree.

Palko may not have been vexed, but he was executed. His case was significant because the Supreme Court appeared to settle on a legal formula for determining what procedures were required by the Due Process Clause. As Cardozo wrote, those rights that were "of the very essence of a scheme of ordered liberty" were incorporated. Anything else the states were free to experiment with, vary, or discard.

There were alternate views that would compete for the Court's allegiance for the next 30 years, most notably the "total incorporation" theory championed by Justice Hugo Black, the first of President Franklin Delano Roosevelt's eight appointments to the Court. Appointed in 1937 after serving in the Senate, Justice Black had been a faithful supporter of the New Deal and a strong advocate of the position that the Supreme Court should defer to Congress when it came to economic legislation. Justice Black believed that the historic purpose of the Fourteenth Amendment was precisely to incorporate the Bill of Rights into a body of law binding on the states as well as the federal government. Justice Black's reading of the Fourteenth Amendment never commanded a majority of the Court, but case by case, the process of selective incorporation ended up with almost all of the provisions of the Bill of Rights being considered essential to ordered liberty.

In Franklin Delano Roosevelt's second term, the Supreme Court came to concede that extensive government economic regulation was constitutional and that deference to the legislature should be the Court's normal role. Some of the Roosevelt appointees believed that their deference to Congress extended to all legislation. Others drew a distinction between economic affairs and other areas like criminal law. In *United States v. Carolene Products Corporation* (1938), an otherwise routine case sustaining the prosecution of a company for shipping skim milk adulterated with coconut oil, Justice Harlan Fiske Stone wrote what is probably the most famous footnote in the Court's history. After reciting the new orthodox position that Congress had almost complete power to regulate interstate commerce, Justice Stone, later to be promoted to Chief Justice by President Roosevelt, observed that:

There may be narrower scope for operation of the presumption of constitutionality when legislation appears on its face to be within a specific prohibition of the Constitution, such as those of the first ten Amendments, which are deemed equally specific when held to be embraced within the Fourteenth.

Both parts of the theoretical structure for the "due process revolution" that would reach a high point in the 1960s were now in place. In *Palko* the Supreme Court said that the Due Process Clause of the Fourteenth Amendment compelled them to ask whether a state's practices affected truly fundamental criminal procedures, while *Carolene Products* asked whether a piece of legislation was embraced by the Bill of Rights. The intersection of these two doctrines resulted in the Court asking the obvious next question: did a state's criminal procedures infringe on the Bill of Rights? The next 30 years would see the Court oscillate between two positions on what can loosely be called civil rights issues, which came to include the issue of capital punishment. One bloc of justices, typically led by Justice Felix Frankfurter, President Roosevelt's third appointment to the Court in 1939 after a quarter century as a professor at Harvard Law School, would counsel a broad policy of judicial restraint. Another bloc of justices including Justice Black and Justice William Douglas (also appointed in 1939) and eventually Justices William Brennan (appointed in 1956) and Thurgood Marshall (appointed in 1967), would advocate judicial intervention on behalf of constitutional rights they thought were being infringed. This philosophical split did not necessarily dictate support of or opposition to the death penalty: Justice Black, for example, though believing that the Bill of Rights was absolutely binding on the states, also reasoned that since the death penalty had co-existed with the Eighth Amendment from the beginning, it could not itself be considered cruel or unusual punishment. Justice Frankfurter, though he personally opposed the death penalty, cast the deciding vote against incorporating the Eighth Amendment in *Louisiana ex rel. Francis v. Resweber* (1947), refusing to block the execution of teenager Willie Francis. As an example of the sort of zigzag the competing views could produce, an example that sheds light on the death penalty controversies to come, consider the two "flag salute cases" of the 1940s, *Minersville School District v. Gobitis* (1940) and *West Virginia State Board of Education v. Barnette* (1943). In the first case, the Court sustained the expulsion from a Pennsylvania public school of two children who, as Jehovah's Witnesses, refused on religious grounds to salute the American flag as part of a daily school exercise. Justice Frankfurter wrote the majority opinion. Three years later in *Barnette*, the Court, again considered the identical claims of expelled Jehovah's Witnesses but this time overturned a statute West Virginia adopted after *Gobitis* that required daily recitation of the Pledge of Allegiance and flag salute. In dissent, Justice Frankfurter chided the Court and especially Justices Black and Douglas, who, by switching sides, had reversed the Court's position. Justice Frankfurter's words describe the conservative view of the role of the Court:

One's conception of the Constitution cannot be severed from one's conception of a judge's function in applying it. The Court has no reason for existence if it merely reflects the pressures of the day. Our system is built on the faith that men set apart for this special function, freed from the influences of immediacy and form the deflections of worldly ambition, will become able to take a view of longer range than the period of responsibility entrusted to Congress and legislatures. We are dealing with matters as to which legislators and voters have conflicting views. Are we as judges to impose our strong convictions on where wisdom lies? That which three years ago had seemed to five successive Courts to lie within permissible areas of legislation is now outlawed by the deciding shift of opinion of two Justice. What reason is there to believe that they or their successors may not have another view a few years hence? Is that which was deemed to be of so fundamental a nature as to be written into the Constitution to endure for all times to be the sport of shifting winds of doctrine?

The contrary view was not formally stated for another generation. In *Robinson v. California* (1962), an otherwise unimportant case, the court held that the Eighth Amendment was incorporated and therefore binding on the states. Later in 1962, Justice Frankfurter retired and was replaced by President Kennedy's second appointment, Arthur Goldberg, long-time counsel to the AFL-CIO and briefly the Secretary of Labor. In 1963, Justice Goldberg took the unusual step of circulating a lengthy memorandum to the other justices discussing whether capital punishment might violate the Eighth Amendment and proposing that the Court take up the issue in one of the six death penalty cases pending before it, even though none of the defendants had even made an argument to that effect.[35] Justice Goldberg set forth the alternative to Justice Frankfurter's philosophy:

It may be suggested that since the death penalty is a mode of punishment about which opinion is fairly divided, a state does not violate the Constitution when it treats the prisoner by such a mode. . . . With all deference, this reasoning does not seem persuasive here. In certain matters—especially those relating to fair procedures in criminal trials—this Court traditionally has guided rather than followed public opinion in the process of articulating and establishing progressively civilized standards of decency. If only punishments already overwhelmingly condemned by public opinion came within the cruel and unusual punishment proscription, the Eighth Amendment would be a dead letter; for such punishments would presumably be abolished by the legislature. The Eighth Amendment, like the others in the Bill of Rights, was intended as a countermajoritarian limitation on governmental action; it should be applied to nurture rather than to retard our "evolving standards of decency." Can there be any doubt that if this Court condemns the death penalty as cruel and unusual—whatever the initial effect—before too long that penalty will no longer be "a mode of punishment about which opinion is fairly divided." As the Court recognized in Weems: "Our contemplation cannot be only of what has been but of what may be."[36]

Justice Goldberg's memorandum failed to convince the Court to take any of the pending cases, but he drafted a dissent from the denial of *certiorari* in one, *Rudolph v. Alabama* (1963), that was joined by Justices Douglas and Brennan. With three members of the Court signaling their willingness to declare capital punishment unconstitutional as a penalty for rape, the crime for which Rudolph had been sentenced, the invitation to criminal defense lawyers was open: challenge your state's death penalty law in federal court. And in *Chapman v. California* (1967), the Court held that the burden was on the state to prove beyond a reasonable doubt that a constitutional error did not contribute to a guilty verdict if the state wished to block a writ of *habeas corpus*.

Only a couple of years after Justice Goldberg's memorandum and *Fay v. Noia*, execution of prisoners for violating state law was limited almost entirely to death row inmates who did not wish to fight their convictions in federal court or who actually sought death. The only death penalty carried out in 1966 was against James French, who had murdered a man in Oklahoma in 1958, pleaded guilty, and requested execution. His counsel negotiated a life sentence, so in 1961, French strangled his cellmate and again requested the death penalty. After being found sane, French died in the electric chair. In 1967, only two executions took place, Aaron Mitchell in California and another volunteer, Luis Jose Monge, in Colorado, who pleaded guilty to murdering four family members and fired his attorney to speed up the execution process.

The federal government had already made capital punishment practically extinct as a matter of executive branch policy: in the 36 years between 1927 and 1963, only 24 federal executions had been carried out, and eight of these had been for espionage or wartime sabotage. In 1957, George Krull and Michael Krull had been hanged for a rape committed in a national park, and in 1963, Victor Feguer was hanged for a 1960 kidnaping and murder in Iowa. Feguer's execution took place in Iowa over the objections of Iowa's governor, but after these three cases, the federal government would not even seek the death penalty for another 30 years. By then the Supreme Court had completely reversed the stance it took in 1812 in *Hudson v. Goodwin.* From *Furman v. Georgia* (1972), the Justices would tell Congress and state legislatures what acts could be considered crimes, what punishments could be imposed for those crimes, and what procedures could be used to impose those punishments. It was plain to Justice Goldberg in 1963 that the eventual discussion of the capital punishment question would involve not just the legal issues but also the examination of the political relationship between the states and the federal government. After reading Justice Goldberg's memorandum, it was also plain that once the issue was brought to the Court, the conversation that would be relevant would go on between and among the Justices and not between the Court and counsel. We present the history of that conversation in Appendix 1.

NOTES

1. See Joseph Melusky, *The American Political System: An Owner's Manual* (Boston, MA: McGraw-Hill, 2000), 41. Much of the ensuing discussion is drawn from Melusky and Pesto, *Cruel and Unusual Punishment: Rights and Liberties Under the Law,* 8–12.

2. Melusky, 42. See Chapter 3, "Constitutional Rights and Liberties," 40–65, for an extended discussion of a "living" constitution and related matters.

3. See William J. Brennan, "The Constitution of the United States: Contemporary Ratification." *South Texas Law Review* 27 (1986): 433.

4. See Robert Bork, "The Case Against Political Judging," *National Review,* 8 December 1989, for an argument that judges should be bound by the original intent of the framers. See also Bork, *The Tempting of America: The Political Seduction of the Law* (New York: Free Press, 1990).

5. See Melusky, 60–61.

6. The latter grievance may also have been aimed at Parliamentary efforts to prevent a repeat of the trial of the British soldiers involved in the 1770 Boston Massacre. In the Administration of Justice Act of 1774, Parliament provided that trials of government officials accused in the colonies could be removed to other colonies or to England, removing a potential check on tyranny.

7. Controversies of this type were slavery and voting rights. The Framers were unable to reach acceptable compromises and finally provided that each state would set its own suffrage requirements and that the issue of slavery and the slave trade would remain unaffected by Congress's power over the slave trade until 1808.

8. Neil H. Cogan, ed, *The Complete Bill of Rights* (New York: Oxford University Press, 1997), 613–17.

9. Saul K. Padover, ed., *The Complete Jefferson* (New York: Duell, Sloan, & Pearce, Inc., 1943), 90–102. The proposal failed to pass the Virginia legislature by one vote in 1785. After a change of the penalties for noncapital crimes from public labor to prison labor, the bill passed in 1796.

10. Cogan, 619.

11. Cogan, 619.

12. The Federalist Papers have been compiled in many places since their original publication in 1788. Our quotes are from Roy P. Fairfield, ed. *The Federalist Papers*, 2nd ed. (Garden City, NY: Anchor Books, Doubleday & Co., 1961).

13. Twelve amendments were submitted to the states. One of the two unratified amendments, preventing Congress from raising its own salaries between elections, lay dormant for 200 years before being ratified in 1992 as the Twenty-seventh Amendment.

14. Cogan, 618. Hamilton wrote under the pseudonym "Publius." The generation from the Declaration of Independence to the ratification of the Bill of Rights was raised on the classics and, in many respects, held an idealized image of Rome of the later Republic as a model for how politicians should act. Adoption of pseudonyms like Publius, Brutus, and Agricola to claim a mantle of classical patriotism was a widespread practice on both sides of the ratification debates. The Roman influence went in the other direction as well: The more imaginative founders thought of the United States as the purified, more worthy successor to England as the world's lawgiver.

15. Cogan, 618.

16. An aerial photograph of Washington, D.C., is worth a thousand words. Streets radiate from Capitol Hill, the home of the legislature. At a safe distance and off to one side is the president's residence, with the prosaic title given to it by its paint color. The Supreme Court building is tucked into a corner in the backyard of the Capitol, a home given to the Court only in the 1930s. For the first 140 years of its existence, the Supreme Court heard cases in the Capitol, and its budget and personnel were the responsibility of the Justice Department. Recall that Thomas Jefferson gave the jury, not the judge, the power to decide the punishment for fortunetelling. The penalties for other crimes were similarly fixed and not subject to judicial discretion.

17. James Madison argued, in *Federalist No. 10*, that faction opposing faction in the legislature would be the safeguard of liberty in the new republic. Judges rated not even a mention. Madison explained the theory of checks and balances in more detail in *Federalist No. 51* and described how this would operate in the House of Representatives in *Federalist No. 52* and in the Senate in *Federalist No. 62*.

18. Americans were torn between wanting to keep up with the mother country and emphasizing America's sense of exceptionalism. Thomas Jefferson was a typical critic of the practice of sending American youths to England for education where, according to him, they would learn "drinking, horse-racing, and boxing" and "acquire a fondness for European luxury and dissipation." Quoted in Ted J. Smith, ed., *In Defense of Tradition, Collected Shorter Writings of Richard M. Weaver* (Indianapolis, IN: Liberty Fund, 2000), 643.

19. Russell Kirk, *The Roots of American Order* (Washington, D.C.: Regnery Gateway, 1991), 368.

20. H. Wayne House, "A Tale of Two Kingdoms: Can There Be Peaceful Coexistence of Religion with the Secular State?" *B.Y.U. Journal of Public Law* 13 (1999): 203.

21. Parliament's Quartering Act of 1774 was deemed to be part of the "Intolerable Acts," but it did not authorize quartering of trooping in private homes. Boston had chafed under military occupation, but those troops were in barracks or on leased property.

22. Alexis de Tocqueville's classic explanation of the United States, *Democracy in America,* expressed the conventional wisdom of the early nineteenth century:

In no country is criminal justice administered with more mildness than in the United States. While the English seem disposed carefully to retain the bloody traces of the dark ages in their penal legislation, the Americans have almost expunged capital punishment from their codes. North America is, I think, the only one country upon earth in which the life of no one citizen has been taken for a political offense in the course of the last fifty years.

Alexis de Tocqueville, *Democracy in America*, Part II, Henry Steele Commager, ed. (New York: Oxford University Press, 1947 [1840]), Henry Reeve translation, 368.

23. Rory K. Little, "The Federal Death Penalty: History and Some Thoughts About the Department of Justice's Role," *Fordham Urban Law Journal* 26 (March 1999): 347, 364.

24. The opinions of the Court in *Marbury v. Madison* and in *United States v. Goodwin and Hudson* were written by John Marshall, who served as the fourth Chief Justice from 1801 to 1835 and who is generally regarded as the greatest justice in the court's history. Marshall and Jefferson cordially detested one another's politics and each suspected the other of undermining the Constitution. This is one of the few Marshall opinions that Jefferson could agree with, even if it meant that the newspaper was free to defame Jefferson.

25. Joseph Story, *Commentaries on the Constitution of the United States* (Durham, NC: Carolina Academic Press, 1987), 710–11.

26. By 1927, *Constitutional Limitations* was in its eight edition, but its analysis of the Eighth Amendment was unchanged. Thomas M. Cooley, *A Treatise on the Constitutional Limitations Which Rest Upon the Legislative Power of the States of the American Union* (8th ed., Walter Carrington) (Boston: Little, Brown, and Company, 1927), Vol. 1, 694.

27. Charles Fairman, "Does the Fourteenth Amendment Incorporate the Bill of Rights? The Original Understanding," *Stanford Law Review* 2 (1949): 5.

28. Meghan S. Skelton, "Lethal Injection in the Wake of *Fierro v. Gomez*," *Thomas Jefferson Law Review* 19 (Spring 1997): 1, 11 n. 65.

29. Guy Cheli, *Sing Sing Prison* (Charleston, NC: Arcadia Publishing, 2003), excerpted at http://www.correctionhistory.org/html/chronicl/state/singsing/html/chair.html (March 1, 2009).

30. Field, who served on the Court from his appointment by Lincoln in 1863 until 1897, correctly assessed O'Neil's sentence as unusually severe. Early in his tenure, the Court had decided in *Pervear v. Commonwealth* (1866) that a fine of $50 and three months' imprisonment was not cruel and unusual punishment for selling liquor without a license. Vermont's hostility to New York's liquor was symptomatic of the growing cultural conflict that would culminate in Prohibition.

31. State courts were deferential to the legislature's choice of criminal punishment as well. For example, New Mexico's territorial court, in *Territory v. Ketchum* (1901), upheld a statute imposing the death penalty for an attempted train robbery. Even in the rare case in which a sentence was overturned for being too harsh, the courts did so in deference to the legislature. In *State v. Driver* (1878), the Supreme Court of North Carolina overturned a five-year sentence of imprisonment in the county jail for a man convicted of whipping and kicking his wife. The court noted that the legislature only permitted such a sentence to be served in the state penitentiary.

32. Justice McKenna served on the Supreme Court from 1898 to 1925 after a career in the California legislature and in the House of Representatives. One evaluation of Supreme Court performance describes his tenure as "a long career of opinions that were striking for their poor grammar and jumbled reasoning." William D. Bader and Roy M. Mersky, *The First One Hundred Eight Justices* (Buffalo, NY: William S. Hein & Co., Inc., 2004), 68.

33. Note. "What is Cruel and Unusual Punishment?" *Harvard Law Review* 24 (1910–11): 54–55.

34. Affirming the death sentences of Julius and Ethel Rosenberg, Judge Jerome Frank, himself an opponent of the death penalty, noted in 1952 that in the 40 years after *Weems*, "No federal decision seems to have held cruel and unusual any sentence imposed under a statute which itself was constitutional." *United States v. Rosenberg*, 195 F.2d 583, 607 (2d Cir.1952).

35. Arthur J. Goldberg, "Memorandum to the Conference Re: Capital Punishment," *South Texas Law Review* 27 (1986): 493 (reproducing the 1963 Goldberg memorandum verbatim).

36. *Id.* at 500–1.

4

Arguments For and Against the Death Penalty

As we said at the beginning of this book, one of the functions the death penalty debate serves is to allow people and especially politicians to signal their positions on other controversial issues. As you read what the Supreme Court has decided in the relatively short time since Justice Goldberg called for the justices to rule that capital punishment was prohibited by the Eighth Amendment, we suggest two ways to evaluate their reasoning. First, to organize our thinking about whether the death penalty as enacted in a particular state at a particular time is good or bad, we have to begin by deciding what are our standards for judging. Second, the Supreme Court has rarely, and at the present time almost never, conducted the debate head on: the justices are usually talking about quite different and often obscure points of law that end up having dispositive impact on the way sentences are actually carried out. We take these points in order.

FIVE WAYS TO JUDGE CRIME AND PUNISHMENT

To judge the merit of a capital punishment system, we must consider there are at least five competing ends served by the punishments in a criminal justice system: expiation, rehabilitation, retribution, interdiction, and deterrence. The last three are relevant to how we think about the death penalty today, but a word should be said about the other two.

Expiation is the belief that crime makes the criminal, in some spiritual sense, unfit to live in society and renders the society he lives in unclean.

Punishment acts to cleanse or "expiate" that stain. In the words of the Old Testament book of Numbers: "You shall accept no ransom for the life of a murderer . . . for blood pollutes the land, and no expiation can be made for the land, for the blood that is shed in it, except by the blood of him who shed it."[1] To offer what may be the most familiar literary illustration of the concept, consider the Biblical short story of Jonah. Jonah is commanded by God to preach to Nineveh but takes a ship in the opposite direction. When a storm threatens to sink the ship, Jonah admits to the crew that he is the cause and advises them that they must cast him into the sea to drown. The crew, although reluctant to kill Jonah, does not question that throwing the sinner overboard is exactly the right thing to do to calm the tempest.[2] If it is not the oldest justification for the death penalty, expiation is certainly the most archaic, and it was practically extinct by the time Christianity spread through the Roman Empire. A religious, political, or academic commentator who advocated the expiatory effects of the death penalty would not be viewed as credible because expiation is no longer viewed as a possible end of the criminal law, much less a permissible one.[3] Nevertheless, even ideas that we think of as discarded continue to influence our thinking—we still speak of sunrise and sunset long after everyone understands that the Earth rotates on its axis—and the invariable claim by death penalty proponents that an execution that has just been carried out provided "closure" to the families of murder victims may be seen as the expiation argument reframed in modern psychological terms instead of traditional religious ones. Similarly, death penalty proponents often compare the relative peace and orderliness of an execution, especially one by lethal injection, to the usually grisly murder committed by the defendant, as if the death of the murderer in some unspoken way is expected to atone for the death he caused.

Rehabilitation is the use of punishments for what medieval philosopher Thomas Aquinas would have called its "medicinal value," to change the criminal within before he returns to society. Because the very point of the death penalty is to remove the offender permanently from society, death clearly has no ability to rehabilitate. The death penalty could be justified as an attempt to impress upon the person to be executed the reprehensibility of his crime, but while the moral reform of a person about to be executed matters to some death penalty opponents like Sister Helen Prejean of *Dead Man Walking* fame, rehabilitation of the criminal's soul or body is certainly not even a goal of proponents of the death penalty.

There can be no real debate about rehabilitation and the death penalty because retentionists and abolitionists do not agree on the fundamental premise that rehabilitation should be a goal of any criminal sentence. The rehabilitationist view dates back to the founding era of the country with the opening of the Walnut Street Jail in Philadelphia in 1790. In 1790, prisons mostly were places where those awaiting trial were crammed together with debtors, vagrants, the mentally ill or insane, and the few convicted criminals awaiting execution, transportation to servitude elsewhere, or the end of their sentences. English reformers like John Howard began to address the wretched and deadly conditions of their prisons in the late eighteenth century, and the next step after attempting to protect the unfortunates from the criminals was to attempt to reform the criminals themselves.

In the age of reform and optimism that ended the nineteenth century, this rehabilitative ideal moved from a focus on the penitentiary to one on the community as the place of reform. Use of indeterminate sentences coupled with the granting of parole under varying degrees of supervision began around 1890 and became widespread. Criminal reformers drew an analogy between crime and illness and asserted that systematic professional care could result in crime being "cured," at least one criminal at a time. By the middle of the twentieth century, the Supreme Court could assert, in *Williams v. New York* (1949):[4]

Retribution is no longer the dominant objective of the criminal law. Reformation and rehabilitation of offenders have become important goals of criminal jurisprudence.

* * *

[I]ndeterminate sentences and probation have resulted in an increase in the discretionary powers exercised in fixing punishments. In general, these modern changes have not resulted in making the lot of offenders harder. On the contrary a strong motivating force for the changes has been the belief that by careful study of the lives and personalities of convicted offenders many could be less severely punished and restored sooner to complete freedom and useful citizenship. This belief to a large extent has been justified.

The irony of this self-congratulation was that it came in the affirmation of a death sentence for Williams.

The second half of the twentieth century saw external and internal attacks on the parole-based rehabilitation model. Though some criminals did reform, treating criminals in prison like patients in a hospital was a failure. Crime rates rose sharply after 1960. Inmates denied parole complained, sometimes justly, that denial was due to their race, poverty, or lack of pull. Successful cases of reform were, by definition, not visible in the crime statistics that began to be compiled by the federal government after 1930, while every crime committed by a released criminal was an increasingly visible failure. Politicians learned from the "Willie Horton" commercials used to attack Massachusetts governor Michael Dukakis during the 1988 presidential election campaign after Horton committed a rape while on furlough from a life sentence imposed for murder, that failed rehabilitative efforts could end their careers. By the 1990s, heightened publicity for murders committed by recidivists, such as the murder of Polly Klaas in California in 1993 by a parolee and the murder of Megan Kanka in New Jersey in 1994 by a repeatedly "treated" sex offender, accelerated already increasingly harsh state and national legislation. Politicians learned that legislation reinstating capital punishment, abolishing parole, extending the confinement of sex offenders beyond the expiration of their sentences, and creating a range of extremely long sentences for "three-strike" offenders were career boosters. Being on the pro-death penalty side of the debate directly contributed to the election of George Pataki as governor of New York in 1994 and the passing of capital punishment legislation in that state in September 1995.

Congress had already turned the federal government away from a rehabilitative model in the Sentencing Reform Act of 1984, which abolished parole in federal sentences. Now inmates would serve a fixed term of imprisonment, set less according to the judge's view of the defendant and more according to Congress' view of the crime under guidelines to be drawn up by a sentencing commission. Prison would then be followed by a fixed term of supervised release, not parole, that could last the rest of the offender's life. States did the same. Those state legislatures that retained parole in almost every case made parole reviews harder, less frequent, or easier to block by requiring a unanimous vote to parole. As a result the number of persons incarcerated in state and federal prisons rose sevenfold from 1972 to 2009.[5]

Judges learned they were not immune from political change. Although federal judges, once appointed by the president and confirmed by the Senate, were given life tenure by the Constitution, they were not guaranteed confirmation or promotion, and a record on the state or lower federal bench of being "soft on crime," especially by granting *habeas corpus* petitions to overturn death sentences, made it easy for a senator to oppose the president's nominees. State judges in those states where judges were elected similarly learned that ruling against the death penalty was a, potential career ender. In 1986, Chief Justice Rose Bird and two other justices from the California Supreme Court were removed by voters, primarily in a protest against their ruling on death penalty cases. Subsequent campaigns in Texas, Alabama, and Tennessee featured attacks on judges who, whether right or not, voted against executions.[6] There were no corresponding campaigns against judges who, whether right or not, voted to uphold executions.

In prisons themselves, the first half of the century saw many wardens, especially in the new Federal Bureau of Prisons begun under President Hoover in 1930, embrace the rehabilitative ideal and publicly oppose the death penalty as useless. The last quarter of the twentieth century saw a general turning away from the belief that rehabilitation is a goal in a system of punishment, but the remaining advocates of the use of a corrections system to reform criminals oppose the death penalty to remain logically consistent. Cause and effect run in the opposite direction as well, as some opponents of the death penalty assert that every person, no matter what the crime, should be rehabilitated. By contrast, for the last 30 years, death penalty advocates have an easier time with the logic as well as the politics of rehabilitation: they can concede that most criminals deserve a second chance while taking the centuries-old position that the death penalty is appropriate for the worst offenders because some criminals just cannot be rehabilitated.

Retribution is a complex idea that can be simply stated: the criminal is punished because he deserves it. In the popular phrase, it is his "just desserts."[7] Unlike expiation, the focus is on the criminal, not the crime. Like expiation, retribution requires belief in an accepted moral order and has, for that reason, grown less popular in more recent American jurisprudence. The framers of the Constitution and the ratifiers of the Eighth Amendment believed in executing murderers because they generally believed that retribution complied with the will of God (or the laws of Nature) and did not enforce mere manmade experiments in social psychology.[8] This belief has weakened considerably. But so has the belief that murderers are the worst criminals. From the 1930s on, lawyers with political ambitions like Earl Warren of California and Thomas Dewey of New York found that prosecuting racketeers for crimes like tax evasion and bribery was a more certain route to public office than was executing petty criminals. With the death penalty unnecessary for front page coverage, district attorneys like New York's Robert Morgenthau could even oppose capital punishment and be re-elected.

Interdiction means stopping the criminal from committing crimes in the future by incapacitating him in some way. Whether the method is execution of a murderer, imprisonment of a burglar, taking away a scammer's access to the Internet, or even cutting off the hand of a pickpocket, taking away the means of crime prevents future harm to society. Obviously, the death penalty is the ultimate interdiction. Less obviously, the argument that the ultimate sanction should be reserved for the ultimate in crime has become an assumption of death penalty opponents. Death penalty advocates have mostly conceded this point.

Deterrence is the idea that the example of punishing one crime can prevent the future commission of crimes by the criminal or by other would-be criminals. It may be considered, depending on one's beliefs, either as a kind of moral education of society or just as Pavlovian conditioning. Because deterrence can be viewed as an end in itself without any explicit discussion of religious or philosophical beliefs, it is currently the most popular justification for the death penalty. It looks like a dry battle over statistics. Nevertheless, the same religious and philosophical problems remain close to the surface because promoting deterrence requires judgments about its legitimacy as well as its costs and benefits. These days, it seems that almost every prosecutor in a capital case asks the jury to convict—and having convicted, to impose the death penalty—in order to "send a message" to the public. But if educating the public is our goal, is the centuries-old maxim that it is better for 10 criminals to go free than for one innocent person to be convicted still true? How about a hundred to one? And how long should it take and how expensive should it be to keep to the desired ratio? If deterrence is our goal, should any effort be devoted to opposing convictions and sentences beyond the bare minimum necessary to have the justice system *perceived* as legitimate? After all, even an innocent person's execution sends the message (maybe a chillingly effective one) that society will impose the death penalty on suspected offenders. By contrast, a criminal justice system that nominally retains the death penalty but, in practice, hardly ever carries it out because of the risk of executing the innocent may well deter fewer crimes than one in which the death penalty was never authorized to begin with. Also, both those who oppose capital punishment because they believe the risk of executing the innocent is unacceptably high and those who support capital punishment because they believe a particular system is accurate enough fail to confront the spillover costs to cases other than capital murder. Even in the most flawed system, it is certain that death penalty prosecutions receive more scrutiny from judges and lawyers than other cases. And given the rarity of capital murder prosecutions, it is mathematically certain that there are far more innocent persons serving lengthy terms for felonies they did not commit than there are on death row for murders they did not commit. While the risk of executing the innocent presents the starkest challenge to the deterrence rationale, should society accept the life imprisonment of the innocent? Those who want to compromise between abolitionists and retentionists by maintaining a seemingly endless series of procedural safeguards that are applicable *only* in capital cases ultimately devote a disproportionate share of society's resources toward vindicating the rights of those who are most likely to be guilty at the expense of those who are more likely to be innocent.[9] Both Florida and Virginia have conducted DNA testing even after a defendant was executed—in the case of Virginia, almost 14 years after Roger Coleman's 1992 execution for a 1981 rape and murder. The result? Coleman was guilty. Did death penalty foes, disappointed at another failed effort to find an iron-clad example of the execution of an innocent man, even consider the lost opportunity to other inmates to prove their innocence? When both scrapping the death penalty and speeding it up have the same benefit of increasing deterrence, the choice between the two policies cannot itself be based on the goal of deterrence.

THE DEBATE BEHIND THE DEBATE

Religious climate, even when not expressed in the official teaching of a church, plays an enormous role in shaping attitudes toward death and, therefore, indirectly shapes the consensus about the death penalty. Some religious leaders call for the abolition of the death penalty, while others accept its validity. It is fair to say that many Americans are at odds with whatever may be the official position of their religious denominations. This is nothing new. Over time, there have also been changes in what might be called religious style, and those changes have also affected the debate on the death penalty, sometimes in more predictable ways than a particular religious dogma. Through the Middle Ages, both asceticism and the belief that this world was valuable chiefly as a gateway to the next one where some purgation of sins was possible encouraged what has been called a contempt for death. Death and judgment, heaven or hell, were the focus of thought. Because in a real sense, everyone expected to undergo a capital trial when they died, the imagination could hardly grasp a world without capital punishment in this life. Reforming the death penalty might mean humane executions, might mean protecting the innocent, but could hardly mean abolition.

With the Renaissance and the rise of humanism, there was an increased focus on this world as a place of value for its own sake. With the Reformation, there was increased focus on the individual, particularly the personal responsibility of the individual in the salvation of his soul. The first unfortunate result of the emergence of these ideas in a Europe breaking up into competing nations was persecution of whatever religion was in the minority in England, France, and Spain, and genocidal conflict between Catholics and Protestants in Germany, where neither side had a majority. A century and a half of savage religious wars commanded the attention of Europe and pushed offstage any discussion of crime and punishment. An additional historical twist in seventeenth-century England was that the first organized calls for less use of the death penalty and for general reform of the criminal law were made by the parties opposing monarchical government. The collapse of the Commonwealth and the restoration of monarchy meant the shelving of criminal law reform.[10] Though regarded as lenient by observers on the Continent, England's capital punishment statutes actually multiplied during the first part of the eighteenth century.

By the late eighteenth century, the age of religious war was over in Europe and political turmoil had subsided in England. The framers were familiar with the ridicule that religious skeptics like Voltaire poured on the spectacle of religious warfare and with the arguments of religious thinkers like Roger Williams, Baptist leader and founder of Rhode Island, that persecution was contrary to any form of Christianity. The framers were also, with few exceptions, the political heirs of the Parliamentary side in the English Civil War and believed they should not be hanged for speaking in opposition to their king. Both influences led to increasing religious and political tolerance, embodied legally in the United States in the First Amendment.

But no part of America's religious inheritance from Europe, whether Protestant or Catholic, Renaissance or Reformation era, nor its political inheritance from England, whether Whig or Tory, could be considered sympathetic toward the criminal or likely to produce abolition of the death penalty. The traditional Catholic view is represented in Dante's *The Divine Comedy*, written early in the fourteenth century. In the poem, Dante is conducted by the Roman poet Vergil through successively lower rings of Hell until they reach the eighth circle, where sorcerers are condemned for eternity. When Dante weeps at their twisted state, Vergil rebukes him for being a fool and asks, "who's wickeder than one that's agonised by God's high equity?"[11] After judgment, one can either have faith in God's justice or pity for the sinner, but not both, and Dante makes it clear which is the correct choice. The post-Reformation Protestant view was, if anything, even sterner. "There but for the grace of God go I," a phrase commonly attributed to the Anglican cleric John Bradford in 1555 as he watched from his cell in the Tower of London while a criminal was led to execution, does not express Bradford's relief at his good fortune: Bradford himself was burned at the stake for heresy shortly thereafter. But Bradford was not expressing sympathy for the condemned, either, so much as his belief that the eternal damnation to follow will be much worse.

Two centuries later in the American colonies, the New England framers of the Constitution might remember uncomfortably that their great grandparents hanged men and women for heresy and witchcraft but still, as children, sat through sermons like Jonathan Edwards's "Sinners in the Hands of an Angry God." It is small wonder that until the end of the eighteenth century, calls for the abolition of the death penalty were limited mostly to calls for reduction in the number of crimes punishable by death and that death penalty reformers often were from fringe or unorthodox religious groups.

Pennsylvania provides an example. It was settled by the Society of Friends (Quakers), who, from the beginning, had a tradition against killing human beings, whether in war or as punishment for crime. From the colony's beginning in 1682, Pennsylvania's Great Law limited the death penalty to treason and murder. England, officially Anglican, prescribed death for all the common law felonies. By 1718, a political crisis arose from another Quaker tenet, resistance to swearing oaths. Because English law required testimony under oath before sworn juries, this led to the dilemma that either there would be no prosecutions for crimes with Quaker witnesses or jurors, or there would be trials before unsworn juries. Hugh Pugh and Lazarus Thomas were convicted of the murder of Jonathan Hayes. There was no question of their guilt, and their appeals were rejected by Lieutenant Governor Keith and the Privy Council, but the anti-Quaker party sought to use, for political advantage, the fact that the jury had eight Quakers (and the grand jury 17) who served without having taken the oath prescribed by statute. They threatened to ask the Crown to exclude Quakers from government altogether. The political crisis was settled by both parties sacrificing the rights of criminal defendants: the Quakers could continue to affirm, while Pennsylvania adopted the orthodox criminal laws of England, with death for a dozen more crimes.[12] At a stroke, William Penn's experiment in limiting capital punishment came to an end, not to be revived until after independence.

Just as the eighteenth century's physical exhaustion with the previous century's carnage led to the end of outright religious wars, the nineteenth century's spiritual exhaustion with the rigor of Dante's and Edwards's traditional points of view was moderated in most denominations in the United States by an increasingly optimistic religious view of the possibility of salvation for everyone. Children were not encouraged so much to view death as a terrible judgment. They were more likely to be told it was a passing to a better world. Whatever the moral effect of this view, the thinking that death was not so awfully certain as a gateway to punishment not only weakened the attachment of society to death as a punishment but also made earthly punishments relatively more dreadful.

This change in religious climate coincided with the effect of unrelated political changes: the rise of party politics and other popular movements in the era of Andrew Jackson had its effect on crime and punishment, too. While the punishment of crime in England and throughout Europe had, for centuries, been something the rulers did to the ruled, in the new democracy in America, the punishment of crimes was something the government of the people did by the people to the people. Leniency in criminal punishments (at least to free men) could be tinged by unacknowledged self-interest as well as by sentiment of mercy. From the other direction, the abolition during the middle third of the nineteenth century of imprisonment for debt meant that in the social scale of punishments, prison sentences were now able to be reserved for what we would call today "real criminals."

These same decades offered another influence from Europe on thinking about crime and punishment from the newly minted discipline of sociology.

Adolphe Quetelet was a nineteenth-century Belgian mathematician and sociologist who stud-
ied criminal behavior through statistical analysis. (Library of Congress)

Adolphe Quetelet, a Belgian mathematician (who not only tutored the young
Prince Albert, future husband of Queen Victoria, but also corresponded with
amateur mathematician and future president James Garfield) found from his
statistical researches that there was an amazing regularity in criminal behavior.
He drew the conclusion that "Society prepares the crime, and the guilty person
is only the instrument."[13] To those influenced by Quetelet's works, as they
filtered through academia into society, it would seem doubly unfair to execute
someone for committing a crime for which society at large bore at least some of
the responsibility. Pioneering French sociologist Emile Durkheim went even
farther in his 1895 work *Rules of Sociological Method*. Durkheim asserted that

crime, even if abhorrent, was inseparable from society itself because all criminal law did was to mark where society was in the normal evolution of morality and law. He suggested that as we got better, more trivial offenses would be made crimes. His followers in American academies could be expected to draw the conclusion that the great danger of modern society was overpunishing crime, and although it was not logically necessary, the association between academics in the social sciences and a generally anti-death penalty stance continues with few exceptions to this day.

Earlier in the nineteenth century, direct opposition to capital punishment came from English society, where politicians like Samuel Romilly and utilitarian philosophers like Jeremy Bentham called for abolition of the death penalty for theft and other minor crimes. Bentham's policies were not based on any concept of human rights or love of liberty but, rather, on the mathematical and mechanistic flavor of contemporary philosophy: Bentham asserted that "the greatest good of the greatest number"—a phrase taken from Beccaria—was better served by less severe but more certain punishments. Even the defenders of the death penalty in Europe probably contributed to American opposition to capital punishment. Consider the defense of the death penalty published in 1821 by Joseph de Maistre, ambassador of the kingdom of Piedmont-Sardinia to the Russian court and known for his philosophical writings opposing the ideals of the French revolution. Maistre wrote his essay in the form of a conversation among noblemen, one of whom asserts that the prerogative of sovereigns to punish the guilty requires the post of public executioner, who was an outcast precisely because he faithfully executed his duties:

A dismal signal is given. An abject minister of justice knocks on his door to warn him he is needed. He sets out. He arrives at a public square packed with a pressing and panting crowd. He is thrown a poisoner, a parricide, a blasphemer. He seizes him, stretches him out, ties him to a horizontal cross, and raises his arms. Then there is a horrible silence; there is no sound but the crack of bones breaking under the crossbar and the howls of the victim. He unties him and carries him to a wheel. The broken limbs are bound to the spokes, the head hangs down, the hair stands on end, and the mouth, gaping like a furnace, occasionally emits a few bloody words begging for death. He has finished; his heart is pounding, but it with joy. He congratulates himself. He says in his heart: "No one can break men on the wheel better than I."

After this intentionally revolting description, Maistre's fictional Count explains:

And yet all greatness, all power, all subordination rests on the executioner; he is both the horror and bond of human association. Remove this incomprehensible agent from the world, and in a moment order gives way to chaos, thrones fall, and society disappears. God, who is the author of sovereignty, is therefore also the author of punishment.[14]

American readers of Maistre's work could be expected to be relieved and perhaps more than a little smug about the relatively humane attitude embodied in Anglo-American experiments in partial abolition of the death penalty.

After Darwin's publication of the *Origin of Species* in 1859, what might be called a wave of religious skepticism led to another paradox: if a man was the product of Nature's impersonal selection process and not an eternal soul destined for judgment by God, then death was the end of existence, and capital punishment was the most terrible of penalties. It was a small and almost unconscious next step to the belief that it should be applied as sparingly as possible. The tide of social and religious optimism, therefore, combined with that of pessimistic materialism to make the death penalty an increasingly rare penalty. It is no surprise that the death penalty was increasingly restricted in the nineteenth century to more serious types of homicide.

However, materialist religions have their changes in dogma too, and at the end of the nineteenth century, evolution sprouted its ugliest flower: scientific racism. In 1889, Cesare Lombroso published a text translated from the Italian into English as *The Criminal Man*. Lombroso asserted that within the evolving race, there were evolutionary throwbacks, natural-born criminals who could be detected by their immutable physical characteristics. Lombroso's contemporaries and successors in criminological theory such as Enrico Ferri and Raffaele Garofalo likewise believed in the inheritability of criminal types and recommended the death penalty for those convicted of murder as a way to protect society from contamination by its inferior members.[15] After the Holocaust, the motive behind this pseudoscience is as laughably transparent to us as the concept of religious war was to Voltaire, but in the early part of the century, it was quite in tune with its time with its implicit suggestion that by "pruning" the race of its "criminal element," we could evolve toward a brighter future even faster.[16] In the United States, the new scientific and pseudoscientific study of innate physical and racial characteristics found welcome in Progressive Era academic and legal circles. In an 1897 address marking the dedication of a new building at Boston University Law School, then Massachusetts Supreme Judicial Court Justice Oliver Wendell Holmes, Jr. mused:

Does punishment deter? . . . [T]he inquiries which have been started look toward an answer of my questions based on science for the first time. If the typical criminal is a degenerate, bound to swindle or murder by as deep seated an organic necessity as that which makes the rattlesnake bite, it is idle to talk of deterring him by the classical method of imprisonment. He must be got rid of; he cannot be improved, or frightened out of his structural reaction. If, on the other hand, crime, like normal human conduct, is mainly a matter of imitation, punishment fairly may be expected to help keep it out of fashion. The study of criminals has been thought by some well known men of science to sustain the former hypothesis.[17]

Holmes, having hinted that he believed that criminals were probably "degenerate rattlesnakes," would go on to serve on the United States Supreme Court for the first three decades of the twentieth century.

At the same time, in entirely different communities of discourse, religious conservatives were becoming alarmed at the enthusiasm of their liberal brethren to criticize or explain away parts of scripture, including the plain approval of the death penalty throughout the Old Testament. To the new fundamentalists, literal acceptance of the Bible appeared to compel support for capital punishment. Meanwhile, many political conservatives feared the impact of what seemed like a wave of lawless and anarchist immigrants: this was the era of Sacco and Vanzetti, executed in 1927 after what, for the times, was a lengthy review in the Massachusetts courts of their 1920 convictions for murder, and of Bruno Hauptman, executed in 1936 after trial in New Jersey the year before for the 1932 Lindbergh baby kidnaping. Once again, a paradoxical alliance of ends resulted as the scientific racist, the xenophobe, and the religious traditionalist all moved to maintain or strengthen criminal penalties. Accurate national statistics were not compiled before 1930, but it appears that the early part of the twentieth century marked a reversal in the decline in the use of the death penalty in the United States, as several states that had repealed their death penalty statutes—Kansas, Colorado, Washington, Oregon, South Dakota, Tennessee, Arizona, and Missouri—reinstated capital punishment. The federal government added the death penalty for a variety of offenses during wartime in the Espionage Act of 1917, and many states followed the federal government's 1932 adoption of the "Lindbergh law" by imposing or restoring the death penalty for kidnaping. Debates of the period focused on retribution and deterrence, as academics and politicians wondered whether the threat of the death penalty would cause an "ordinary" kidnaper to be more or less likely to kill his hostage.

ADDITIONAL PARADOXES

It is safe to anticipate that capital punishment will continue to generate impassioned debate and controversy. Some of the arguments are direct. For example, a critic might say that it is morally unacceptable and that it fails to deter crime: "Capital punishment is wrong. Always. Period." Alternatively, a proponent might say that it is morally right or, at least, that it is a necessary evil: "An eye for an eye, a life for a life. Always. Period." But some of the arguments are complex and nuanced. Sometimes an argument begins in a particular way but takes an unexpected turn along the way. Knowing the premise of an argument does not always allow one to predict the conclusion. Consider the following examples:

- Premise One—"A sentence of life without the possibility of parole promises a lifetime of anguish and suffering." A proponent of capital punishment would conclude that it is, therefore, more humane to execute the convicted criminal. On the other hand, an opponent of capital punishment might observe that such a life sentence is a more severe and fitting penalty for a heinous criminal than the momentary and fleeting pain of execution. In other words, we should eliminate capital punishment because the death penalty lets the criminal "get off" too easily!
- Premise Two—"Public executions are barbaric spectacles." An opponent of capital punishment would be expected to be especially opposed to public executions. On the other hand, some death penalty foes actually *supported* public executions for a time. Why? They hoped that such public executions would vividly demonstrate the wanton cruelty of capital punishment, thus rallying public opposition to its continued use.
- Premise Three—"Scientific evidence can conclusively demonstrate guilt or innocence." An opponent of capital punishment can point to proven examples of wrongful convictions and the risk that an innocent man will be executed in urging that the death penalty be eliminated. On the other hand, supporters of capital punishment can point to the same evidence and conclude that advances in DNA testing and the increasingly inexpensive blanketing of public places with surveillance cameras make it increasingly unlikely that wrongful executions will occur in the future. In other words, we can stop worrying so much about making mistakes.

In short, it is important to pay attention and to follow arguments from their beginnings to their ends. Do not assume any conclusions.

A SAMPLING OF ARGUMENTS AGAINST CAPITAL PUNISHMENT

When the modern death penalty reform movement began in Europe in the 1750s, there were two significant differences between the arguments of leading opponents of capital punishment, like the Italian jurist Cesare Beccaria, the French philosopher Voltaire, and, later, British reformers Jeremy Bentham and Samuel Romilly, and those of present-day abolitionists. Early opponents often argued that the death penalty was too frequently applied but accepted it in principle for some crimes. Second, they argued from the perspective of supporters of law enforcement, not of leniency. While making the points that the death penalty as applied was often excessively cruel, that it was an ineffective deterrent, and it had, on occasion, been erroneously applied, they advocated life imprisonment as a suitable alternative for most crimes not solely out of mercy but out of a desire to punish the criminal effectively.[18]

As mentioned previously, Beccaria's essay, "Of Crimes and Punishments," was very influential in the era of the framers.[19] "What right," Beccaria asked, "have men to cut the throats of their fellow creatures?" He answered that no individual can give others the right to take his life. In light of the fact that no man has a right to kill himself, no man can give this right to others. It follows that since the death penalty is not authorized by any right, it is a "war of the whole nation against a citizen whose destruction they consider necessary or useful to the general good." Beccaria argued that the death penalty is neither necessary nor useful except when a criminal still has connections that threaten society. Presumably Beccaria, unlike some who quote him today, would have accepted the 2005 execution of Stanley "Tookie" Williams for four murders in California, since even in the final clemency process before Governor Arnold Schwarzenegger, the evidence was that Williams, a founder of the gang known as the crips, had continued to threaten and assault inmates and guards in prison.

Beccaria also questioned the effectiveness of capital punishment as a deterrent, contending that it is not the intensity of the pain that has the greatest impact on the mind, but its continuance. The execution of a criminal is merely a "momentary spectacle" and is, therefore, a less effective method of deterring others than "the continued example of a man deprived of his liberty, condemned, as a beast of burden, to repair by his labour, the injury he has done to society." The spectator says to himself, if I commit such a crime, I will be "reduced to that miserable condition for the rest of my life." By contrast, the violent impressions made by the terrors of capital punishment produce only momentary effects on spectators.

For a punishment to be just, Beccaria maintained, it should have only the degree of severity necessary to deter others. Some can look upon the prospect of death with "intrepidity and firmness." Some criminals reason that their crimes will enable them to live "free and happy" lives, enjoying the fruits of their actions until they are apprehended, convicted, and sentenced. A day of "pain and repentance" may come, but it will be short. The criminal may willingly exchange an hour of grief for years of "pleasure and liberty." On the other hand, the "perpetual slavery" of imprisonment has the degree of severity necessary to deter even the most hardened and determined criminal. Extended imprisonment is a more severe punishment than the death penalty and it serves as a more effective deterrent.

Beccaria criticized the "barbarity" of the death penalty and its attendant formal pageantry. He found it "absurd" that laws against homicide are, in turn, enforced by the imposition of the death penalty. Through capital punishment, a people "publicly commit murder themselves" in order to signify that murder is wrong. When confronted with the argument that almost all nations have used the death penalty at some point in their histories, Beccaria replied that "the history of mankind is an immense sea of errors." After all, human sacrifices have also been common in many nations—hardly a compelling argument to reinstate the practice.

The timeless character of Beccaria's arguments against capital punishment can be seen in a paper presented at a 1914 meeting of the Men's International Theosophical League of Humanity.[20] One argument addresses the deterrent effects of capital punishment. Although it does remove a particular culprit from society and prevents him from committing similar crimes, it does little to deter other potential murderers. Murders are usually committed in fits of passion or temporary insanity, without "consideration of reason or self-interest." Furthermore, the death penalty denies the reformative character of punishment. Our duty is to isolate the dangerous man from society for so long as he remains dangerous. The only way to destroy a criminal is to reform him. Execution of the criminal takes away our chance to reform him and is nothing but "a stupid blunder." In addition, innocent persons have been hanged. Capital punishment is "irrevocable" and the "errors of justice" cannot be remedied. Capital punishment also repudiates the divine nature of man. Anger, fear, and retribution are passions that are to be left to eternal justice. As such, we should not accept a procedure that, if committed privately, would be regarded as murder "pure and simple."

After England abolished the death penalty in 1965, debates about whether the death penalty should be reinstated there brought forth numerous arguments on both sides of the issue that replayed themes sounded during the reforms of 1859.[21] Arguments against the death penalty included the possibility that innocent people would be executed, economic and racial disparities in the application of capital punishment, and the inherent brutality associated with executions, regardless of the method chosen. Two additional arguments presented the perspective of criminals and their families. First, consider the hell that the innocent family and friends of the criminal must endure in the time leading up to the execution and during the execution itself. It is difficult for people to accept that their loved one could have been guilty of such a serious crime and even more difficult to accept the imposition of the death penalty. The victim's family surely suffers, but the suffering of the murderer's family is real, too. Two wrongs do not equal one right. Further, keep in mind that criminals also have the capacity to feel fear, pain, and loss. Reflect upon the extreme mental anguish that the criminal suffers as the time of execution approaches. How would you feel knowing that you were slated to be put to death tomorrow morning at dawn? It is relatively easy to set aside such concerns when considering perpetrators of heinous offenses. It is less so when considering an 18-year-old girl sentenced to death for being a drug trafficking mule.[22] Since the Supreme Court has limited eligibility for the death penalty to a subset of murderers that excludes very young, very impaired, and mere accomplice defendants, it has been paradoxically easy to set aside such sympathy. Consider Karla Faye Tucker, executed in Texas in 1998 for her role in a grisly double murder in 1983. Tucker was widely considered to have sincerely reformed after becoming a born-again Christian while on death row, but Governor George W. Bush suffered no political ill effects from declining Tucker's request for a reprieve. During his campaign for President in 1992, Governor William J. Clinton of Arkansas was widely seen as benefiting from approving the execution of Ricky Rector despite Rector's admitted brain damage.

Public arguments against capital punishment today are generally based on one of three claims: (1) capital punishment is immoral because all killing is immoral; (2) capital punishment is unjust because the death penalty is irrevocable; (3) capital punishment fails to deter capital crimes. Philosopher Roy Weatherford has recently added a "nonpacifist" argument against capital punishment, claiming that it is immoral because of the *kind* of killing it is.[23] Weatherford agrees with British philosopher David Hume that one of the chief roots of morality is our sympathy for our fellows. But murderers do not arouse much sympathy: our sympathies lie not with the killer but with the pathetic victim. Weatherford believes, however, that the main reason moralistic critiques of capital punishment usually fail is that the moral teaching of the Judeo-Christian religious tradition is that capital punishment is not murder. The Biblical injunction "thou shalt not kill" has been widely interpreted to mean "Thou shalt not murder." Only murderous killing is forbidden. It is acceptable to kill in self-defense or in a just war. Weatherford concedes that deadly force is justifiable in self-defense or in just war. He, nevertheless, denies that capital punishment constitutes a similarly justified form of killing.

Weatherford's argument rejects the claim that capital punishment can be defended as society's version of the individual right of self-defense. For a killing to be justified, individuals or nations must be in "imminent danger of destruction" and deadly force must be the only reasonable available means for self-preservation. Neither criterion is met with respect to the death penalty. Capital punishment differs from self-defense in important ways. Weatherford presents several examples. The first involves killing in a just war. It is permissible for a soldier to kill an enemy soldier who poses a threat to the platoon or mission.

However, once an enemy soldier is captured and disarmed, the justification for killing vanishes. Killing unarmed prisoners of war is murder and is legally and morally prohibited. Another relates to justified killing to defend one's family. But suppose that a burglar invades my house and threatens my family, but instead of killing him, I knock him out and tie him up. I then have a drink, ponder the situation, become angry, pick up a gun, and shoot him. At this point, after the burglar has been incapacitated and no longer poses a threat, the killing is no longer justified. In fact, it is murder. Another example of justified killings involves the use of deadly force by police officers attempting to prevent a crime or the escape of a criminal. Police are justified in shooting a fleeing felon if he cannot be stopped by other available means. But suppose that this fleeing felon trips and breaks his leg. The pursuing police officers then capture, disarm, and handcuff him. If, upon reflection that perhaps a lenient judge will let him off with a light sentence, they decide to shoot and kill the criminal, the action is no longer justified. Once again, this killing is murder. The common feature of the unjustified killings in these examples is that the person killed has already been captured and incapacitated and no longer poses an immediate threat to anyone.

If the killing of unarmed prisoners who pose no immediate threat is murder, not justified killing, then applying this principle to capital punishment leads Weatherford to conclude that "the death penalty is murder." As the immediacy of the threat recedes, as the criminal is rendered nondangerous, as the time between the threatening action and the response of killing increases, the killing becomes less an urgent form of self-defense and more an instance of reflective premeditated murder. Although the death penalty has some of the characteristics of justified killing, it also has the characteristics of delay, disarming, and premeditation that make such killings unjustified. In sum, Weatherford agrees that self-defense and just wars provide examples of justified killing, but the elements of delay, disarming, and premeditation transform capital punishment into murder.

Weatherford's argument is a more elaborate presentation of the position of the Roman Catholic Church. In the first official Catechism issued by the church in several centuries, Paragraph 2267 admits the possibility of moral capital punishment but then, quoting from *Evangelium Vitae*, an 1995 encyclical letter by Pope John Paul II, limits those cases in practice to exclude any imaginable sanction for use of the death penalty in the United States:

Assuming that the guilty party's identity and responsibility have been fully determined, the traditional teaching of the Church does not exclude recourse to the death penalty, if this is the only possible way of effectively defending human lives against the unjust aggressor.

If, however, non-lethal means are sufficient to defend and protect people's safety from the aggressor, authority will limit itself to such means, as these are more in keeping with the concrete conditions of the common good and more in conformity with the dignity of the human person.

Today, in fact, as a consequence of the possibilities which the state has for effectively preventing crime, by rendering one who has committed an offense incapable of doing harm—without definitely taking away from him the possibility of redeeming himself—the cases in which the execution of the offender is an absolute necessity "are very rare, if not practically non-existent."

The possible execution of the innocent has been a perennial theme of death penalty opponents, but it has grown in prominent in public debates since the 1990s, when developments in DNA testing have made it possible in many cases where conviction rested on circumstantial evidence to establish that someone other than the accused was responsible for the crime. For most Americans, the potentials and pitfalls of DNA testing were placed in the spotlight for the first time during the murder trial of football player and actor O. J. Simpson in the summer of 1995. On July 15, 1997, Richard Dieter, executive director of the Death Penalty Information Center, announced the results of the Center's study. The report identified 69 people as of that writing who had been released from death rows since 1973 "after evidence of their innocence emerged." The study concluded that "[t]he current emphasis on faster executions, less resources for the defense and an expansion of the number of death cases mean that the execution of innocent people is inevitable."[24] Periodic and well-reported additions since then to the number of defendants condemned to death for crimes but later exonerated when evidence showed someone else committed the crime continue to fuel opposition to the death penalty.

Law professor Jack Greenberg, who, as counsel to the NAACP Legal Defense Fund from the late 1940s until the 1980s, opposed capital punishment in court and in academic publications, offered a version of Beccaria's empirical argument against capital punishment tailored to the United States.[25] Proponents of capital punishment, he says, describe an ideal system in which the death penalty is inflicted only upon reprehensible criminals and is carried out with sufficient frequency to deter other would-be capital offenders. But the reality in America, according to Greenberg, is that the death penalty is inflicted rarely and erratically. It is employed almost exclusively against killers of Whites and almost never against killers of Blacks.[26]

According to Greenberg, through the mid-1980s, an average of 19,000 homicides were committed in the United States, while the average number of executions hovered at about 20 per year, which reflects the public's ambivalence about capital punishment. Courts overturn capital convictions at a high rate, often on grounds unrelated to the seriousness of the crime. Reprehensible criminals have escaped the death penalty while less heinous criminals have been executed because their trials avoided technical or procedural errors. Greenberg concludes that the current system of capital punishment violates a central principle of justice: the most reprehensible criminals deserve the most severe sentences.[27] Consider the Green River killer. In November 2003, Gary Ridgway pleaded guilty to almost 50 strangling deaths in the Seattle area under a plea agreement that precluded prosecutors from seeking the death penalty in exchange for information about unsolved crimes. If Ridgway can get life, who can prosecutors in Washington credibly say deserves death?

Modern critics update Beccaria's questioning of the deterrent effects of capital punishment. Does the threat of execution deter crime more effectively than life imprisonment? For capital punishment to deter, they argue, the criminal would have to pause and anticipate likely consequences. What are the odds of being caught? Convicted? Executed? Such rational reflection does not occur when homicides happen in the heat of passion or anger or under the influence of drugs or alcohol. These are factors that have distinguished murder from manslaughter since Cain killed Abel, but in the late-twentieth-century advances in the study of the biological basis of behavior[28] brought this argument new weight. Many killers, though not so impaired as to be exempt from execution under *Atkins v. Virginia* (2002), are disturbed or are of low intelligence. Even if, legally speaking, they premeditate their crimes sufficiently to be convicted of capital murder, common sense says they kill impulsively. Most killers do not engage in the kind of cost-benefit analysis that the deterrence argument requires. And if they did, abolitionists like Greenberg say, the conclusion would be: you may in rare cases be executed if you commit murder in the deep South, especially in Texas, and kill a White person.[29]

In the most extreme form of this antideterrence argument, abolitionists assert that the death penalty actually can act as a crime magnet. Just as law enforcement personnel have coined the phrase "suicide by cop" as a grim way to describe mentally disturbed individuals who seek out armed confrontation with police, many judges in death penalty states can recall at least one murderer who proclaimed that he committed the crime precisely to receive the death penalty. In addition to those successful volunteers for suicide by murder, consider David Paul Hammer. In April 1996, Hammer was in the federal prison in Lewisburg, Pennsylvania, serving a 1,000-year prison term imposed by the state courts of Oklahoma, when he persuaded his cellmate that if Hammer pretended to injure him in an altercation, the cellmate would be transferred to a better prison. When the cellmate was tied, Hammer strangled him to death. Hammer initially claimed he was insane, then pleaded guilty to the murder. After a jury recommended the death sentence in 1998, he waived all appeals and asked for the death penalty. This use of the death penalty as an incentive provoked one appeals court judge to write that "Hammer wholly frustrates the underlying justifications for capital punishment." Four years later, after being confined at the federal death row at Terra Haute, Indiana, Hammer changed his mind again. Only days before the statute of limitations ran out on his opportunity to challenge his execution, Hammer moved to vacate his sentence on the grounds that his attorneys had failed to defend him effectively and the prosecution failed to turn over evidence. On December 27, 2005, a federal district court judge issued a 278-page opinion vacating Hammer's death penalty. The government did not appeal. As this book went to print, Hammer was reportedly posting content to a website dedicated to news about the death penalty. It is uncertain whether he has a cellmate.

If severe punishment does deter crime, then the prospect of life imprisonment would be severe enough to deter most rational persons from committing serious crimes. A form of punishment can be an effective deterrent only if it is carried out consistently and promptly. Abolitionists say a sentence of life imprisonment can meet these conditions. Capital punishment cannot meet them without reducing delays by eliminating procedural safeguards for suspects and defendants.[30]

Another rhetorical argument against capital punishment attacks its justification as a form of retributive justice. Retribution is held out as a morally permissible use of the power of the state, and capital punishment pays back the offender with the only punishment of equal severity. Does the rule that the punishment must fit the crime, abolitionists ask, permit capital punishment for the crime of murder any more than it would require the corrections system to rape rapists, torture torturers, betray traitors, and kill mass murderers over and over again? Even if such punishments were not impossible, justice and human dignity would impose limits on the severity of punishment. It is but a short step to the conclusion that the death penalty is similarly abominable. As Coretta Scott King, widow of slain civil rights leader Martin Luther King, Jr. and death penalty opponent, once observed: "An evil deed is not redeemed by an evil deed of retaliation. Justice is never advanced in taking of human life. Morality is never upheld by legalized murder."[31]

Abolitionists attack the retributive basis of capital punishment in more concrete terms. If similar severe condemnations should befall offenders who commit similar reprehensible crimes, what of the capital punishment system's regional, racial, and gender biases? This last point is an exceptionally fertile topic for abolitionist rhetoric because it avoids the more controversial topics of race and crime, and because the statistics are so skewed. During the 1980s and 1990s, only about 1 percent of those on death row were women, even though women committed about 15 percent of criminal homicides.[32]

Law professor Victor Streib conducted a study covering the period from 1973 through 2007 and found that at every stage of the process, women are less likely to be on the way to execution: they represent 10 percent of arrests for murder, but only 2 percent of the capital sentences. After appeals, only 1.4 percent of death row inmates are women, and after pardons and commutations, ultimately only 1.1 percent of those executed are women.[33] And of course, socio-economic class also has important effects: approximately 90 percent of those on death rows were unable to afford to hire their own lawyers when they were tried.[34]

The American Civil Liberties Union is probably the most widely known public organization seeking to abolish capital punishment as an "intolerable denial of civil liberties."[35] Philosophy professor Hugo Adam Bedau first authored "The Case Against the Death Penalty" for the ACLU's Capital Punishment Project in 1973. In subsequent revisions, Bedau offers, in capsule form, all the modern arguments against the death penalty:

- Capital punishment is cruel and unusual. It is a relic of the days when slavery, branding, and other forms of corporal punishment were common. Like these barbaric practices, capital punishment is outmoded.
- Opposition to the death penalty is not the same as sympathy for convicted murderers. The murderer demonstrates disrespect for human life. Legal execution does the same: it demonstrates the inefficiency and brutality of violence as a solution to social problems.
- Capital punishment denies due process of law because its imposition is often arbitrary. It is always irrevocable, depriving an individual of the opportunity to benefit from any new evidence that might prove his innocence.
- The death penalty violates constitutional guarantees of equal protection because it is applied in a random and discriminatory fashion. It is imposed most often upon those whose victims are White, on offenders who are minorities, and on those who are poor and uneducated.
- Changes in death sentencing have been superficial. The Supreme Court in the early 1970s identified various defects in capital statutes that have not been remedied. The shift from "unrestrained discretion" to "guided discretion" in sentencing has not made the process less random.
- The death penalty is not a viable form of crime control. When police chiefs were asked to rank factors that reduce violent crime, they mentioned curbing drug use, putting more police officers on the street, longer sentences, and gun control. They ranked the death penalty as least effective.
- Capital punishment wastes the time and energy of courts, prosecuting attorneys, defense counsel, juries, and courtroom and correctional personnel. It depletes legal and law enforcement resources.

Italy's minister for European Union affairs, Emma Bonino, walks to St. Peter's Square with an execution device strapped to her back during a rally for the United Nations to put a moratorium on the death penalty in Italy on April 8, 2007. The United Nations General Assembly adopted a resolution to abolish the death penalty on December 18, 2007. (AP/Wide World Photos)

- A society that respects life does not deliberately kill human beings. An execution is an official homicide. It endorses killing to solve problems and provides a damaging example of using violence to resolve conflicts: "The benefits of capital punishment are illusory, but the bloodshed and resulting destruction of community decency are real."

Abolitionists also stress that the international community generally rejects capital punishment. Half of all nations, including every nation in Western Europe, have abolished the death penalty. Canada abolished it in 1976. Between 1989 and 1995, two dozen other countries abolished the death penalty. The United Nations General Assembly formally urged nations to abolish the death penalty in a resolution adopted (by a 104-to-54 vote with 29 abstentions) on December 18, 2007. The resolution was opposed by the United States, as well as by Zimbabwe, Saudi Arabia, North Korea, and Iran. Abolitionists proclaim that this is not company we should be keeping.

Abolitionists, generally speaking, are more liberal across the board than proponents, but a new feature of the death penalty debate in the past two decades has been the appeal by abolitionists to fiscal conservatives. Matthew Stephens, a prison chaplain, cites a report from the *Miami Herald* computing that keeping a prisoner in jail for life would cost the state in excess of $500,000, based on a 40-year life span in prison. By contrast, the newspaper reported that each execution costs more than $3 million when costs associated with trial and sentencing, mandatory state review, additional appeals, jail costs, and the actual execution are taken into account.[36] Richard Viguerie, the pioneer of direct mail fundraising by political conservatives since the 1970s, who is credited with contributing to the birth of the modern conservative movement, announced his support for a moratorium on executions in 2009 with the appeal to conservatives that the death penalty process is "no different from any politicized, costly, inefficient, bureaucratic, government-run operation" except that the "end result is the end of someone's life."[37]

Eric M. Freedman, a law professor, also argues that the death penalty is a failure as a deterrent because it is more expensive than keeping murderers in prison for life. A New York study estimated that the death penalty costs three times more than life imprisonment. In Florida, each execution costs the state more than $3 million—approximately six times the cost of life imprisonment. California could save about $90 million per year by abolishing the death penalty and resentencing death row inmates to life terms. Extensive investigations and lengthy appeals account for many of these expenses, but the idea of providing less searching review in capital cases is contrary to common sense. Freedman also maintains that the death penalty reduces public safety because money spent on capital punishment could otherwise be spent on bulletproof vests for police officers, drug treatment programs, and other beneficial programs.[38]

Should the death penalty be shelved as too expensive? Abolitionists point to some of the current dollars-and-cents considerations:[39]

- In 2009, legislators in Colorado, Kansas, Maryland, Montana, Nebraska, New Hampshire, and New Mexico were urged to abolish the death penalty to curb the burden of rising costs on already tight state budgets.[40] New Mexico's lawmakers agreed.
- Lengthy appeals processes add particularly to the costs of capital punishment. This reflects our fear of making a mistake and sentencing an innocent person to death. These lengthy appeals monopolize much of the time of judges, attorneys, and other court employees, clogging court systems. New Jersey had reinstated its death penalty in 1982 but became the first state to repeal capital punishment by legislation signed in December 2007. Death

penalty opponents grounded their appeal on dollars and cents by proposing that the costs savings from abolition be used for benefits and services to the families of murder victims. An internal study by the legislature showed immediate savings of more than $125,000 per inmate simply from eliminating the final stay on death row and the mandatory state judicial review of the circumstances of the crime to determine whether the penalty was proportionate.[41]

- One incontrovertible objection to the death penalty is that mistakes cannot be undone.

Abolitionists stress that if we, as a society, wrongly convict and execute an innocent person, we cannot fix the error. Mistakes *do* occur. Human judgment is fallible. A 1998 conference at Northwestern University Law School focused on 74 cases of men and women who were freed from death row on the likelihood—and in many cases the absolute certainty—that they were not guilty. The conference led to the establishment of the Northwestern Center on Wrongful Convictions, which notes that Anthony Porter was exonerated in 1999, after 16 years on death row, when journalism students tracked down and videotaped the confession of the real killer. At one point Porter came within 48 hours of being executed.[42] Efforts to reduce costs and to speed up the process by limiting appeals should be considered in this context. Had the system moved faster, some wrongly convicted people would have been executed.[43] At its 1997 meeting, the American Bar Association House of Delegates passed a resolution calling for a halt on executions until courts nationwide can ensure that these cases are administered fairly and impartially, in accordance with due process, and with minimum risk of executing innocent people.[44]

Justice Blackmun summed up virtually all the objections to the death penalty in *Callins v. Collins*,[45] a 1994 decision in which the Court denied review in a Texas death penalty case. In the following excerpt from Justice Blackmun's dissenting opinion, he announced that he would no longer "tinker with the machinery of death":

Bruce Edwin Callins will be executed [tomorrow] by the state of Texas. Intravenous tubes attached to his arms will carry the instrument of death, a toxic fluid designed specifically for the purpose of killing human beings. The witnesses . . . will behold Callins . . . strapped to a gurney, seconds away from extinction. Within days, or perhaps hours, the memory of Callins will begin to fade. The wheels of justice will churn again, and somewhere, another jury or another judge will have the . . . task of determining whether some human being is to live or die.

We hope . . . that the defendant whose life is at risk will be represented by . . . someone who is inspired by the awareness that a less-than-vigorous defense . . . could have fatal consequences for the defendant. We hope that the attorney will investigate all aspects of the case, follow all evidentiary and procedural rules, and appear before a judge . . . committed to the protection of defendants' rights . . .

But even if we can feel confident that these actors will fulfill their roles . . . our collective conscience will remain uneasy. Twenty years have passed since this court declared that the death penalty must be imposed fairly and with reasonable consistency or not at all, and despite the effort of the states and courts to devise legal formulas and procedural rules to meet this . . . challenge, the death penalty remains fraught with arbitrariness, discrimination . . . and mistake . . .

From this day forward, I no longer shall tinker with the machinery of death. For more than 20 years I have endeavored . . . to develop . . . rules that would lend more than the mere appearance of fairness to the death penalty endeavor . . . Rather than continue to coddle the court's delusion that the desired level of fairness has been achieved . . . I feel . . . obligated simply to concede that the death penalty experiment has failed. It is virtually self-evident to me now that no combination of procedural rules or substantive regulations ever can save the death penalty from its inherent constitutional deficiencies . . . Perhaps one day this court will develop procedural rules or verbal formulas that actually will provide consistency, fairness and reliability in a capital-sentencing scheme. I am not optimistic that such a day will come. I am more optimistic, though, that this court eventually will conclude that the effort to eliminate arbitrariness while preserving fairness 'in the infliction of [death] is so plainly doomed to failure that it and the death penalty must be abandoned altogether.' I may not live to see that day, but I have faith that eventually it will arrive. The path the court has chosen lessens us all.[46]

A SAMPLING OF ARGUMENTS IN FAVOR OF CAPITAL PUNISHMENT

During the post–1965 debates in England and the post-*Furman* debates in the United States about whether the death penalty should be reinstated, the arguments advanced by proponents were the mirror images of those previously made by abolitionists. One argument made in support of the death penalty is that it permanently removes the worst criminals from society. A dead criminal cannot commit additional crimes, either in prison or outside after escaping or being released. Furthermore, while opponents of capital punishment frequently stress that it costs more than life imprisonment, executions in the United States are relatively expensive precisely because of the costs attributable to lengthy appeals and delays in carrying out the sentence. These costs could be lowered by limiting appeals. In twentieth-century England before abolition, for example, the average time spent on death row was from three to eight weeks and there was only one appeal.

Another argument proponents for the death penalty advance is that it is a very real punishment, not some attempt at rehabilitative treatment.

A murderer subject to capital punishment suffers in direct proportion to the offense: an eye for an eye, a life for a life. Retribution for murder is seen by many as a legitimate justification for the death penalty. Some go so far as to support capital punishment for offenses other than murder.

In addition, the supporters of capital punishment point to its deterrent effects. Some concede that it is difficult to provide conclusive proof that the death penalty deters criminals—other than the one who is executed. However, it appears that in countries where death sentences are almost always carried out, serious crime declines. In other words, the death penalty deters if execution is seen as certain or at least likely. Capital punishment is most likely to deter where the potential criminal has time to plan and consider the potential consequences of the crime. On the other hand, when a crime is committed in the heat of the moment, it is unlikely that any punishment could serve as a deterrent. For this reason, some supporters of capital punishment concede that it should be reserved only for cases of murder with premeditation.

Ernest van den Haag, a professor of jurisprudence and public policy, and until his death one of the few academic voices unabashedly for capital punishment,[47] acknowledged in 1986 that fewer than 30 murderers were at that time being executed every year, and most convicts sentenced to death are likely to die of old age. Nevertheless, he maintained, the death penalty raises important questions because it is society's harshest punishment, it is irrevocable, and it is the only corporal punishment still applied to adults.

Van den Haag rejected the claim that capital punishment is immoral because it allegedly is applied in a discriminatory fashion: maldistribution of any punishment among those who deserve it does not affect the justice or morality of the *punishment itself.* Because punishments are imposed on individuals, not on racial or ethnic groups, to van den Haag the relevant question is: does *this* individual deserve the punishment? If one person who deserves to be executed escapes the punishment, the guilt of another individual who *is* executed is in no way diminished. At its starkest, van den Haag's argument means that if the death penalty were imposed on guilty Blacks but not on guilty Whites, this irrational and discriminatory distribution would not result in the execution of any individual who did not deserve it. To let some guilty persons escape punishment does not do justice to them or to society, but it is not unjust to those guilty persons who were executed.[48]

Most academics are not proponents of capital punishment, and most proponents of capital punishment are not academics. As a result, van den Haag is rather alone in the abstract intellectual exercise of hypothesizing that racial discrimination is irrelevant to the justice of capital punishment. Most proponents of capital punishment would concede that it was precisely the racial disparity in the way the death penalty was applied for rape that caused the

Supreme Court to abolish capital punishment for rape in *Coker v. Georgia* (1977), whether the Justices admitted it or not. But proponents of capital punishment do embrace almost every other version of van den Haag's distribution thesis: that Texas puts murderers to death but Massachusetts does not does not mean that anyone in Texas is executed who does not deserve to be executed. To death penalty proponents, the abolitionists have a problem with federalism as much as capital punishment, and that tacit disagreement over how much diversity is tolerable in a nation of 50 states ends up being the fuel for a large part of the capital punishment debate.

Proponents of capital punishment, for the most part, will concede the possibility of miscarriages of justice, even in capital cases. Their reply to abolitionists is twofold. First, nearly all discretionary policies, whether mandating installation of airbags in automobiles or permitting concealed carrying of firearms, will cost the lives of some innocent bystanders. Those policies are chosen despite risks because the benefits outweigh the unintended costs. For those who think the death penalty is just, miscarriages of justice should be reduced as much as is reasonable but must be weighed against the moral benefits of capital justice. To proponents, it is abolitionists who are being unreasonable in claiming the death penalty is unjust even when it does not miscarry.[49]

The second response proponents of capital punishment make to the argument against the possibility of wrongful execution is to point to the spillover effect of ensuring zero error in other parts of the justice system. If a million dollars is spent re-examining the DNA evidence in a murder case on the chance that doubt can be cast on the verdict or in retrying the murderer because an appellate court, years after the fact, deems that the trial attorney missed a gambit, that is a million dollars unavailable to clear a backlog of evidence at a police crime lab that might have freed several persons unjustly accused of lesser crimes. It is hypocritical, capital punishment advocates say, to turn over every stone and pebble for those criminal defendants who are already likely to have had the most reliable determination of facts humanly possible while ignoring other potential injustices because the defendant is "only" serving a life sentence.

Proponents of capital punishment can conclusively argue that execution rules out any chance of recidivism in a way that life imprisonment, with its chance of parole, commutation, pardon, or escape, cannot. Beyond that specific case, there is no conclusive statistical evidence that the death penalty is a deterrent, much less a better deterrent than other punishments. Just as most opponents of capital punishment would continue to oppose it even if the death penalty were proven to deter, most proponents would favor retention of the death penalty as retribution even if it could be shown that it did not deter. Just as there are undoubtedly cases of unusually disturbed criminals who kill precisely to gain the 15 minutes of fame being a capital defendant would attract, there are similarly unquantifiable cases of criminals who fear the death penalty because of its finality more than imprisonment. Proponents differ from abolitionists precisely in their "hunch" about which of these groups is larger. To a proponent, sparing the lives of even a few prospective victims by deterring their murderers is valuable. Death penalty proponents also point out that the deterrent effect of the death penalty is just as firmly a hunch as the claim that tough sentencing means less crime. Crime in the United States began dropping sharply in the early 1990s as incarceration rates rose. The murder rate dropped as executions rose to a peak in 1994. To death penalty advocates neither of these is a coincidence.

Proponents reply with derision to the argument that executing a murderer endorses or legitimizes killing. Just as imprisonment is not thought to legitimize kidnaping, and fines are not thought to legitimize robbery, execution is a deserved punishment for an unlawful act. And further, proponents assert, the abolitionist argument that harsh criminal penalties inspire brutal crimes is tantamount to arguing that if criminal punishments were less harsh, criminal conduct would follow suit. That is fatuous.

Is the death penalty, in Justice Brennan's words, "uniquely degrading to human dignity"?[50] Some capital punishment proponents, echoing eighteenth-century philosopher Immanuel Kant, maintain that holding the murderer responsible to the contrary affirms his humanity by recognizing his rationality and responsibility for his actions.[51] He learns through his punishment that his fellow men and women have found him unworthy of living. Less theoretically inclined proponents often embrace a system that includes capital punishment precisely to have a credible ultimate deterrent: proponents claim that abolitionists are usually not interested in the real-world worthiness of the criminals they are ostensibly championing, nor are the criminals themselves satisfied with being held accountable for their crimes through punishments less than death. In fact, proponents point out, where the death penalty is not available, abolitionists make the exact same arguments about life without parole.[52] In short, to a proponent, the abolitionist argument is neither anchored to the real world nor sincerely advanced.

These arguments appear in letters to the editor every month in papers across America. They were summarized more than a century ago by John Stuart Mill, one of the most influential of nineteenth-century English liberals, in a speech before Parliament on April 21, 1868, in opposition to a bill banning capital punishment. (Reforms in previous decades had left the death penalty only for those convicted of aggravated murder.) Mill argued that where there is conclusive proof of guilt, depriving the criminal of "the life of which he has proved himself to be unworthy" is the most appropriate punishment.[53] Mill, generally considered a liberal champion because of the defense of individual freedom in his essay *On Liberty* (1859), defended the death penalty on the ground on which Justice Brennan attacked it: humanity to the criminal. The death penalty, Mill reasoned, is the *least* cruel method of deterring murderers. Subjecting a murderer to imprisonment with hard labor for life places him in "a living tomb" long after memory of his crime has faded. Compared to the "short pang of a rapid death," a long life of arduous and monotonous toil is more cruel. Human laws merely hasten death. The criminal would have died eventually at any rate, and in all likelihood, with a greater amount of bodily suffering.[54]

Mill's arguments recall the instances used by Cesare Beccaria to illustrate the cruelty and severity of life imprisonment in an attempt to persuade Europe's rulers in the previous century to *abolish* capital punishment. The elimination of the death penalty, Beccaria contended, would not mean that murderers would get away with their crimes. Instead, they would face the even harsher punishment of life imprisonment. Mill asserted that life imprisonment is harsher so that the presumably more compassionate members of Parliament would draw the opposite conclusion and *preserve* death by hanging as a humane punishment.

Who has the better of this argument? Both are still used, and it may be a case of the grass is always greener on the other side of the barbed wire fence. Italy is one of the nations most vocal against the use of the death penalty in the United States.[55] There is virtually no chance capital punishment will ever return to Italy. In 2007, 311 prisoners serving life sentences in Italy petitioned the government for the "right to be executed." They claimed that a life sentence without the possibility of parole was a "living death" where they died a little every day.[56] Would they have petitioned if they were in a state like Texas where executions occur with some regularity?

To those who say that capital punishment does not always deter, Mill answered that its influence should not be measured by its effect on hardened criminals. Those whose way of life keeps them "within sight of the gallows" become hardened and care little about the prospect of capital punishment. It is said that old soldiers are little affected by the chance of dying in battle. Similarly, professional criminals become indifferent to their possible executions. But the effectiveness of capital punishment should be judged by its deterrent effects on those who are still innocent and who are motivated to resist temptation. Does capital punishment deter? On one hand, we know that *some* murders occur. The perpetrators of these crimes have not been deterred. But we cannot know how many people it *succeeded* in deterring. We cannot know how many human beings have been saved from those who would otherwise have murdered them. It is reasonable to conclude that at least *some* innocent lives have been saved by the death penalty.[57]

Capital punishment, Mill argued, loses its effectiveness when it is threatened for lesser offenses. It ceases to intimidate if criminals do not believe in it. Pickpockets worked the crowds during public executions. They did not fear that they would be executed. As such, capital punishment should be reserved for the most serious crimes.[58] On this point, Mill repeated the position taken by another champion of liberalism, Jean Jacques Rousseau, almost a century earlier. Rousseau would have been considered an abolitionist in his day because he believed:

> ... frequent punishments are a sign of weakness or slackness in the government. There is no man so bad that he cannot be made good for something. No man should be put to death even as an example if he can be left to live without danger to society.[59]

But from a modern perspective, Rousseau would certainly be a death penalty advocate because:

> ... every wrongdoer attacks the society's law, he becomes by his deed a rebel and a traitor to the nation; by violating its law he ceases to be a member of it; indeed he makes war against it. And in this case, the preservation of the state is incompatible with *his* preservation; one or the other must perish; and when the guilty man is put to death it is less as a citizen than as an enemy. ... and therefore the right of war makes it legitimate to kill him.[60]

To the abolitionist argument that it is illogical to try to teach respect for life by destroying it, Mill observed that the same argument could be made about any form of punishment. The criminal justice system is designed to make criminals suffer to deter them from inflicting suffering upon innocent people. We fine criminals. Doing so does not show disrespect for property. We imprison criminals. Doing so does not show disrespect for personal freedom. In the same way, executing a murderer does not show disrespect for human life. To the contrary, it demonstrates our high regard for human life as we enforce the rule that he who takes a life deserves to forfeit his own.[61]

Mill conceded that if an innocent person is erroneously executed, this mistake can never be remedied. This argument is convincing where the criminal justice system is dangerous to the innocent. But Mill believed that the defects of the criminal justice system of his time favored the accused. Courts were inclined to allow 10 guilty persons to escape before a single innocent person suffered. Prisoners were afforded the benefit of the "merest shadow of a doubt." The impossibility of correcting errors in capital cases, he thought, made judges and juries even more reluctant to find a defendant guilty.[62] Similar arguments are made today.

Political essayist Robert Lee is a contemporary supporter of capital punishment. He observes that capital punishment *does* deter. It deters at least one person, the person who has been executed, from ever again committing a crime. But deterrence is not the point. First, it is wrong to punish one person merely to serve as an example to others. Second, deterrence has nothing to do with the condemned person's guilt or innocence. Deterrence could be achieved by executing an innocent person. To Lee and proponents like him, the question is, has the accused *earned* this penalty? Was this penalty deserved?[63]

Lee also addresses the financial expense of today's capital punishment system. Lee believes that high costs are due to excessive appeals and delay tactics employed by defense attorneys. In a 1990 speech to the American Law Institute, then Chief Justice William H. Rehnquist recommended that death row inmates be given one chance to challenge their sentence in state courts and one chance to challenge it in federal courts. Congress substantially adopted his recommendations in 1996.

To proponents like Lee, life imprisonment is an unsatisfactory alternative to the death penalty. Lifers endanger guards and other prisoners. What do they have left to lose? Further, these prisoners sometimes escape. Only capital punishment adequately protects society.[64]

Some proponents even reject mercy-based arguments. Mercy does not supersede justice. The state does not have the right to extend mercy on the part of a murder victim because the wrong was done to the victim, not to the state. Justice is the only standard for assigning punishment.[65]

Lee also contends that capital punishment appropriately reflects society's need for retribution. As British jurist Lord Denning said in 1953, " . . . it is essential that the punishment for grave crimes . . . adequately reflect the revulsion felt by a great majority of citizens for them."[66]

Should the death penalty be discarded as the punishment of a time now past, or retained because it has the same value that it always did? The arguments in favor of the death penalty can be summarized as follows:

- Expiation: Family members of the victim may take years to recover from the death of a loved one. Some may never recover. The death penalty can contribute to their recovery by providing a form of closure. A life sentence leaves the criminal alive to haunt the thoughts and memories of the grieving family. The death penalty provides finality.
- Deterrence: While prison time is an effective deterrent for some would-be criminals, for others, imprisonment has not only lost the ability it had to inspire fear but may, in fact, be an improvement over their precarious circumstances on the street. Many wardens will candidly report that their

populations go up in the winter as parolees go "back inside" for "three hots and a cot." There is every reason to believe that this decline in the deterrent effect of prison has had a trickle-up effect on more serious criminals, for whom a more severe punishment is needed. The death penalty can serve as an effective deterrent, and prosecutors should have this option at their disposal. Does the death penalty in fact deter? Statistics cannot reveal the number of people who decided not to commit a capital offense because of the death penalty. Without it, even more serious crimes might be committed.

• Retribution. A fundamental principle of justice is that the punishment should fit the crime. When someone commits a premeditated murder, it makes sense that the perpetrator should forfeit his life as well. To death penalty proponents, support for the death penalty is part of an effort to have the criminal justice system place more emphasis on protecting the victim than the accused. Connecticut's legislature voted to repeal that state's little-used death penalty in 2009, but the repeal was successfully vetoed by Governor Jodi Rell in part due to testimony by William Petit, Jr., whose wife and children were murdered by two paroled felons. Dr. Petit's plea to the legislature was, "My family got the death penalty and you want to give murderers life. That is not justice."[67] Without death as a sanction, proponents argue, the system shows relatively more sympathy for criminals than it does for victims. A person who is on death row is there for a reason. And because as a practical matter, every jurisdiction that uses capital punishment requires more than "mere" premeditated murder before a defendant can be sentenced to death, in many cases he has committed other heinous crimes, too. To proponents, a long line of victims await justice: capital punishment provides it.

• Interdiction. Prisoners who receive life sentences are by definition very dangerous. Prisoners already serving life sentences when they commit crimes are even more dangerous. What prevents them from murdering others while they are in prison? Threatening them with a longer sentence or with the loss of some privileges will not protect other prisoners and guards. In fact, one of the most dangerous places for prison guards is California's death row, where prisoners have little expectation of being executed and less expectation of improved conditions. Corrections officers are routinely assaulted with homemade weapons and even feces and urine hurled by inmates.[68] The real prospect of facing the death penalty can serve as a deterrent for such prisoners. Prisoners who are serving life sentences have decades to plan escape attempts and even to commit additional crimes. Without the death penalty as an additional sanction, what incentive is there to prevent such a prisoner from attempting to escape? And, of course, proponents constantly point out that if the death penalty were promptly executed in the first place, escape would be a nonissue.

- Innocence. One of the main arguments against the death penalty is the possibility of error. DNA tests have revealed that some innocent prisoners had been placed on death row. But DNA testing and other methods of modern crime-scene science cut both ways. They can eliminate almost all uncertainty about a person's guilt or innocence. It is already difficult to convict an innocent person. A unanimous jury must conclude that there is evidence of guilt beyond a reasonable doubt. Multiple appeals are provided. Add to these precautions that DNA testing is more than 99 percent reliable, and it is extremely unlikely that an innocent person will be executed. Proponents can point to the ever-increasing number of exonerations from death row with the same enthusiasm as do abolitionists, because the fact of exonerations can be contrasted with the extremely sketchy and anecdotal claims by abolitionists that innocent men have actually been executed. Proponents of the death penalty admit the possibility of error but point out that innocent defendants are convicted of noncapital crimes as well, and that no one even advances the argument that imprisonment is somehow cruel because innocent defendants are imprisoned.[69] If abolitionists are sincere about exonerating the innocent, proponents suggest that the last place to focus is defendants sentenced to capital punishment because there is an almost complete absence of evidence for the abolitionist claim that any innocent person has been executed in the United States since 1976.

- Spillover effects. Just as some proponents believe that the death penalty balances the books for the taking of life, so other supporters of capital punishment point to its effect on the criminal justice system generally. While opponents of the death penalty talk about the expense of particular cases, proponents point out that most criminal cases, murders included, are settled through plea bargains. The accused admits guilt in exchange for a reduced sentence. Plea bargains are important in cutting costs and relieving an overcrowded court system. The death penalty gives prosecutors another important bargaining chip that they can use in the plea-bargaining process. A prosecutor who believes that a defendant deserves a life sentence may be unable to force a defendant to plead guilty and accept this sentence without the threat of the death penalty.

Recall Justice Blackmun's dissenting opinion in *Callins v. Collins*. In the following excerpt from his concurring opinion, Justice Scalia responded to Justice Blackmun:[70]

The Fifth Amendment provides that '[n]o persons shall be held to answer for a capital . . . crime, unless on a presentment or indictment of a Grand Jury . . . nor be deprived of life . . . without the due process of law.' This clearly permits the death penalty to be imposed, and establishes beyond doubt that the death penalty is not one of the 'cruel and unusual punishments' prohibited by the Eighth Amendment. [H]owever, over the years since 1972 this court has attached to the imposition of the death penalty two quite incompatible sets of commands: the sentencer's discretion to impose death must be closely confined (see *Furman v. Georgia*, 1972), but the sentencer's discretion not to impose death (to extend mercy) must be unlimited (*Eddings v. Oklahoma*, 1982; *Lockett v. Ohio*, 1978). These commands were invented without benefit of any textual or historical support; they are the product of just such 'intellectual, moral, and personal' perceptions as Justice Blackmun expresses today, some of which . . . have been made part of what is called 'the court's Eighth Amendment jurisprudence.'

Though Justice Blackmun joins those of us who have acknowledged the incompatibility of the court's *Furman* and *Lockett-Eddings* lines of jurisprudence . . . he unfortunately draws the wrong conclusion from the acknowledgment . . . Surely a different conclusion commends itself, to wit, that at least one of these judicially announced irreconcilable commands which cause the Constitution to prohibit what its text explicitly permits must be wrong. Convictions in opposition to the death penalty are often passionate and deeply held. That would be no excuse for reading them into a Constitution that does not contain them, even if they represented the convictions of a majority of Americans. Much less is there any excuse for using that course to thrust a minority's views upon the people.

Justice Blackmun begins his statement by describing with poignancy the death of a convicted murderer by lethal injection. He chooses, as the case in which to make that statement, one of the less brutal of the murders that regularly come before us, the murder of a man ripped by a bullet suddenly and unexpectedly, with no opportunity to prepare himself and his affairs, and left to bleed to death on the floor of a tavern. The death-by-injection which Justice Blackmun describes looks pretty desirable next to that. It looks even better next to some of the other cases currently before us, which Justice Blackmun did not select as the vehicle for his announcement that the death penalty is always unconstitutional, for example, the case of the 11-year-old girl raped by four men and then killed by stuffing her panties down her throat. How enviable a quiet death by lethal injection compared with that!

CONCLUSIONS: LOOKING TO THE FUTURE?

The decisions of the Court and the competing arguments of thinkers off the Court reflect the development of the debate. At the birth of the country, with the exception of the Pennsylvania Quakers and Benjamin Rush, there was hardly any dispute about the validity of capital punishment in the abstract. The objections were to how painfully it was carried out and to how many crimes less than murder, violent rape, or treason should be punished by death. Because the United States was expressly founded on the theory that government was by the consent of the governed, there never could be the objection like the one Thomas Paine made to capital punishment in England, that criminal penalties were imposed on the people, and not enacted by the people. So long as traditional beliefs about right, wrong, and the nature of crime remained stable, for the first hundred years of this country, there could be arguments about whether the punishment fit the crime, but not over what those punishments could be.

With the growth of the government and especially of the federal government, all sorts of unplanned consequences could and did come about. One was that the traditional notion of deterrence, once the federal government began to keep reliable statistics, could be tested by examining the evidence to see whether criminal punishment was, in fact, deterring anyone. In the 1950s, primitive statistical examination of the correlation between use of the death penalty and crimes in the same jurisdiction hardly provided support for the notion that the death penalty was a deterrent to crime overall or even to murder in particular. When more extensive data sets and more sophisticated statistical tools became available at the end of the twentieth century, the verdict of the statisticians was mixed: it seemed that the death penalty was a slight deterrent if regularly used, but it was ineffective in halting most headline-grabbing and grisly murders, and in some cases, the prospect of notoriety on death row appeared to be the motive for murder. The tendency of academics on both sides to find that statistics support their stance on the death penalty and the lure of publicity from making controversial deterrence arguments perhaps clouded the debate.[71]

When issues of racial discrimination and equal protection came to the forefront after World War II, unsurprisingly, the racial disparities in the imposition of death became matters for public discussion as well. One reason for the practical disappearance of the death penalty in the years well before *Furman* was the sense, not just on the Court, that the death penalty was being disproportionately imposed on Black men. The Supreme Court never expressly stated that this was the reason behind its condemnation of unguided jury determination of eligibility for death, and *McCleskey v. Kemp* (1987) specifically rejected the notion that slight disproportions in the race of death row inmates had constitutional significance, but the pattern of Supreme Court decisions in the 30 years before and after *Furman* are illuminated by the Court's push to achieve a color-blind criminal justice system. With controversies such as whether prosecutors or defendants were barred from using peremptory challenges to shape the racial diversity of a jury settled in the 1980s and 1990s, more recently, the Court has turned to the question of poverty and eligibility for the death penalty in its examination of whether death row defendants received adequate representation.

Once the worst excesses in biased jury selection procedures and sentencing schemes were identified and eliminated, and after repeated forays into questions of whether victim-impact evidence could be permitted before a jury, the Court, however, had to confront two inescapable facts. First, it is impossible to have a jury make a decision that allows someone outside the jury room to be certain that there was no bias or arbitrariness unless the rules for imposing the death sentence are tightly circumscribed to make the death sentence possible only for the worst kinds of murders. Second, if the evidence is so tightly controlled, the jury's ability to hear (possibly mitigating) evidence relating to the defendant's deservingness of death is limited, and the jury ceases to be the voice of the community and merely checks off boxes on a verdict slip. Judges disagree where the line should be drawn, but almost all of them recognize that juries cannot do two incompatible things at once.

The possibility of executing an innocent defendant has troubled judges and juries since the beginning of the criminal justice system, but the issue took on heightened relevance in the last two decades of the twentieth century with the development of DNA testing and other technologies that could, in some cases, exclude persons as possible suspects. At the same time, the experience of the federal and state courts in the previous decades with repetitive filing of *habeas corpus* petitions solely for purposes of staving off execution led to a profound sense that the judicial system needed to be made less susceptible to manipulation.

Again, the two goals of a final decision and a certain decision are in diametric opposition to each other. Since one cannot have one without sacrificing the other, the Court has repeatedly drawn and redrawn the line between the two. At first, the Court's decisions in the 1990s in *Gomez* and *Herrera* carried the Court in the direction of cutting off review in order to stop the endless *habeas corpus* litigation that, as of 2007, made the average stay on death row 13 years. Congress provided some statutory relief from repetitive filings in the Antiterrorism and Effective Death Penalty Act in 1996 (known within the death penalty bar as "AEDPA"). The Court more recently has announced, in *House v. Bell* (2006), that an inmate who can demonstrate that new scientific evidence exists that would give a reasonable jury a reasonable doubt about his guilt is entitled to review of his claims. President George W. Bush and Congress came to the aid of the Court by enacting the Innocence Protection Act of 2004, which permits controlled scientific testing of evidence in support of plausible claims that a defendant was actually innocent. Forty-six state legislatures had done likewise by 2009. The Court recently has held, in *District Attorney's Office for the Third Judicial District v. Osborne* (2009), that judges are not free to supplement these statutes by inventing a new constitutional right to DNA testing. It appears that this portion of the debate about certainty versus finality has come to a close.

What is certain is that with the attempt to do so many incompatible things at once, the death penalty has become a costly one. The Supreme Court is unlikely to mention the cost of the death penalty as a factor that affects its constitutionality, but legislators certainly are aware of the bottom line: unsurprisingly, all three states that have repealed the death penalty since *Gregg v. Georgia* have cited economic reasons as among the chief reasons. In an era when DNA evidence has exonerated well over 100 death row inmates, death penalty opponents are finding more success as fiscal conservatives than as social liberals: the argument that an innocent man might be executed is less and less convincing to the public, and the argument that a criminal might suffer during lethal injection is, for the most part, more likely to be met with jeers rather than sympathy.

Even death penalty opponents may be surprised that the most effective check on executions, at present, seems to be through litigation over the cocktail of drugs used in lethal executions. In a law review article shortly after Charlie Brooks was executed by Texas on December 7, 1982, in the nation's first use of lethal injection, law professor Victor Streib touched on death penalty issues that were "hot" in the 1980s, namely racial fairness and personal responsibility. Streib noted that Brooks was the first Black to be executed since 1967, Brooks was a Black man convicted of murdering a White man, and Brooks's codefendant pleaded guilty and received a 40-year sentence even though he may have actually fired the murder weapon. In passing, Streib noted that Brooks's execution "prompted a minor and unresolved controversy about the medical ethics involved and whether lethal injection is a more humane and/or more desirable form of accomplishing capital punishment."[72] Twenty-five years later, the "minor unresolved controversy" has, as a practical, matter taken sole position at center stage, with the decision in *Baze v. Rees* (2008) that lethal injection using a three-drug protocol was not cruel and unusual punishment. As lower courts wrestle with the caveat by Chief Justice Roberts that it might be cruel to refuse to adopt an alternative that is readily available and can be proved to significantly reduce the risk of severe pain, it appears that litigation over the different lethal combinations of drug cocktails will continue for years. Meanwhile, in early 2011, the sole domestic supplier of the thiopental sodium used in executions announced that it would halt production of the drug and the Italian government also banned the export of the drug for any such use.[73] Death penalty opponents have threatened medical personnel with professional ethics charges for participating in lethal injections, even if the only connection is that the governor signing the execution warrant has a medical degree.[74] Like the guillotine, electrocution, and the gas chamber, at the outset, lethal injection was hailed as a humane way to induce a peaceful death. It appears, however, that the controversy over this method of execution will not itself be "put to sleep" any time soon.

As the country moves forward, the debate over capital punishment on the Court most resembles that on the Court of the 1960s: the issue divides the Justices but has moved to the back burner. Unlike the Warren Court and the Burger Court of the 1960s and 1970s, the tenures of Chief Justice Rehnquist and now Chief Justice John Roberts seem marked by their attempts to keep the Court out of the spotlight. Despite the biting exchange we quoted from *Callins v. Collins,* Justice Scalia and Justice Blackmun wrote just for themselves in a case the Court as a whole declined to review. Conflict within the Court over capital punishment was muted by a lack of turnover on the Court. For 11 years, from 1994 to 2005, the Court had the same nine Justices, one of the longest stable periods in the Court's history. By contrast, during President Franklin Delano Roosevelt's time in office, there were eight new Justices in seven years; in the turbulent 10 years just before *Furman,* there were also eight new Justices. In recent years, the Court's members have been very familiar with each other and each other's judicial style. At least in capital punishment and other criminal law decisions, opinions appeared to be written in an attempt to achieve as large a degree of consensus as possible. Reliance on personal opinion about the death penalty as a basis for making constitutional law, like Justice Blackmun in *Callins,* has not been imitated even by the Justices most opposed to the death penalty. The days are over when bumper stickers responded to the Court's criminal procedure rulings with "Impeach Justice Douglas," and in fact, retired Justice Sandra O'Connor and other judges are working hard to attempt to educate the public about what it is the Court does out of a concern that too many persons are unaware of, or indifferent to, any role the Court has under the Constitution. With the Court taking a lower profile, the center of the debate has moved to state legislatures and to Congress.

Nevertheless, the Court keeps the last word on the death penalty, and on the Court, the most important principle of jurisprudence is the aphorism attributed to Justice Brennan that "it takes five votes to do anything around here." To paraphrase Justice Frankfurter's observation, the Court's decisions cannot be separated from the Justices' concept of their role, and the Justices have reliably divided into two distinct groups for the last 30 years. In the 1970s, the Court contained two reliable death penalty abolitionists, Justices Brennan and Marshall, who made the ruling in *Furman* possible. Until their departure from the Court in the early 1990s, and with the conversion of President Nixon's appointee Justice Harry Blackmun to the abolitionist position until his retirement in 1994, the antiexecution wing of the court only needed to convince two Justices that in a particular case, the death penalty

The U.S. Supreme Court building in Washington, D.C. The relative stability of Supreme Court Justices in recent years has moved the spotlight on the capital punishment issue to state legislatures and governors. (Franz Jantzen/Collection of the Supreme Court of the United States)

was unreliably or improperly imposed. President Ronald Reagan's appointment of Sandra O'Connor, Antonin Scalia, and Anthony Kennedy as Justices and the promotion of William Rehnquist to be Chief Justice moved the Court in the 1990s toward greater deference toward state capital punishment legislation and led to a curtailment of some of the more extreme examples of condemned inmates resorting to federal courts to delay executions. Justice O'Connor's and Justice Kennedy's position in the middle of the Court made them the swing votes in many of the Court's closer decisions.

President William Clinton's two appointees, Justices Ruth Ginsburg in 1993 and Stephen Breyer in 1994, joined Justice John Paul Stevens, the last sitting justice from the Court that issued *Gregg*, and, Justice David Souter, President George H. W. Bush's first appointee, as four reliable votes in opposition to the death penalty. George H. W. Bush's second appointee, Justice Clarence Thomas, hearkens back to Justice Hugo Black's historical analysis of the Eighth Amendment as consistent with the death penalty. President George W. Bush's two appointees, Chief Justice John Roberts in

2005 and Justice Samuel Alito in 2006, take deferential positions to state capital punishment laws similar to those of the justices they replaced, Chief Justice Rehnquist and Justice O'Connor. The swing vote in 5–4 cases now and for the foreseeable future appears to be Justice Kennedy.

Many assumed that Sonia Sotomayor, President Barack Obama's appointment to replace Justice Souter after his retirement in 2009, would follow Justice Souter's generally anti–death penalty leanings. But Justice Sotomayor may disappoint abolitionists hoping to maintain a bloc of four Justices opposed to the death penalty. Before being named to the district court by President George H. W. Bush, Justice Sotomayor was a prosecutor in New York City for five years early in her career, and her first opinion in a capital case, *Wood v. Allen* (2010), affirmed the denial of a writ of *habeas corpus* to an Alabama inmate on death row for murdering his ex-girlfriend. Writing for seven members of the Court, Justice Sotomayor demonstrated no discomfort at upholding a death sentence on fairly narrow technical grounds without any questioning of the legitimacy of capital punishment itself.

Justice Stevens, who retired in 2010, dissented in *Wood v. Allen*, but also on fairly narrow technical grounds. Justice Stevens announced in his concurrence in *Baze v. Rees* (2008) that he had come to the *personal* conclusion that the death penalty was a pointless extinction of life and therefore cruel and unusual, but that he also felt constrained to find that under the law as it stood the death penalty was not unconstitutional. By contrast with Justice Blackmun in *Callins*, Justice Stevens found support for his frequent votes against the death penalty in the Constitution and precedents of the Court, not his personal preferences. In one of his last opinions, Justice Stevens agreed with the other eight members of the Court to uphold an Ohio death sentence in *Smith v. Spisak* (2010). Stevens objected that Spisak's attorney was wrong to argue to the jury that his client, who took the stand and admitted three murders, was "sick," "twisted," and "never going to be any different," but conceded that not even Clarence Darrow could have persuaded a jury to spare him.[75]

Even if Elena Kagan, Stevens's successor on the Court, shares an abolitionist disposition on the death penalty, it is highly unlikely that she will be an open opponent of capital punishment. The confirmation process has been formally conducted only since the 1950s and televised since the 1980s but, after the defeat of President Reagan's nominee Robert Bork and the unsuccessful attempt to derail President George H. W. Bush's nomination of Justice Thomas, candidates for the Supreme Court tend to be selected for their absence of documented opinions on controversial issues, and hearings are more of an opportunity for Senators to display their support or opposition for the nominating President's policies. It is unlikely that an open abolitionist in the mold of Brennan, Marshall, and later Blackmun will even be nominated. Recently, presidents have confounded the stereotypes that Democrats are abolitionists and Republicans are the opposite: President Clinton signed a federal death penalty act creating dozens of death-eligible offenses in 1994, and President George W. Bush signed a federal DNA testing statute 10 years later. Unless a politically powerful abolitionist president is presented with several vacancies on the Court, we are highly unlikely to see another *Furman*.

Most cases never reach the Justices, of course. Rising caseloads overall and the recent trend of the Supreme Court to review fewer decisions than in the 1960s and 1970s mean that an increasing share of death penalty decisions will finally be made in the lower federal courts. There, matters have become more routinized as the federal courts of appeals and district courts have almost universally adopted procedures to handle death penalty cases and last-minute appeals to avoid the all-night rush to decision that sometimes took place in previous decades. Most courts have a law clerk or law clerks who specialize in capital punishment *habeas corpus* petitions to provide consistent research and memoranda to the judges. In many cases, these obscure clerks exercise enormous influence on the reasoning behind whether a sentence of death is upheld, if not on the decision itself. Most judges take the bench at middle age or later and rely on the ideas or philosophies they were exposed to a quarter- or half-century earlier, so that whether conservative or liberal, judges for the most part acted as a brake on the latest fads in legal and political thought. The introduction of law clerks a century ago did little at first to change this. From the 1920s to the 1990s, however, the rapid turnover of young lawyers fresh from elite law schools, especially Harvard and Yale, helped spread new trends in legal philosophy more rapidly, especially to the Supreme Court. Conservative Justices like former professors Felix Frankfurter and Antonin Scalia or liberal Justices like former professors William Douglas or Ruth Bader Ginsburg retained close ties to the academy. Appeals court and Supreme Court law clerks often became professors and sent their protégés back as a new generation of law clerks and sometime as judges. At the Supreme Court today, there is a three-generation illustration of this: Chief Justice Roberts began his career by clerking for Chief Justice Rehnquist, and Chief Justice Rehnquist began by clerking for Justice Robert Jackson. Justice John Paul Stevens clerked for Justice Wiley Rutledge. After Stevens' retirement, clerks remain well represented: Justice Stephen Breyer clerked for Justice Arthur Goldberg, Justice Samuel Alito clerked for a judge on the Court of Appeals, and Justice Elena Kagan clerked for both a circuit judge and Justice Thurgood Marshall.

Until the 1980s the model clerk served a brief apprenticeship before he went into practice for himself. Increasingly, however, a law clerk may spend many years or even her (the change in gender is deliberate: while law was a male preserve as late as Justice O'Connor's law school days, today most new lawyers are female) whole career as a clerk. As judges retire or, more recently, leave the lower federal courts in increasing numbers to pursue more lucrative careers staff law clerks are in many cases more familiar with the thick records and complex proceedings in death penalty appeals. The proliferation of staffs and the gradual change in the role of the law clerk has led to several well-publicized criticisms of judges delegating too much decision making to unappointed bureaucrats,[76] but the only noticeable effect of the change is that the interchange between academics and judges, especially in the lower federal courts, has greatly diminished. Cases from the middle of the twentieth century, such as *Trop v. Dulles* (1958), which held that loss of citizenship for desertion was unconstitutional,[77] were often heavily influenced by law school scholarship, but to take only one example, federal courts that cited the *Harvard Law Review* 4,410 times in the 1970s did so only 1,956 times in the 1990s, and only about 1,000 times in the current decade.[78] There is a chasm between the academy and the bench, and regardless of the politics of the judges themselves, it appears to be widening.[79]

And, whatever the influences on them, in the end, final decision making clearly remains with the judges.[80] They may issue fewer literary works as the pressure on the lower courts to keep up with increasing caseloads continues,[81] but a death row inmate and even the lawyers on the case care less about scholarship and bureaucracy[82] than the simple yes or no to the question "am I going to die this month?" The answer to that is mixed. There was a public clash in 1992, widely known as the "battle of the faxes," between the Supreme Court and the Court of Appeals for the Ninth Circuit over the lower court's unsuccessful attempt to block California's execution of Robert Alton Harris. That clash continues in dozens of lower-profile cases, many of which pit the Supreme Court's limited ability to supervise the lower courts against the apparent determination of some judges on the courts of appeals to prevent capital punishment in all cases. Consider the case of *Wong v. Belmontes* (2009), in which the Supreme Court issued a *per curiam* opinion reversing the Ninth Circuit. A *per curiam* ("by the court") opinion is a form of opinion often used by the Court to signal that the Justices believe that an issue is so well settled that no individual Justice needs to write an opinion. Fernando Belmontes bludgeoned a woman to death in 1981 to get $100 dollars to buy drugs, and his conviction and death sentence had been repeatedly upheld in California's state courts. A federal district judge likewise denied a writ of *habeas corpus*. In 2003, the Ninth Circuit ruled that Belmontes' jury had been incorrectly instructed, moving him off death row. The Supreme Court reversed that decision in 2006. Upon receiving the case back, after two more years, the Ninth Circuit then found that the death penalty must be reversed, this time because Belmontes' attorney had been so ineffective as to deny Belmontes a fair sentencing.

In *Wong v. Belmontes,* the Supreme Court pointed out, in as close to a scolding as the Supreme Court gives, that the Ninth Circuit had previously considered Belmontes' attorney's work "substantial" until its first ruling was overturned, then reinterpreted the same evidence to find his work a "cursory" effort that failed to defend Belmontes. The Supreme Court, calling the Ninth Circuit's assessment of the evidence "fanciful," again reversed. Twenty-nine years after the murder, it is unclear whether the Ninth Circuit will review the matter again, and if it does, whether the Supreme Court will have the time to supervise its performance.

It appears that the Supreme Court at least has the will. While Justice Kagan's views are yet to be disclosed, all the other Justices (except Justice Ginsburg, who wrote a separate concurrence, not a dissent) joined the Court's most recent public scolding of the Ninth Circuit in *Harrington v. Richter* (2011),[83] which reversed a grant of *habeas corpus* in a noncapital murder conviction. Justice Kennedy wrote, in language that could have come from *Moore v. Dempsey* almost 90 years earlier:

[H]abeas corpus is a guard against extreme malfunctions in the state criminal justice system, not a substitute for ordinary error correction through appeal. . . . As a condition for obtaining habeas corpus from a federal court, a state prisoner must show that the state court's ruling . . . was so lacking in justification that there was an error well understood and comprehended in existing law beyond any possibility for fairminded disagreement.

Since the days of President Eisenhower, who is reputed to have said that he only made two mistakes as President, and "both [Brennan and Warren] are on the Supreme Court," presidents have grown increasingly hands-on in deciding who is nominated to the Supreme Court, maybe their longest-lasting impacts on the nation's laws. But the political reality is that federal district court judges, though formally nominated by the president just like Supreme Court Justices, are chosen largely by the senators of the states in which their federal courts sit, especially when they are from the same party as the president. As a result, the position of federal judges on the death penalty tends to mirror the politics of citizens of their states, not the president's views. Court of Appeals judges tend to be selected by the president with more input from the Department of Justice and less input from the senators, but very often they are chosen from the ranks of district judges, so the local political influence remains a strong one. Despite the Supreme Court's more recent commands to federal courts to be more deferential to state courts, individual district judges are in the position to be the single most influential brake on the actual carrying out of a death sentence, and because senators from the South tend to be more supportive of capital punishment than senators from California or Pennsylvania, it is not surprising that a defendant's chance of getting off death row is lower in the belt from Texas to Florida.

Federal judicial politics can provide cover to politicians not even interested in federal judgeships. Prosecutors in large metropolitan areas like Los Angeles and Philadelphia have long found it politically advantageous to run campaigns promising to pursue the death penalty. They also find being able to ask for the death penalty to be a valuable bargaining chip. The Supreme Court has held that such plea bargaining is part of acceptable criminal practice.[84] Prosecutors also charge capital crime to "death-qualify" the jury in the belief that pro–death penalty jurors are proprosecution jurors.[85] So death rows continue to grow, particularly in California, creating ever-increasing costs and the unique risks to corrections officers from dealing with inmates who have little or nothing to lose. On the other hand, as most attorneys who practice criminal law will admit, a prosecutor who pursues the death penalty can, by excluding those jurors who cannot pass the *Witherspoon* test, increase the likelihood that the jury will convict the defendant of at least a crime warranting a life sentence. Even if there is little chance outside Texas that a death penalty sentence will be carried out, district attorneys throughout the country have political and tactical reasons to continue to pursue capital punishment in murder cases.

The debates continue, raising the same issues that Beccaria and Mill were familiar with, and much in the same terms. It takes four Justices to grant review to a petition for a writ of *certiorari*. In March 2009, in *Thompson v. McNeil,* the Court denied review to the petition of William Lee Thompson, on death row in Florida for 32 years after committing a brutal torture murder in 1976, the same year *Gregg* held once more that the Eighth Amendment permitted capital punishment. Justices Stevens and Breyer dissented from the denial of *certiorari*, believing that such a long delay might itself be cruel and unusual punishment. Justice Thomas responded by recounting the gruesome details of the crime and reminding the other Justices that the long delay was in large part caused by "this Court's Byzantine death penalty jurisprudence."[86] All three of the Justices quoted themselves, and properly so because they have been having this argument in similar form in similar cases since the argument first was raised in *Lackey v. Texas* (1995). In December 2009, Justices Stevens and Breyer and Justice Thomas considered the same issue again after the Court denied review to Cecil Johnson's claim that Tennessee had taken too long to execute him in *Johnson v. Bredesen* (2009). No one budged. Cecil Johnson was executed for three murders committed during a robbery 29 years earlier. That is the current death penalty debate in miniature. Separate debates go on in the legislature, on the Court, and in jury rooms across the United States. That everyone is counting heads but not changing minds on the issue means that the stage is set for continued gridlock. Whether you are for or against capital punishment, consider as a last word Justice Potter Stewart's concurrence in *Furman* that the death penalty, if applied only rarely, was unconstitutional:[87]

These death sentences are cruel and unusual in the same way that being struck by lightning is cruel and unusual. For, of all the people convicted of rapes and murders in 1967 and 1968, many just as reprehensible as these, the petitioners are among a capriciously selected random handful upon whom the sentence of death has in fact been imposed. . . . [T]he Eighth and Fourteenth Amendments cannot tolerate the infliction of a sentence of death under legal systems that permit this unique penalty to be so wantonly and so freakishly imposed.

Have we made progress, or have we come full circle?

NOTES

1. Numbers 35:31–33, Revised Standard Version.
2. Jonah had his sentence commuted to a three-day term of imprisonment. The belief in crime and sin as requiring expiation by punishment appears in other cultures beside the Jewish one. The Greek cycle of plays known as the Oresteia, not to mention the myth of Oedipus, similarly presents crime as a stain on society. This was not merely a literary convention. The Greek colony of Massalia (modern Marseilles, France) maintained the condemned criminal at public expense for one year, then executed him as a public purification of the city. Michael Grant, *The Rise of the Greeks* (New York: Charles Scribner's Sons, 1988), 251. Among the Celts, condemned criminals were executed every five years, often by burning. James G. Frazer, *The Golden Bough* (New York: Macmillan Publishing Co., 1963 [1922]), 757–58.
3. Most American essays, even by theologians such as Cardinal Avery Dulles, do not even mention the subject. Cardinal Dulles does discuss the other four ends of punishment. Avery Dulles, "Catholicism and Capital Punishment," *First Things* 112 (April 2001): 30.
4. *Williams v. New York*, 337 U.S. 241, 240–49(1949).
5. Issue Brief, The Pew Center on the States. "Prison Count 2010" (March 2010), www.pewcenteronthestates.org.
6. Penny J. White, "Errors and Ethics: Dilemmas in Death," *Hofstra L. Rev.* 29 (2001): 1265–99.
7. About 1625, the Dutch jurist Hugo Grotius wrote, in *The Law of War and Peace*, Book II Chapter 20 Section II:
For as a seller, though no express stipulation be made, is understood to have bound himself by all the usual and necessary conditions of a sale, so, punishment being a natural consequence of crime, every heinous offender appears to have

voluntarily incurred the penalties of law. In this sense some of the Emperors pronounced sentences upon malefactors in the following manner: "you have brought this penalty upon yourselves."

8. The distinction between *malum in se*—things like murder, which are bad in themselves—and *malum prohibitum*—things like failure to drive at the posted speed limit, which are bad because they are prohibited—has long been a part of legal education. Blackstone drew the sharp distinction between the two, arguing that the death penalty should never be imposed for what he called mere offenses against municipal law.

9. As a minor example, in *Ake v. Oklahoma* (1985), the Supreme Court supplemented the right to effective assistance of counsel it recognized in *Powell v. Alabama* (1932) by holding that a defendant in a capital case who makes a showing that his sanity is likely to be at issue must be provided a psychiatric expert as well. The Court has not applied this right to other crimes.

10. Donald Veall, *The Popular Movement for Law Reform 1640–1660* (London: Oxford University Press, 1970) 95–96, 127–41.

11. Dante Alighieri, *The Divine Comedy, 1: Hell* (London: Penguin Books, 1949 [c. 1314]), Dorothy Sayers translation, 195–96.

12. Daniel J. Boorstin, *The Americans: The Colonial Experience* (New York: Random House, 1958.), 46–48; Joseph H. Smith, *Appeals to the Privy Council from the American Plantations* (New York: Octagon Books, Inc., 1965), 243–44.

13. I. Bernard. Cohen, *The Triumph of Numbers: How Counting Shaped Modern Life* (New York: W.W. Norton & Co., 2005), 124–33.

14. Joseph comte de Maistre, *St. Petersburg Dialogues* (Montreal: McGill-Queen's University Press, 1993), Richard A. Lebrun translation, 19–20. Just in case anyone is left in doubt of Maistre's position, his Count goes on to explain that errors in inflicting capital punishment are not only "excessively rare," they are balanced out by the "happy" possibility "that a man "tortured for a crime he did not commit really merited punishment for an absolutely unknown crime."

15. J. Robert Lilly, Francis T. Cullen, and Richard A. Ball, *Criminological Theory: Context and Consequences*, 2d ed. (Thousand Oaks, California: SAGE Publications, 1995) 21–26.

16. Enrico Ferri, who in his own right became an influential political figure in early-twentieth-century Italy, wrote:

It seems to me that the death penalty is prescribed by nature. . . . [P]rogress of every kind is due to continual selection, by the death of the least fit in the struggle for life. . . . It would therefore be in agreement with natural laws that human society should make an artificial selection, by the elimination of anti-social and incongruous individuals.

Quoted in Stephen Jay Gould, *The Mismeasure of Man* (New York: W. W. Norton & Co., 1981), 140.

17. Oliver W. Jr. Holmes, "The Path of the Law," *Harvard Law Review*, 110 (March 1997 [1897]): 991, 1002. The "well known men of science" Holmes cited were Ferri and Garofalo.

18. "Arguments For and Against Capital Punishment," http://www.capital punishmentuk.org/thoughts.html (6 November 2008).

19. Cesare Bonesana, Marchese Beccaria, "Of Crimes and Punishments," translated from the French by Edward D. Ingraham, second American edition, Philadelphia, published by Philip H. Nicklin (1819), http://www.constitution.org/cb/crim_pun28.txt (15 November 2008).

20. "A summary of Arguments Presented at a Meeting of the Men's International Theosophical League of Humanity, March, 31, 1914," included in *To Abolish Capital Punishment: A Plea to the Citizens of Every Country,* Point Loma, California, 1914, from *Sunrise Magazine,* April/May 1998. See http://www.theosophy-nw.org/theosnw/issues/pu-vscap.htm (6 November 2008).

21. "Arguments For and Against the Death Penalty," http://www.capitalpunish mentuk.org/thoughts.html (6 November 2008).

22. Singapore executed two 18-year-old girls for this crime in 1995. China did the same in 1998.

23. Roy Weatherford, "A Non-Pacifist Argument Against Capital Punishment," 20th WCP: A Non-Pacifist Argument Against Capital Punishment, *Applied Ethics,* http://www.bu.edu/wcp/Papers/OApp/OAppWeat.htm (6 November 2008).

24. Melusky, 61.

25. Jack Greenberg, "Against the American System of Capital Punishment," *Harvard Law Review,* 99 (1985–86): 1670–80.

26. Greenberg, 1670. The death penalty is not applied evenly across the United States. It is used most frequently in southern states. See previously cited "Facts and Figures About the Death Penalty."

27. Greenberg, 1673.

28. See, e.g., Adrian Raines, "The Biological Basis of Crime," in *Crime: Public Policies for Crime Control,* J.Q. Wilson and J. Petersilia, eds. (Oakland, California: ICS Press, 2002). 43–74.

29. Greenberg, 1677.

30. Hugo Adam Bedau, "The Case Against the Death Penalty," The American Civil Liberties Union Freedom Network, http://www.aclu.org/capital/general/10441pub19971231.html (13 March 2009).

31. Coretta Scott King, Speech to National Coalition to Abolish the Death Penalty, Washington, D.C., September 26, 1981, as cited by Bedau, note 30. Note this argument is the same as the one used by Thomas Paine almost 200 years earlier in *The Rights of Man.* Writing in reply to Edmund Burke's denunciation of the murder of French officials in the seizing of the Bastille at the beginning of the French Revolution, Paine denounced English and French capital punishment and the practice of publicly exhibiting the bodies of the executed. As for the crimes of the rebels:

They learn it from the governments they live under; and retaliate the punishments they have been accustomed to behold.... Lay then the axe to the root, and teach governments humanity. It is their sanguinary punishments which corrupt mankind.

Thomas Paine, *The Rights of Man,* in *Two Classics of the French Revolution* (New York: Anchor Books, 1989 [1791]), 294.

32. Bedau, citing U.S. Bureau of Justice Statistics, "Capital Punishment," 1980–1994 and *Uniform Crime Reports,* 1980–1994. Of roughly 20,000 capital sentences carried out since colonial times, fewer than 600 involved women. Eric Felten, a writer for the *Washington Times,* observed that of 108 White women executed in the past 350 years, 27 were found guilty of witchcraft, the only crime women have been executed for in greater numbers than men. Eric Felten, "The Death Penalty's Glass Ceiling," *Wall Street Journal* (January 24, 1996), A15.

33. Harry Greenlee and Shelia Greenlee, "Women and the Death Penalty: Racial Disparities and Differences," *William & Mary Journal of Women and the Law,* 14 (Winter 2008): 319, 321.

34. Bedau citing Ronald J. Tabak and J. Mark Lane, "The Execution of Injustice: A Cost and Lack of Benefit Analysis of the Death penalty" *Loyola of Los Angeles Law Review* 23, Issue 1 (November 1989), 59–146.

35. Bedau, at note 30.

36. Matthew L. Stephens, "Instrument of Justice or Tool of Vengeance?" *Christian Social Action* 3 (10, November 1990), reprinted in McKenna and Feingold, *Taking Sides: Clashing Views on Controversial Political Issues* (Guilford, Connecticut: Dushkin/McGraw-Hill, 2007), 160–64.

37. Richard A. Viguerie, "When Governments Kill," *Sojourners Magazine* 38 (7, July 2009): 10.

38. Eric M. Freedman, "The Case Against the Death Penalty," *USA Today Magazine* (March 1997), reprinted in McKenna and Feingold, *Taking Sides: Clashing Views on Controversial Political Issues* (Guilford, Connecticut: Dushkin/McGraw-Hill, 2007), 150–55.

39. The BalancedPolitics.org website on the topic, "Should the Death Penalty Be Banned As a Form of Punishment? In a Nutshell" serves as the source for this summary. See http://www.balancedpolitics.org/death_penalty.htm (6 November 2008).

40. Ian Urbina, "In Push to End Death Penalty, Some States Cite Cost-Cutting," *New York Times* (February 25, 2009), A1.

41. Robert J. Martin "Killing Capital Punishment in New Jersey: The First State in Modern History to Repeal its Death Penalty Statute," *University of Toledo L.R.* 41 (Spring 2010): 485–543, 522, 531.

42. Steven A. Drizin and Beth A. Colgan, "Let the Cameras Roll: Mandatory Videotaping of Interrogations Is the Solution to Illinois' Problem of False Confessions." *Loyola University Chicago Law Journal* 32, Issue 2 (Winter 2001) 337–424, 302.

43. Bedau estimated that since 1900 there have been on the average four cases per year of innocent persons convicted of murder, and 23 wrongful executions. Hugo Bedau and Michael L. Radelet, "Miscarriages of Justice in Potentially Capital Cases." *Stanford Law Review* 40, Issue 1 (November 1987) 21–180, 84.

44. "ABA Calls for Moratorium on Executions Until Death Penalty Fairness Assured," http://www.pbs.org/wgbh/pages/frontline/angel/procon/aba.html

(15 March 2009). For the full text of the resolution, see http://www.abanet.org/irr/rec107.html (15 March 2009).

45. 510 U.S. 1141, 1143–59 (1994).

46. According to Linda Greenhouse, the *Callins v. Collins* dissent was a joint project of Justice Blackmun's law clerks, kept on file until a generic death penalty case that raised no unusual issues came along. Linda Greenhouse, *Becoming Justice Blackmun: Harry Blackmun's Supreme Court Journey* (New York: Henry Holt and Company, LLC, 2005), 176–81.

47. Ernest van den Haag, "The Ultimate Punishment: A Defense," *Harvard Law Review* 99 (1985–86) 1662–69.

48. van den Haag, 1663.

49. van den Haag, 1665.

50. *Furman v. Georgia*, 408 U.S. 238, 291 (1972) (Brennan, J., concurring).

51. van den Haag, 1669.

52. For the argument that life without parole is as cruel as the death penalty, see Bruce Ledewitz, and Scott Staples, "No Punishment Without Cruelty," *George Mason University Civil Rights Law Journal* 4 (Winter, 1993): 41. The Supreme Court held in *Graham v. Florida* (2010) that life without parole is a cruel and unusual punishment for juveniles except in the case of homicide.

53. John Stuart Mill, "Speech In Favor of Capital Punishment," In Melusky and Pesto, 209–13.

54. Mill, 210.

55. Thomas Cahill, *Mysteries of the Middle Ages*, (New York: Random House 2006), 36–37

56. "Italian Inmates seek death penalty," http://news.bbc.co.uk/2/hi/6707865.stm (May 31, 2007).

57. Mill, 211.

58. Mill, 211.

59. Jean Jacques Rousseau, *The Social Contract* (London: Penguin Books, 1968 [1762]), Maurice Cranston translation, 79.

60. Rousseau , 79.

61. Mill, 212.

62. Mill, 212.

63. Robert W. Lee, "Deserving to Die," *The New American*, 13 August 1990, reprinted in McKenna and Feingold (2007), 142–49.

64. Lee, 146.

65. Alan Brudner, "Retributivism and the death penalty." *University of Toronto Law Journal*, 30, Issue 4 (Fall 1980), 337–55, 352.

66. Brudner, 348.

67. Amanda Falcone, "Petit favors death penalty for justice, not revenge." (Meriden, CT) *Record Journal* (4 March 2009), http://myrecordjournal.com/latestnews/article_61537f84-76da-5764-a668-e557bc6861ec.html.

68. John M. Glionna, "Hazard pay." (Johnstown, PA) *Tribune-Democrat* (11 May 2001), page A-20.

69. James Bain was released in December 2009 after DNA evidence excluded him as the rapist in an assault on a child in 1974. Bain served 35 years, the longest period of wrongful imprisonment known in the 245 DNA-based exonerations known to the Florida Innocence Project. http://floridainnocence.org/content/?tag=james-bain (December 17, 2009). Bain's requests for forensic testing of the evidence against him had repeatedly been turned down. It is unknown how many repeat analyses of DNA in capital cases were conducted by federal and state courts in Florida during Bain's imprisonment, but it is almost certain that the evidence that freed Bain would have been tested sooner if Bain had been sentenced to death.

70. 510 U.S. 1141, 1141–43.

71. In one case, Chapter 4 of Steven D. Levitt and Stephen J. Dubner's 2005 hit *Freakonomics: A Rogue Economist Explores the Hidden Side of Everything* (New York: HarperCollins Publishers), asserted that the reason homicide rates fell in the 1990s was not the quadrupling of the capital punishment execution rate but, rather, the availability of abortions to eliminate those boys who would have become murderers. That the shock value was intentional can be seen from reading Chapter 2 of the same book, which asserted that the lynchings carried out by the Klan effectively thwarted civil rights for African-Americans for decades. The authors do not explain how 281 lynchings in the 1920s completely deterred desegregation while 478 capital executions in the 1990s failed to deter murder.

72. Victor L. Streib, "Executions under the Post Furman Capital Punishment Statutes: The Halting Progression from 'Let's Do It' to 'Hey, There Ain't no Point in Pulling So Tight,'" *Rutgers Law Journal*, 15 (2, Winter 1984): 443–87, 460.

73. Nathan Koppel, "Hospira to Stop Making Lethal-Injection Drug" *Wall Street Journal* (21 January 2011) http://online.wsj.com/article/SB100014240527487 04754304576095980790129692. html.

74. Brett Barrouquere, "Kentucky Gov. May Have Risked Medical License," *Pittsburgh Post-Gazette* (November 19, 2004), A-12. Kentucky's governor Ernie Fletcher signed the warrant for the execution of Thomas Bowling in 2004, prompting the challenge ruled on by the Supreme Court in *Baze v. Rees*, but also prompting Arthur Zitrin, a retired New York psychiatrist who opposes the death penalty, to charge Dr. Fletcher with violating AMA guidelines. As this book goes to print, Bowling remains on Kentucky's death row.

75. *Smith v. Spisak*, 130 SCT, 676, 693 (2010).

76. Penelope Pether, "Sorcerer, Not Apprentices: How Judicial Clerks and Staff Attorneys Impoverish U.S. Law," *Arizona State Law Journal*, 39 (Spring 2007): 1–67.

77. See Appendix 1.

78. Adam Liptak, "When Rendering Decisions, Judges Are Finding Law Reviews Irrelevant," *New York Times* (March 19, 2007), A1.

79. Richard A. Posner, *How Judges think*, (Cambridge, MA: Harvard University Press 2008), 221–29.

80. See, e.g., Todd C. Peppers et al., "Inside Judicial Chambers: How Federal District Court Judges Select and Use Their Law Clerks," *Albany Law Review*, 71 (2008): 623–40.

81. Because the Supreme Court can dictate its own workload, the length of opinions from that court has risen steadily for decades. In the lower courts, however, the typical Court of Appeals judge must decide more than three times as many appeals each year as in the days of *Furman*. See Walter K. Stapleton, "The Federal Judicial System in the Twenty-First Century," *Delaware Lawyer* (Fall, 1995): 34.

82. See Stephen J. Choi and G. Gulati, *Which Judges Write Their Opinions (and Should We Care)?* New York University Law School Law and Economics Research Paper Series, Working Paper No. 05–06. (May 2005) http://ssrn.com/abstract=715062 (15 March 2008). The authors conclude that available analytical tools can sometimes distinguish between judges who write their own opinions and those who have law clerks draft them.

83. 131 SCT, 770, 786–87 (2011).

84. In *United States v. Jackson* (1968), the Court invalidated the death penalty provisions of the Lindbergh law because a kidnaper who pleaded guilty faced a maximum life sentence, while a kidnaper found guilty after a jury trial could be executed. The law coerced all defendants into giving up the right to a jury trial. Plea bargains allow prosecutors to do the same on an individual basis, but the Supreme Court has repeatedly held that this is permissible.

85. In *Witherspoon v. Illinois* (1968), the Court held opponents of capital punishment could not be excluded from jury service in a capital case unless they could not set that belief aside and follow a judge's instructions. The effect on death penalty opponents is obvious: the more thoughtful and honest one's opposition, the less likely one is to be seated on a jury.

86. 129 SCT, 1299, 1302 (2009).

87. 408 U.S., 238, 309–10 (1972).

Appendix 1

An Annotated List of Cases: Evolving Standards of Decency and the U.S. Supreme Court's Treatment of Capital Punishment

INTRODUCTION

Numerous cases have come to the Supreme Court of the United States over the years in which the Court was asked to address the constitutional status of capital punishment itself or its application under particular circumstances. These cases reveal that the Court's views of the death penalty have evolved to reflect changing societal norms and mores. Some of the Court's most important decisions in this area are summarized here. These summaries are intended to provide a convenient overview of the Court's decisions. We encourage you, however, to read the full opinions of the justices themselves. Cases can be accessed online at http://www.oyez.org (the U.S. Supreme Court Media Oyez Project at the Illinois Institute of Technology Chicago–Kent College of Law), http://www.law.cornell.edu (the Legal Information Institute at Cornell University Law School), or http://www.supremecourt.gov (the official Website for the Supreme Court of the United States).

PART ONE—THE ROAD FROM *WILKERSON* TO *FURMAN*: 1878–1971

Question: Is death by firing squad a cruel and unusual punishment?
Wilkerson v. Utah, 99 U.S. 130 (1878)

The Territory of Utah provided that a person convicted of murder in the first degree would "suffer death, or, upon the recommendation of the jury, may be imprisoned at hard labor in the penitentiary for life at the discretion of the court." Wilkerson was convicted of murder in the first degree and was sentenced by the proper court to be publicly shot until he was dead. Writing for the Supreme Court, Justice Clifford concluded that death by firing squad did not violate the Constitution's prohibition of cruel and unusual punishments.

Question: Does death by electrocution constitute cruel and unusual punishment?
In re Kemmler, 136 U.S. 436 (1890)

This case involved the first execution by electrocution conducted in New York. In 1888, the New York state legislature provided that "[t]he punishment of death must in every case be inflicted by causing to pass through the body of a convict a current of electricity of sufficient intensity to cause death." Kemmler maintained that his electrocution would constitute cruel and unusual punishment. Writing for the Court, Chief Justice Fuller observed that electrocution is not "inhuman and barbarous." The state legislature had determined that electrocution was "a more humane method" than hanging and that it would produce "instantaneous" and "painless" death.

Question: Does a second execution attempt, following the malfunction of an electric chair, violate constitutional protections against double jeopardy and cruel and unusual punishment?
Louisiana ex rel. Francis v. Resweber, 329 U.S. 459 (1947)

The question whether the Eighth Amendment was incorporated as part of the Due Process Clause came to the Court in 1947. Willie Francis was sentenced to die in the Louisiana electric chair for a murder committed when he was 15. The first attempt to electrocute Francis failed due to a malfunction in the chair. He was strapped into the electric chair, the switch was thrown, and a mechanical failure prevented the machine from working. Would a second attempt to electrocute Francis be cruel and unusual punishment? Four members of the Court (Justice Reed, joined by Justices Black and Jackson and Chief Justice Vinson) said no: it was just as if Francis had suffered from an accidental fire in his cell. Four members (Justice Burton, joined by Justices Douglas, Murphy, and Rutledge) said yes: Louisiana could not torture a prisoner to death by repeated shocks, and it made no difference whether the first attempt was an accident. Justice Frankfurter, who as a law professor, had called for the abolition of capital punishment, cast the deciding vote: since the first failure was not intentional, a second attempt would not be unconstitutional. Francis was executed at age 17.

Question: Is stripping a man of his citizenship as punishment for a crime cruel and unusual punishment?
Trop v. Dulles, 356 U.S. 86 (1958)

In 1958, the Court decided an Eighth Amendment case that seemed at first to have little to do with due process or the death penalty. Albert Trop was a 20-year-old private in the United States Army who, in 1944, deserted for one day. He was court-martialed and dishonorably discharged. Under a federal law passed in 1865 to stem the flood of desertions from the Union Army during the Civil War, Trop was stripped of his citizenship. Writing for the Court, Chief Justice Warren held that the forfeiture of citizenship was unconstitutional. Justices Black, Douglas, and Whitaker joined Warren. Justice Brennan, concurring, supplied the fifth vote for Trop. Warren said that desertion "does not necessarily signify allegiance to a foreign state" and that "[c]itizenship is not a license that expires upon misbehavior." Furthermore, Trop did not voluntarily "renounce or abandon his citizenship." Finding that Trop's denationalization was a "cruel and unusual punishment," Warren stated that these words must draw their meaning from "the evolving standards of decency that mark the progress of a maturing society"—a concept that would figure prominently in subsequent Eighth Amendment cases.

Question: Can states exclude from juries all persons who are opposed to the death penalty?
Witherspoon v. Illinois, 391 U.S. 510 (1968)

The Supreme Court held that states could not exclude from juries all persons opposed to the death penalty because doing so would result in juries that were not fairly representative of the community. Exclusion of jurors was permissible only if it could be shown that the juror's personal opposition to the death penalty was so strong as to prevent him or her from making an impartial decision on the defendant's guilt. Justice Stewart delivered the opinion of the Court. A jury "[c]ulled of all who harbor doubts about the wisdom of capital punishment" falls "woefully short" of the impartiality to which defendants are entitled under the Sixth and Fourteenth Amendments. Stewart found that the State had "stacked the deck" against the petitioner: "In its quest for a jury capable of imposing the death penalty, the State produced a jury uncommonly willing to condemn a man to die." Justice Douglas wrote a concurring opinion. Justice Black, joined by Justices Harlan and White, dissented.

Question: Can states give juries complete discretion over the imposition of the death penalty?
McGautha v. California, 402 U.S. 183 (1971)

McGautha was convicted of first-degree murder in California. He was sentenced to death pursuant to State statutes that left the decision whether he would live or die to the complete discretion of the jury. The Supreme Court, by a vote of six to three, upheld the challenged law. Justice Harlan wrote for the majority. Justice Black concurred separately, emphasizing that history showed that the Eighth Amendment permitted the death penalty. Justices Brennan, Marshall, and Douglas dissented. One year later, Justices Harlan and Black had retired, and *McGautha* was reversed in *Furman v. Georgia.*

PART TWO—FROM *FURMAN* TO *GREGG:* 1972–1976

Introduction

During the 1960s, the death penalty appeared to be falling into disfavor. Executions declined and doubts grew about its legality. Following *Witherspoon v. Illinois* (1968), where the Supreme Court ruled that jurors could not be excluded from serving on juries on the ground that they had reservations about the death penalty, an unofficial moratorium on executions went into effect as additional challenges were brought to the Court.

Question: Is capital punishment constitutionally permissible or must states carefully limit jury discretion in such cases?
Furman v. Georgia, 408 U.S. 238 (1972)

During 1970s, the death penalty was invalidated and later reinstated. In 1972, the Supreme Court appeared to eliminate capital punishment when it struck down Georgia's death penalty statute. The law gave juries complete discretion in imposing the death sentence. In *Furman v. Georgia,* the Court held that this practice of unguided jury discretion violated the Eight Amendment's ban on cruel and unusual punishment. Had the death penalty been dealt a death blow?

Furman revealed a badly divided Court. The case was decided by the narrowest of margins: five to four. The majority was unable to agree on a single opinion and presented five separate concurrences by Justices Douglas, Brennan, Stewart, White, and Marshall. Only Brennan and Marshall went so far as to conclude that the death penalty *itself* had become constitutionally impermissible. The others took issue with how it had been *applied.* The four members appointed by President Nixon—Chief Justice Burger and Justices Powell, Rehnquist, and Blackmun—dissented. The immediate effect was to strike down existing death penalty statutes in 40 states. A close reading of *Furman* shows that the Court held that *particular* death penalty laws were unconstitutional if they were arbitrary, disproportionate to the crime, offended society's sense of justice, or were not more effective than less severe penalties. However, as Burger pointed out in dissent, the Court's decision permitted states to make a "thorough re-evaluation" of the subject and to enact new death penalty laws that limited jury discretion.

Question: Is the imposition of the death penalty *always* constitutionally impermissible?
Gregg v. Georgia, **428 U.S. 153 (1976)**

In 1976, the Supreme Court decided *Gregg v. Georgia* and two companion cases, *Jurek v. Texas* and *Proffitt v. Florida*. Responding to Burger's invitation in *Furman*, 35 states enacted revised capital laws. Ten states attempted to eliminate jury discretion by making the death penalty mandatory for certain crimes. Twenty-five states implemented two-stage procedures in capital cases: the first stage of the trial would determine guilt or innocence and the second stage would determine punishment. In *Gregg* and the companion cases, the Court upheld new death-penalty statutes in Georgia, Texas, and Florida. Justice Stewart announced the Court's judgment that the death penalty itself was constitutionally permissible as long as its application avoided the defects noted above. In spirited dissents, Justices Brennan and Marshall reaffirmed their *Furman* positions that the death penalty was constitutionally impermissible "for whatever crime and under all circumstances."

The unofficial moratorium on executions that began with *Witherspoon* ended after 10 years when Gary Gilmore was executed by a firing squad in Utah on January 17, 1977. Gilmore did not challenge his death sentence. His last recorded words were. "Let's do it." Capital punishment had returned.

PART THREE—*AFTER GREGG*: 1976–1989

Introduction

Following the Court's decision in *Gregg,* executions resumed in the United States. Controversy and public debate ensued. Some supporters of capital punishment cite it as a deterrent to crime. A study focusing on the deterrent effects of capital punishment from 1976 through 1989 concluded that the death penalty does little to deter capital crime. The study used statistics from the FBI Uniform Crime Report and concluded that regions that use the death penalty the least are the safest for police officers. Conversely, police officers are in most danger in the South, where executions are carried out most frequently.[1] During this same time period, the Supreme Court was busy refining its views on the death penalty. The period was marked by mixed signals.

Question: Is a mandatory death penalty for first-degree murder constitutionally permissible?
Woodson v. North Carolina, 428 U.S. 280 (1976)

In a number of cases, the Supreme Court found fault with death penalty practices and applications. In *Woodson v. North Carolina* (1976) and the companion case, *Roberts v. Louisiana,* the Court struck down state laws that provided mandatory death sentences for those convicted of murder if the character of the defendant and the circumstances of the crime were not taken into account. The Court voted five to four with Justice Stewart, joined by Justices Brennan, Marshall, Powell, and Stevens in the majority and Chief Justice Burger and Justices Blackmun, White, and Rehnquist in the minority.

Question: Is death an excessive penalty for the crime of rape?
Coker v. Georgia, 433 U.S. 583 (1977)

In *Coker v Georgia,* the Court reviewed state laws that made rape a capital offense. The Court ruled that although rape is a serious, reprehensible, and violent crime, death is a "disproportionate and excessive punishment" for a rapist who does not take human life. Justice White, joined by Justices Stewart, Blackmun, and Stevens, announced the judgment of the Court. Citing history and objective evidence in support of his conclusion, White noted that Georgia was the only state that "authorizes a sentence of death when the rape victim is an adult woman, and only two other jurisdictions provide capital punishment when the victim is a child." Justices Brennan and Marshall concurred, repeating their view that the death penalty is always cruel and unusual punishment. Justice Powell concurred in part and dissented in part. Chief Justice Burger, joined by Justice Rehnquist, dissented.

Question: Must state death penalty laws permit consideration of a wide variety of mitigating factors?
Lockett v. Ohio, 438 U.S. 586 (1978)

An Ohio statute limited the range of mitigating factors that could be considered by a sentencing judge in capital cases. The United States Supreme Court ruled that the State death penalty law was unconstitutional because it did not permit consideration of a wide range of relevant mitigating factors. In *Bell v. Ohio,* decided on the same day, the Court also held that a judge must be permitted to consider relevant mitigating factors. Announcing the judgment of the Court, Chief Justice Burger said that a trial judge must not be precluded by a state law "from considering as a mitigating factor, any aspect of the defendant's character or record and any of the circumstances of the offense that the defendant proffers."

Question: Is a state law permitting the death penalty in cases where the crime is "outrageous or wantonly vile" too vague?
Godfrey v. Georgia, 446 U.S. 420 (1980)

Cases like *Furman, Gregg,* and *Woodson* established that states could retain the death penalty if aggravating circumstances were present, a defendant was permitted to present all evidence of mitigating factors, and juries did not act arbitrarily. *Godfrey v. Georgia* focused on *aggravating* factors. Here, the Court invalidated as unconstitutionally vague a state law that permitted a death sentence if the crime was "outrageous or wantonly vile." In announcing the judgment of the Court, Justice Stewart, joined by Justices Blackmun, Powell, and Stevens, said that "[t]here is no principled way to distinguish this case, in which the death penalty was imposed, from the many cases in which it was not." Concurring, Justices Brennan and Marshall reiterated their belief that "the death penalty is in all circumstances cruel and unusual punishment." Chief Justice Burger and Justice White, joined by Justice Rehnquist, dissented.

Question: Can relevant mitigating factors be excluded in a capital case?
Eddings v. Oklahoma 455 U.S. 104 (1982)

Monty Lee Eddings, a juvenile in Oklahoma, was tried as an adult on a first-degree murder charge. The judge considered the defendant's age as a mitigating factor, but he refused to consider the defendant's turbulent family history and emotional disturbance as mitigating factors. The Supreme Court struck down the death sentence, emphasizing that relevant mitigating factors cannot be excluded from consideration by the sentencing judge. Justice Powell delivered the opinion of the Court. Justice Brennan concurred, as did Justice O'Connor. Chief Justice Burger, joined by Justices White, Blackmun, and Rehnquist, dissented.

Question: Is a death sentence for the driver of a getaway car disproportionate to the crime?
Enmund v. Florida, 458 U.S. 782 (1982)

In *Coker v. Georgia,* the Supreme Court ruled that the death penalty is excessive for the crime of rape of an adult female. In *Enmund,* the Court returned to the issue of disproportionality. Earl Enmund aided and abetted felony murder by serving as the driver of a getaway car. He neither killed anyone nor did he witness the killings. Writing for the majority, Justice White held that the focus must be on "[Enmund's] culpability, not on that of those who committed the robbery and shot the victims." In light of the fact that he neither killed nor intended to kill, his culpability was plainly different from that of those who killed and a death sentence for Enmund's offense was excessive. Justice Brennan concurred, repeating his unconditional rejection of capital punishment. Justice O'Connor, joined by Chief Justice Burger and Justices Powell and Rehnquist, dissented.

Question: Is a life sentence without possibility of parole for a nonviolent repeat offender too severe?
Solem v. Helm, 463 U.S. 277 (1983)

In *Solem*, the Court again ruled that the Eighth Amendment prohibits sentences that are disproportionate to the crime. Jerry Helm was convicted of writing a bad check for $100—his seventh nonviolent felony. Under a South Dakota recidivist statute, he was sentenced to life imprisonment without possibility of parole. The Court found this sentence to be excessive. Writing for the majority, Justice Powell noted that "a criminal sentence must be proportionate to the crime for which the defendant has been convicted." Although a state may be justified in punishing repeat offenders more severely, Helm's offenses were all "relatively minor." His sentence of life without parole was the most severe punishment authorized by South Dakota law for any crime. As such, the sentence was "significantly disproportionate" to the crime. Chief Justice Burger, joined by Justices White, Rehnquist, and O'Connor, dissented.

Question: Is it constitutionally permissible to execute a person who has been declared legally insane?
Ford v. Wainwright, 477 U.S. 399 (1986)

In this case, the Supreme Court held that the Constitution prohibits the execution of a prisoner who is insane. The Court identified shortcomings in Florida's procedures for determining sanity and ordered further evidentiary hearings on the question of Ford's competence to be executed. Writing for the majority, Justice Marshall pointed to a centuries-old tradition in common law barring execution of a prisoner who has lost his sanity as "savage and inhuman." Consistent with this common-law heritage, Marshall concluded that the Constitution also prohibits the execution of a prisoner "whose mental illness prevents him from comprehending the reasons for the penalty or its implications."

Question: Is the death penalty constitutionally permissible for accomplices if their participation in a crime was major and if they displayed reckless indifference to the value of human life?
Tison v. Arizona, (1987)

The Supreme Court narrowed *Enmund v. Florida* in *Tison*. In this case, the Court upheld the death penalty for accomplices if their participation in the crime was "major" and if they displayed "reckless indifference to human life." Writing for the majority, Justice O'Connor found that the petitioners "actively participated" in events leading up to and following the murders of four members of a family. In *Enmund*, the defendant had not actively participated in the killing and was not present when it occurred. Here, the Tisons' level of personal culpability was much greater. Petitioners were "actively involved in every element of the kidnaping-robbery and [were] physically present during the entire sequence of criminal activity culminating in the murder of the Lyons family and the subsequent flight." Petitioners' own personal involvement in the crimes was "substantial" and "sufficient to satisfy the *Enmund* culpability requirement." Justice Brennan, joined by Justices Marshall, Blackmun, and Stevens, dissented.

Question: Are statistics showing racial disparities in the imposition of the death penalty sufficient to sustain constitutional challenges to state death penalty laws?
McCleskey v. Kemp, 481 U.S. 279 (1987)

Warren McCleskey argued that Georgia's death penalty system was racially biased. He presented a study by Professor David Baldus showing that Blacks who murdered White victims were the most likely defendants to receive the death penalty. The Supreme Court ruled that the *general* data contained in the Baldus study were not sufficient to sustain McCleskey's challenge. Instead, it would have been necessary for him to demonstrate that decision makers in this *particular* case acted with a racially discriminatory intent. Writing for the majority, Justice Powell concluded that "the Baldus study does not demonstrate a constitutionally significant risk of racial bias affecting the Georgia capital sentencing process" and that McCleskey's arguments would be "best presented to the legislative bodies." Justices Brennan, Marshall, Blackmun, and Stevens dissented.

Note: In a 1991 interview, Justice Powell said that, if he could, he would change his vote to find the death penalty unconstitutional. Powell stated, "I would vote the other way in any capital case. ...I've come to think that capital punishment should be abolished." He added that he did not think the death penalty could be fairly administered, and lengthy delays breed cynicism about the law, courts, and judicial processes. See David L. Gregory, "Legal Arguments Against the Death Penalty," http://www.vincenter.org/95/gregory.html, (15 November 2008).

Question: Is it constitutionally permissible to execute a person who was under the age of 16 when he committed a capital crime?
Thompson v. Oklahoma, 487 U.S. 815 (1988)

William Wayne Thompson participated in a murder when he was 15 years old. The Supreme Court ruled that a defendant cannot be executed for a crime

committed when he was below the age of 16. Justice Stevens, joined by Justices
Brennan, Marshall, and Blackmun, observed that many respected professional
organizations, other nations sharing our Anglo-American heritage, and leading
members of the Western European community find that "it would offend civilized standards of decency to execute a person who was less than 16 years old at
the time of his or her offense." Punishment should be "directly related to the personal culpability of the criminal defendant." There is broad agreement that ado-
lescents as a class are "less mature and responsible than adults." For this reason,
"less culpability [attaches] to a crime committed by a juvenile than to a comparable crime committed by an adult." Teenagers are "less able to evaluate the consequences" of their conduct. They are "more apt to be motivated by mere
emotion or peer pressure" than are adults. Given the lesser culpability of juvenile
offenders and their capacity for rehabilitation and growth, the retributive and
deterrent purposes of capital punishment are not well served by executing a 15-
year-old offender. Execution of such juvenile offenders is constitutionally impermissible. Justice O'Connor concurred. Justice Kennedy did not participate.
Justice Scalia, joined by Chief Justice Rehnquist and Justice White, dissented.

Question: Is it constitutionally permissible to execute persons who were 16 and 17 years of age, respectively, at the time that they committed capital crimes?
Stanford v. Kentucky, 492 U.S. 361 (1989)

Kevin Stanford was 17 years old when he committed a murder in Kentucky.
Heath Wilkins was 16 years old when he committed a murder in Missouri.
Unlike *Thompson,* involving a 15-year-old murderer, here the Court *upheld* death
sentences that had been imposed on both juvenile defendants. Justice Scalia delivered the opinion of the Court. Chief Justice Rehnquist and Justices White,
Kennedy, and O'Connor—who switched sides from *Thompson*—also voted to
uphold the capital sentences. Scalia pointed out that "a majority of the States
that permit capital punishment authorize it for crimes committed at age 16 or
above." Concurring, O'Connor explained that the sentences imposed on Wilkins
and Stanford should not be set aside because "no national consensus forbids the
imposition of capital punishment on 16- or 17-year-old capital murderers."
Justice Brennan, joined by Justices Marshall, Blackmun, and Stevens, dissented.
In sum, as of 1989, *no* 15-year-old capital offender could be sentenced to death,
but *some* 16- and 17-year-old capital offenders could be sentenced to death.

Question: Does the death penalty for mentally retarded murderers *always* constitute cruel and unusual punishment?
Penry v. Lynaugh, 492 U.S. 302 (1989)

The Supreme Court held that executing mentally retarded individuals
who are convicted of capital crimes does not necessarily violate the Eighth

Amendment. In this case, however, the Court struck down Johnny Paul Penry's death sentence because the jury had not been properly instructed about how to take into account his mental retardation and other mitigating factors. Justice O'Connor, delivering the opinion of the Court, noted that in *Ford v. Wainwright*, a clear national consensus supported the conclusion that "the Eighth Amendment prohibits execution of the insane." Here, however, there was "insufficient evidence of a national consensus against executing mentally retarded people convicted of capital offenses for us to conclude that it is categorically prohibited by the Eighth Amendment." Mental retardation is a factor that may "lessen a defendant's culpability for a capital offense" and such mitigating circumstances must be considered in determining appropriate punishment for individual offenders. In *some* such cases, a capital sentence may be constitutionally permissible. Justices Brennan, Marshall, Stevens, Blackmun, Scalia, Rehnquist, White, and Kennedy concurred in part and dissented in part.

To summarize, during these post-Gregg years (1976–1989), the Court ruled that it is constitutionally impermissible to execute some accomplices, 15-year-old criminals, and the insane. However, the Court also ruled that it may be constitutionally permissible to execute other accomplices, 16-year-old criminals, and the mentally retarded. The Court "refined" its approach to the death penalty during these years. Whether or not it "clarified" the legal status of capital punishment is another question.

PART FOUR–FROM *HARMELIN TO RING*: 1991–2002
Introduction

The years leading up to and immediately following the turn of the century featured continued ambivalence in thinking about the death penalty and about the concept of cruel and unusual punishment in sentences under "three strikes" and "zero tolerance" laws. Political developments reflected similar ambivalence. For example, in 1992, Governor Bill Clinton found it politically prudent to interrupt his presidential campaign to return to Arkansas for the execution of Ricky Ray Rector. Congress passed the 1994 Violent Crime Control Act, providing the death penalty for numerous federal crimes. The same year, Illinois executed the high-profile serial killer John Wayne Gacy. In 1995, New York Governor George Pataki signed a measure reinstating the death penalty in the state. The following year, Congress passed the Antiterrorism and Effective Death Penalty Act, restricting federal and state inmates in most cases to one *habeas corpus* petition, imposing a one-year statute of limitations on the filing of petitions, and commanding federal courts to defer to state court rejection of inmate claims unless the state court's findings were not just wrong but "unreasonable." The Supreme Court declared the Act constitutional in *Felker v. Turpin* (1996). In 1997, Timothy McVeigh was convicted and sentenced to death for the 1995 bombing of a federal building in Oklahoma City. He was executed in 2001.

However, in 1999, Nebraska funded a study of the fairness of the application of the death penalty in the state. In 2000, Illinois Governor George Ryan announced a moratorium on executions in the state following several exonerations and reversals of death sentences. In 2002, Maryland Governor Parris Glendening imposed a moratorium on executions in the state and announced a study to determine whether there were racial biases in Maryland's application of the death penalty. Nationwide, the Death Penalty Information Center reported that 53 death-row inmates had been exonerated between 1991 and 2002, following the presentation of new evidence.[2]

Public opinion was also mixed. Public support for the death penalty reached 80 percent in 1994 Gallup polls—an all-time high. In May of 2001, Gallup showed public support for the death penalty at 65 percent— the lowest level in 20 years. In May of 2002, approximately eight months after the terrorist attacks of September 11, 2001, public support for the death penalty was back up to 72 percent.

Question: Will the Court revise the "proportionality rule"?
Harmelin v. Michigan, 501 U.S. 957 (1991)

In *Solem v. Helm*, the Court held that sentences that are disproportionate to the crime committed are prohibited by the Eighth Amendment. In *Harmelin,* five members of the Court voted to uphold a sentence of life imprisonment without possibility of parole for possession of 650 grams of cocaine. Justice Scalia, joined by Chief Justice Rehnquist, wanted to overturn *Solem's* proportionality rule in noncapital cases. Justice Kennedy, joined by Justices O'Connor and Souter, distinguished *Harmelin* from *Solem*. Harmelin's crime, possession of a large amount of cocaine, was "far more grave" than the crime at issue in *Solem*: writing a bad check. For this reason, Harmelin's sentence was not "grossly disproportionate" to the crime. Justices White, Blackmun, Stevens, and Marshall dissented.

Question: Will Justice Blackmun continue to "tinker with the machinery of death"?
Callins v. Collins, 510 U.S. 1141 (1994)

This Texas death penalty case involved lethal injections. It merits special mention because here Justice Blackmun, who had voted to uphold the death penalty in a number of cases earlier in his career, expressed his personal frustration with the death penalty itself and with attempts to devise rules to make capital punishment fair and constitutionally workable. Concluding that the "death penalty experiment has failed," he announced that he would "no longer tinker with the machinery of death." Like Justices Brennan and Marshall (and, based on his 1991 interview, Powell) before him, Blackmun now regarded the death penalty as categorically prohibited by the Constitution. Justice Scalia took issue with Blackmun in a strongly worded opinion of his own.

Question: Can a state precommit an individual in order to prevent him from endangering others if he is released from custody?
Kansas v. Hendricks, **521 U.S. 346 (1997)**

Kansas' Sexually Violent Predator Act provided for the civil commitment of persons who were likely to engage in predatory sexual violence. Leroy Hendricks, a convicted pedophile who was scheduled to be released from prison, admitted that he continued to harbor sexual desires for children. Under the Kansas Act, he was committed in order to prevent him from endangering others if he were to be released. The Supreme Court upheld this precommitment. Writing for the Court, Justice Thomas stressed that states "may take measures to restrict the freedom of the dangerously mentally ill. This is a legitimate non punitive governmental objective and has been historically so regarded." Justice Kennedy wrote a concurring opinion. Justices Breyer, Stevens, Souter, and Ginsburg dissented.

Question: Will the Court reexamine *Penry*? Is it cruel and unusual to execute mentally retarded individuals?
Atkins v. Virginia, **536 U.S. 304 (2002)**

Should the death penalty ever be imposed on a mentally retarded criminal? Here, the Supreme Court reversed its position from *Penry v. Lynaugh* and ruled that it is a cruel and unusual punishment to execute mentally retarded individuals. Justice Stevens, joined by Justices O'Connor, Kennedy, Souter, Ginsburg, and Breyer, delivered the opinion of the Court. Noting that mentally retarded persons have "disabilities in areas of reasoning, judgment, and control of their impulses," Stevens said that they "do not act with the level of moral culpability that characterizes the most serious adult criminal conduct." Citing an increase in the number of states banning such executions since *Penry* was decided in 1989, the Court concluded that a national consensus had developed that capital punishment is "excessive" for mentally retarded offenders.

Question: In jury trial cases, can judges, on their own, decide whether to impose the death penalty?
Ring v. Arizona, **536 U.S. 548 (2002)**

This case examined Arizona's capital sentencing procedure where juries determined guilt or innocence and judges alone decided on punishment.

Demonstrating that the Eighth Amendment was not the only relevant constitutional provision, the Supreme Court held that such sentencing procedures violate the Sixth Amendment right to trial by jury: juries, and not judges, must on whether to impose the death penalty. Justice Ginsburg delivered the opinion of the Court. The decision was joined by conservative justices as well as death penalty opponents; the only two dissenters were Chief Justice Rehnquist and Justice O'Connor, both from Arizona.

PART FIVE—ISSUES AND PROSPECTS FOR THE TWENTY-FIRST CENTURY: DEATH THROES FOR DEATH ROWS?

Introduction

Some recent developments suggest that capital punishment will continue to play an important criminological role in the United States. For example, in 2003, Governor Robert L. Ehrlich, Jr. of Maryland rescinded a moratorium on executions that had been imposed by his predecessor, Governor Parris Glendening. In 2008, the Supreme Court upheld Kentucky's lethal-injection protocols and procedures against challenges in *Baze and Bowling v. Rees*. Public support for capital punishment also has remained fairly strong. Gallup poll results showed an increase in support for the death penalty to 74 percent in 2003—the highest level in seven years. There were some fluctuations in public opinion over the next few years, but public support for the death penalty stood at 65 percent in 2009.[3]

Numerous other developments, however, suggest that capital punishment may be on the wane. In 2003, Governor George Ryan declared the Illinois death penalty system to be "arbitrary, capricious, and . . . immoral." He commuted the death sentences of 167 inmates on the Illinois death row. At the same time, speaking in opposition to Governor Ehrlich's position, Maryland Attorney General J. Joseph Curran, Jr. said that mistakes are inevitable and that the death penalty should be eliminated. In 2003, Kentucky Governor Paul Patton commuted the death sentence of Kevin L. Stanford. Stanford was 17 years old when he committed a capital crime, and it was his death sentence that the Supreme Court affirmed in *Stanford v. Kentucky* (1989). In 2004, the governors of South Dakota and Wyoming signed legislation raising the minimum age for imposition of the death penalty to 18 years of age at the time of the crime. In 2005, the Supreme Court handed down a decision in *Roper v. Simmons* that overturned *Stanford v. Kentucky*. The Court ruled that executing murderers who were 16 or 17 when they committed capital crimes was a form of cruel and unusual punishment. In 2006, New Jersey imposed a moratorium on executions in New Jersey, pending results of a comprehensive study of the State's death penalty system. In 2007, Governor Jon Corzine signed legislation abolishing capital punishment in New Jersey. In 2007, the American Bar Association published a report recommending a moratorium on the death penalty in Indiana. In 2007, the General Assembly of the United Nations voted to adopt a moratorium on the death penalty. In 2008, the Supreme Court held in *Kennedy v. Louisiana* that the death penalty is constitutionally prohibited in cases involving the rape of a child if the crime did not result in, nor was intended to result in, the child's death. New Mexico repealed its death penalty in 2009. Illinois formally abolished the death penalty in 2011. There was a 12-percent decrease in executions in 2010 compared to 2009 and more than a 50-percent decrease compared to 1999. Richard Dieter, executive director of the Death Penalty Information Center, said, "[w]hether it's concern about the high costs of the death penalty at a time when budgets are being slashed, the risks of executing the innocent, unfairness, or other reasons, the nation continued to move away from the death penalty in 2010."[4]

The Supreme Court has *not* declared that the capital punishment is flatly prohibited by the Eighth Amendment. Furthermore, public support for the death penalty remains rather strong. But the number of death sentences per year has dropped from 153 in 2003 to 114 in 2010. The number of executions per year has dropped from 65 in 2003 to 46 in 2010. The death penalty is not dead, but it appears to be in decline.

Question: One more time: Is it constitutionally permissible to execute persons who were under the age of 18 when they committed capital crimes?

Roper v. Simmons, 543 U.S. 551 (2005)

Simmons was 17 when he planned and committed a capital murder. After he had turned 18, he was sentenced to death. The Missouri Supreme Court set aside Simmons' death sentence in favor of life imprisonment without eligibility for release. It held that, although *Stanford v. Kentucky* (1989) rejected the claim that the Constitution bars capital punishment for juvenile offenders younger than 18, a national consensus had developed against the execution of those offenders since *Stanford*. The United States Supreme Court agreed, ruling that the Eighth and Fourteenth Amendments forbid imposition of the death penalty on offenders who were under the age of 18 when their crimes were committed. Justice Kennedy, joined by Justices Stevens, Souter, Ginsburg, and Breyer, delivered the opinion of the Court. Kennedy cited the rejection of a juvenile death penalty in most states, the infrequency of its use, the trend towards its abolition, the immaturity and reduced culpability of juvenile criminals, and overwhelming international opinion on the subject in support of the decision. Justices O'Connor, Scalia and Thomas and Chief Justice Rehnquist dissented.

Question: Is execution by lethal injection inhumane?
Baze and Bowling v. Rees, 533 U.S. 35 (2008)

Two inmates challenged Kentucky's four-drug lethal injection protocol, claiming that it was inhumane. They conceded that the procedure was "humane" when performed correctly, but they maintained that incorrect administration of the drugs would amount to cruel and unusual punishment. In a 7–2 decision, the Court disagreed. Chief Justice Roberts delivered the opinion of the Court. Roberts did allow that a state might violate the constitutional ban on cruel and unusual punishment if it continued to use a particular method in the face of superior alternative procedures. Justices Kennedy and Alito joined Roberts. Justices Scalia, Thomas, Breyer, and Stevens concurred in the judgment. Justice Ginsburg, joined by Justice Souter, dissented. In his separate concurring opinion, Justice Stevens, for the first time, stated his opposition to capital punishment. Reminiscent of Justices Blackmun, Powell, Brennan, and Marshall before him, Stevens said that he had become persuaded that current decisions "to retain the death penalty as a part of our law are the product of habit and inattention rather than an acceptable deliberative process that weighs the costs and risks of administering that penalty against its identifiable benefits." The "diminishing force of the principal rationales for retaining the death penalty" led Stevens to the conclusion that the death penalty represents "the pointless and needless extinction of life with only marginal contributions to any discernible social or public purposes." Such a penalty is excessive, cruel, and unusual. In spite of his personal reservations about capital punishment, however, Stevens concurred in the judgment out of respect for established precedents.

Question: Is the death penalty a constitutionally permissible penalty for a defendant who is convicted of raping a child under the age of 12?
Kennedy v. Louisiana, 554 U.S. 407 (2008)

A Louisiana court found Patrick Kennedy guilty of raping his 8-year-old stepdaughter. Louisiana law allowed the death penalty for defendants found guilty of raping children under the age of 12 and the jury awarded a death sentence. In a 5–4 decision, the Supreme Court held that the Eighth Amendment bars states from imposing the death penalty for the rape of a child where the crime did not result, and was not intended to result, in the child's death. Justice Kennedy delivered the opinion of the Court. Justices Stevens, Souter, Ginsburg, and Breyer concurred. Citing *Coker v. Georgia*, where the Court struck down a capital sentence for the rape of an adult woman, Justice Kennedy concluded that applying the death penalty in a rape case would be "cruel and unusual punishment" and would violate a national consensus on the issue. Justice Alito, joined by Chief Justice Roberts and Justices Scalia and Thomas, dissented. Alito argued that *Coker* did not apply in cases involving the rape of a child and that in light of the facts of this case and the heinous nature of the crime, the death penalty was not excessive.

Question: Is a sentence of life without parole for a juvenile convicted of a nonhomicidal offense "cruel and unusual" punishment?
Graham v. Florida, 560 U.S. __ (2010)

Graham was 17 years old when he was convicted of armed robbery and sentenced to life in prison without parole. The Court ruled that sentencing a juvenile offender to life imprisonment without parole for a nonhomicide crime is cruel and unusual punishment. Justice Kennedy delivered the opinion of the Court. Justices Stevens, Ginsburg, Breyer and Sotomayor and Chief Justice Roberts concurred. Citing *Kennedy v. Louisiana* (capital punishment is impermissible for nonhomicide crimes), *Atkins v. Virginia* (capital punishment is impermissible for criminals with low-range intellectual functioning), and *Roper v. Simmons* (capital punishment is impermissible for juveniles), Justice Kennedy found the challenged Florida sentence to be unconstitutional. The fact that life sentences are rarely imposed on nonhomicide juvenile offenders demonstrated to Kennedy that a national consensus opposes such sentences. Furthermore, juvenile offenders have lessened culpability, nonhomicide crimes are less deserving of the most severe sentences than premeditated murders, and such sentences have been widely rejected throughout the world. Justices Thomas, Scalia, and Alito dissented.

CONCLUSIONS

The Court continues to interpret the Eight Amendment's prohibition of cruel and unusual punishment with an eye toward evolving standards of decency. Over the years, several members of the Court—Justices Brennan, Marshall, Powell, and Blackmun—maintained that capital punishment was categorically prohibited by the Constitution. More recently, Justice Stevens also concluded that the death penalty is pointless and unjustified. Nevertheless, he adhered to established precedent and stopped short of striking down the death penalty. The Court continues to scrutinize how the death penalty is applied in particular cases. To survive this scrutiny, it must not be applied in an arbitrary or discriminatory fashion, juries must have an opportunity to consider all relevant mitigating factors, it must be administered as humanely as possible, and it cannot be used against insane, retarded, or juvenile offenders. Capital punishment remains constitutionally permissible if

code. Invading Viking settlers on eastern coast of England establish separate kingdoms.

1066   William of Normandy becomes king of England after Battle of Hastings, halts use of death penalty by local feudal lords.

1166   Henry II of England publishes Assize of Clarendon, providing for indictment by grand jury and eventually leading to trial by jury. Trial by ordeal and trial by battle remain alternatives.

1200s   Justinian's Code enjoys new popularity in western Europe. Roman Catholic Church outlaws trial by ordeal (1215). Use of death penalty to combat treason and heresy increases throughout Europe. Thomas Aquinas defends the death penalty for heresy by comparing the heretic who corrupts the faith to a counterfeiter, who is justly killed for corrupting the currency. In England, common law develops that in addition to treason, felonies punishable by death include murder, manslaughter, mayhem, robbery, rape, sodomy, arson, burglary, and larceny. Benefit of clergy (exemption from secular courts to those claiming to be literate and therefore clergy) increasingly available to defendants to avoid death penalty for crimes other than treason.

1500s–1600s Reformation brings religious conflict to western Europe. In England, Anglicans draw and quarter Catholics. Catholics burn Anglicans. Anglicans again draw and quarter Catholics. On the continent, Catholics, Calvinists, and Lutherans burn or behead one another.

1608–1688   American colonies settled by refugees from English religious wars and the Thirty Years War, which devastates central Europe (1618–1648). In 1649, Parliament beheads Charles I. Virginia executes George Kendall for spying (1608); Daniel Frank for theft (1630).

1636   The Massachusetts Bay Colony lists 13 crimes punishable by death, including idolatry and witchcraft.

1641   Attempts in England to reduce number of capital offenses defeated by opposition of lawyers. Use of torture in English courts forbidden. In Massachusetts, the Body of Liberties (1641) forbids "cruel and inhuman" punishments but permits limited use of torture.

1660–1690s Mary Dyer (1660) and others hanged in Boston for defying laws against Quakers remaining in Massachusetts. Ann Glover (1688) hanged in Boston for being a Catholic and a witch. Eighteen witches (1692) hanged at Salem; Giles Cory is pressed to death for refusing to plead either guilty or not guilty.

1682   Under William Penn's Great Law, the death penalty is prescribed only for murder and treason in Pennsylvania. Under pressure from England, in 1718, Pennsylvania abandons the Great Law.

1688	Bloodless coup known as the Glorious Revolution replaces James II with William III of Orange and Mary II as joint monarchs of England. In 1689, Parliament passes Bill of Rights, forbidding cruel and unusual punishments.
1700s	Mildness of English criminal practice is praised by writers like Montesquieu but criticized by Thomas Paine and others as a "Bloody Code." Jury nullification, the defense of benefit of clergy, and the practice of pardoning and "transporting" convicted criminals to American colonies as indentured servants saves many capital defendants from execution. Parliament makes returning to England after transportation a felony.
1723	Interest in England in modernization of the common law and concern for protection of private property in an era of social unrest lead to enactment of the Waltham Black Act in England. England adds scores of new capital offenses without protection of benefit of clergy.
1764	Cesare Beccaria publishes *Essay on Crime and Punishment*, calling for abolition of torture and capital punishment. European countries abolish judicial use of torture and restrict use of death penalty in response.
1776–91	American states adopt Bills of Rights and Declarations of Rights modeled on English Bill of Rights outlawing cruel and unusual punishments. Northwest Ordinance (1787) outlaws cruel or unusual punishments in Northwest Territory. Constitution proposed (1787), ratified without Bill of Rights (1789). First Congress enacts federal crime bill with mandatory death penalty for murder and rape on federal property or on the high seas and also submits constitutional amendments to states for ratification. Eighth Amendment forbids federal government to impose cruel and unusual punishments (1791).
1787	Dr. Benjamin Rush delivers speech on prison reform at the home of Benjamin Franklin. Published as *An Enquiry into the Effects of Public Punishments upon Criminals and upon Society*, it contains the first American argument for total abolition of the death penalty. In 1788, Rush follows with *An Enquiry into the Justice and Policy of Punishing Murder by Death*, devoted solely to the argument that the death penalty should be abolished.[1]
1800s	Political change in United States and advances in technology influence use of the death penalty. Toward the end of the century, mandatory death sentences replaced in many jurisdictions by death penalty at the discretion of the jury or judge. Fixed terms of imprisonment are increasingly supplemented or replaced by indeterminate sentences with release from prison on parole at the discretion of a court or parole commission.

1830s	Connecticut (1830), Rhode Island (1833), Pennsylvania (1834), and New York, New Jersey, and Massachusetts (1835) pass laws ending public executions. By 1845, eastern and midwestern states end public executions. Hangings increasingly take place in prison with either only official witnesses or a few members of the public chosen as representative witnesses. Public hangings remain popular spectacles.
1859	Abolitionist John Brown is hanged for treason, conspiracy, and murder on December 2, 1859, at Charles Town, Virginia.
1889	New federal law allows, for the first time, an appeal from a death sentence imposed in federal trial court. Supreme Court later holds, in *McKane v. Durston* (1894), that the Constitution does not require a state to allow criminal appeals.
1890	On August 6, 1890, murderer William Kemmler is the first person executed in the electric chair, at New York's Auburn Prison. The chair is later installed at Sing Sing Prison.
	The Supreme Court decides, in *Holden v. Minnesota*, that Minnesota's switch from public hangings to hangings within a county jail or other building designed to "exclude the view of persons outside" violates no constitutional right of Clifton Holden.
1891	Federal law creates Courts of Appeals, an intermediate appeals court below the Supreme Court.
1896	Ohio switches its method of execution to electrocution.
1897	Federal law amended to reduce the number of offenses eligible for the death penalty. The mandatory death penalty is abolished in favor of jury discretion to choose capital punishment or life imprisonment.
1898	Massachusetts switches its method of execution from hanging to electrocution.
1900s	A short-lived abolition movement leads to the repeal of numerous state death penalty statutes.
1907	Kansas abolishes capital punishment. Eight more states (Minnesota, Washington, Oregon, North Dakota, South Dakota, Tennessee, Arizona, and Missouri) follow suit over the next 10 years in abolishing or sharply restricting the death penalty. Eventually, all except Minnesota reinstate some death penalty provisions.
	New Jersey switches its method of execution to electrocution.
1908	Virginia switches its method of execution to electrocution.
1909	North Carolina switches its method of execution to electrocution.
1910	Kentucky switches its method of execution to electrocution.

1910s	Fear of immigrants, radical political movements, racial conflict, and sensational murder cases spark renewed use of and debate over the death penalty.
1912	South Carolina switches its method of execution to electrocution.
1913	Arkansas, Indiana, Pennsylvania, and Nebraska switch their method of execution from hanging to electrocution.
1915	The Supreme Court decides, in *Malloy v. South Carolina*, that South Carolina's switch from execution by hanging to execution in the electric chair violates no constitutional right of Joe Malloy because South Carolina's preference for use of electrocution "is the consequent of a well grounded belief that electrocution is less painful and more humane than hanging."
1923	Nevada's Supreme Court decides *State v. Gee Jon*, upholding Nevada's statute providing for executions in the gas chamber. The court writes: "The Legislature has determined that the infliction of the death penalty by the administration of lethal gas is humane, and it would indeed be not only presumptuous, but boldness on our part, to substitute our judgment for theirs, even if we thought differently upon the matter."
1924	In Chicago, attorney Clarence Darrow pleads Richard Loeb and Nathan Leopold Jr. guilty to the kidnaping and murder of Leopold's 14-year-old cousin. Darrow's defense is that his clients were mentally disturbed as a result of their privileged social environment (both defendants had millionaire parents) and intellects (both defendants, themselves teenagers, had been accepted to law school), and obtains life sentences for his clients after arguing among other things that "it is unfair to hang a 19-year-old boy for the philosophy that was taught him at the university." Loeb was later murdered in jail. Leopold was paroled after 33 years.[2]
1927	On August 27, 1927, Massachusetts electrocutes Nicola Sacco and Bartolomeo Vanzetti, Italian immigrants with anarchist sympathies, for two murders in 1920. Felix Frankfurter, later a Supreme Court Justice, writes *The Case of Sacco and Vanzetti*, claiming that Sacco and Vanzetti were innocent. Debate over Sacco and Vanzetti's guilt or innocence continues for decades.
1930s	U.S. executions reach an all-time peak, averaging 167 a year.
1936	New Jersey electrocutes Bruno Hauptmann for the 1932 kidnaping and murder of the infant son of aviation pioneer Charles Lindbergh. Hauptman maintains his innocence to the end. The media coverage of the trial is widely criticized by judges and lawyers as creating a "carnival atmosphere."[3] Congress enacts the "Lindbergh Law" only months after the kidnaping, making death in the course of an interstate kidnaping a capital offense.

A crowd estimated at from 10,000 to 20,000 watches the hanging of Rainey Bethea in Owensboro, Kentucky.

1937   A crowd estimated at 1,500 watches the hanging of Roscoe Jackson in Galena, Missouri, for murder. The first and only execution in Stone County, Missouri, it is the last known public execution in the United States.[4]

1948   On December 10, 1948, the United Nations adopts by a vote of 48–0 (with 8 abstentions from 6 Soviet-controlled nations, Saudi Arabia, and South Africa) the Universal Declaration of Human Rights. The death penalty is not expressly mentioned, but Article 5 provides, "No one shall be subject to torture or to cruel, inhuman, or degrading treatment or punishment."

1949   West Virginia becomes the last state to switch to electrocution as its method of execution.

1953   Julius and Ethel Rosenberg are electrocuted in Sing Sing Prison by the federal government, for espionage.

1957   Alaska, Hawaii, and Delaware abolish the death penalty.

1959   Sociologist Thorsten Sellin publishes *The Death Penalty,* asserting that statistical comparison of states with and without the death penalty shows that the death penalty does not deter homicide. Over the next decade, Sellin publishes additional studies supporting this view, including a study for the Canadian Parliament showing that the death penalty for murdering police officers does not deter police murderers, and a study showing that the death penalty for life prisoners who murder does not deter prison murders.[5]

1960s   Class-action lawsuits, federal *habeas corpus* petitions, and growing public opposition to the death penalty lead to a decline in executions.

1960   Caryl Chessman, the "Red Light Bandit," is executed in California's gas chamber for kidnaping and sexual assault, but not murder, of women he stopped while impersonating a police officer. Chessman, who died claiming he was innocent, had spent 11 years on death row, with eight stays of execution, seven trips to the Supreme Court, two books authored in prison, and worldwide public petitions for clemency signed by millions.

1961   Delaware readopts the death penalty.[6]

1963   Victor Feguer is hanged on March 15, 1963, for interstate kidnaping and murder at Fort Madison, Iowa, after a plea by Iowa's governor for commutation to life imprisonment is rejected by President Kennedy. Feguer is the last man executed by the federal government for 38 years. Supreme Court Justice Arthur Goldberg circulates a memorandum to the other Justices urging them to grant review to six death penalty cases on the Supreme Court's docket and strike down the death penalty as a violation of the Eighth Amendment. The Court denies review in all six cases.[7]

Lee Harvey Oswald assassinates President Kennedy. Jack Ruby murders Oswald on live television as Oswald is being transported by police. A Texas jury finds Ruby guilty of murder and recommends the death penalty, but Ruby successfully appeals, then dies of cancer in prison in 1967 while awaiting a new trial.

1964   Oregon abolishes the death penalty.

1965   Iowa and West Virginia abolish the death penalty. Great Britain abolishes the death penalty

1966   One person is executed in the United States this year.

1967   Luis Jose Monge dies in the gas chamber at Colorado State Penitentiary on June 2, 1967. Only one other person is executed in the United States this year, Aaron Mitchell in California. An unofficial moratorium on executions begins as class actions challenging the death penalty are litigated nationwide.

Canada sharply restricts the death penalty.

1970s   An eventful decade for capital punishment sees the death penalty invalidated and then reinstated.

1972   On February 18, 1972, California's Supreme Court decides *People v. Anderson*, holding California's death penalty is both cruel and unusual and therefore unconstitutional under California law. Prominent among the 104 inmates taken off California's death row are Charles Manson (the Tate-LaBianca "Helter Skelter murders") and Sirhan Sirhan (the assassination of Robert Kennedy).

On June 29, 1972, the Supreme Court decides *Furman v. Georgia,* holding that the death penalty amounts to cruel and unusual punishment because juries impose sentences arbitrarily. The decision overturns all existing death penalty laws and death sentences.

1972–1976 States re-enact death penalty laws in an attempt to comply with the criticisms made in *Furman*.

1975   Economist Isaac Ehrlich publishes *The Deterrent Effects of Capital Punishment: A Matter of Life and Death,* asserting that statistical studies show that each death penalty execution saves approximately eight lives. Ehrlich's study triggers 30 years of academic debate.

1976   Solicitor General Robert Bork, citing Ehrlich's study, argues to the Supreme Court that re-enacted death penalty statutes are constitutional. On July 2, 1976, the Supreme Court holds in *Gregg v. Georgia* that under the state's new two-stage trial system, the death penalty no longer violates the Eighth Amendment.

Canada, which last executed anyone in 1962, abolishes the death penalty.

1977   On January 17, 1977, a Utah firing squad makes murderer Gary Gilmore the first person executed in the United States in almost 10 years.

Oklahoma becomes the first state to adopt lethal injection as its method of execution.

1984   Six Virginia death-row inmates escape from prison, triggering a massive manhunt. All six are recaptured within three weeks.[8]

1986   Roger "Animal" DeGarmo announces an auction for witness seats to his execution. Although DeGarmo claims he received two $1,500 bids, Texas Department of Correction officials refuse to allow the sales.[9]

The Supreme Court, in *Ford v. Wainwright*, holds that the Eighth Amendment forbids the execution of persons who become insane while awaiting execution.

A retention election in California results in the removal from office of Chief Justice Rose Bird and Justices Joseph Grodin and Cruz Reynoso. It is widely believed that voters were responding to the justices' well-known opposition to the death penalty.

1988   The *Miami Herald* reports that Florida has spent an average of $3.2 million dollars per execution carried out from 1973 to 1988.[10]

1989   The Supreme Court, in *Penry v. Lynaugh*, holds that the Eighth Amendment permits the execution of mentally retarded persons.

The Supreme Court decides, in *Stanford v. Kentucky*, that the Eighth Amendment permits the death penalty for murderers who commit their crimes at age 16 or older. In June 2003, Governor Paul Patton of Kentucky commutes Stanford's sentence to life imprisonment.

1990s   Congress debates the death penalty as part of larger revisions to federal criminal laws.

1990   Pennsylvania, which has not executed anyone since 1962, switches its method of execution from electrocution to lethal injection.

1992   After an all-night exchange of stays and overruling of stays between the Court of Appeals for the Ninth Circuit and the Supreme Court, California executes Robert Alton Harris in the gas chamber at San Quentin Prison for murdering two teenagers.

Peter Neufeld and Barry Scheck begin The Innocence Project at Cardozo Law School to study cases where DNA evidence might be able to exonerate convicted defendants.

The *Dallas Morning Herald* reports Texas has spent an average of $2.3 million dollars per death penalty prosecution.[11]

1993   On June 28, 1993, Kirk Bloodsworth becomes the first person exonerated by DNA evidence. After nine years in prison (two of them on death row) for the 1984 murder of a 9-year-old girl, Bloodsworth was set free by a Maryland judge and later pardoned by the governor of Maryland. The real murderer, Kimberly Ruffner, pleaded guilty and received a life sentence on May 20, 2004.[12]

Washington executes Westley Dodd by hanging.

Helen Prejean, C.S.J., writes *Dead Man Walking: An Eyewitness Account of the Death Penalty in the United States.* Made into a hit movie in 1995 (Academy Award for Best Actress for Susan Sarandon as Prejean, Best Actor nomination for Sean Penn as Matthew Poncelet, the condemned murderer based on Elmo Sonnier, executed by Louisiana in 1984 for the murder in 1977 of two teenagers), the movie changes the actual method of execution used from electrocution to lethal injection.

1994   President Clinton signs Federal Death Penalty Act of 1994 on September 15, 1994, making dozens of federal crimes subject to death penalty "if death results" in the course of the crime.

Illinois executes John Wayne Gacy, convicted in 1980 of 33 murders, mostly of young boys whose bodies were buried under the crawlspace beneath Gacy's residence.

A federal judge holds that Washington may not execute Mitchell Edward Rupe by hanging because Rupe had gained so much weight in prison that he likely would be decapitated during a hanging. Rupe dies in prison of natural causes in 2006.

Kansas reinstates the death penalty as a punishment for murder.

Justice Blackmun dissents from the denial of *certiorari* in *Callins v. Collins*, declares his opposition to any use of the death penalty.

1995   New York reinstates the death penalty as a punishment for murder.

Justice John Paul Stevens, commenting on the Supreme Court's denial of *certiorari* in *Lackey v. Texas*, speculates that excessive time on death row awaiting capital punishment may itself be a violation of the Eighth Amendment. In subsequent cases, Justice Stephen Breyer agrees with Stevens and Justice Clarence Thomas criticizes both, arguing that excessive delays are the result of the Supreme Court's "Byzantine death penalty jurisprudence."

Pennsylvania executes Keith Zettlemoyer by lethal injection for the 1980 murder of a witness against him. A few months later, Pennsylvania executes Leon Moser. Zettlemoyer and Moser are executed only because, over the opposition of their attorneys, they have discontinued all appeals. The third and last Pennsylvania execution (Gary Heidnik in 1999) is likewise a volunteer for death. Depending on the state, executions of inmates who prefer execution over continued appeals are from 8 percent to 100 percent of all executions.

1996   The Antiterrorism and Effective Death Penalty Amendments Act (AEDPA) becomes effective. It limits state prisoners, in most cases, to one federal *habeas corpus* petition, provides for a one-year time limit to file in federal court after state appeals are exhausted, and requires federal courts to defer to state court rulings unless they are unreasonably wrong. In *Felker v. Turpin*, the Supreme Court upholds AEDPA against challenges that it suspends the writ of *habeas corpus* in violation of the Constitution.

AEDPA provides additional procedural limitations to federal review of death sentences for states that are certified to have guarantees of competent counsel for inmates on death row. As of 2010, the federal government still had not adopted guidelines for certifying state guidelines as adequate.

Delaware executes Billy Bailey by hanging after he declines the option of lethal injection.

Utah executes John A. Taylor by firing squad.

The federal Court of Appeals for the Ninth Circuit holds, in *Fierro v. Gomez,* that California cannot execute David Fierro because the gas chamber is cruel and unusual punishment. California amends its law to make lethal injection the primary method of execution. As of 2011, David Fierro remains in prison.

1997   In February, the American Bar Association calls for moratorium on executions until death penalty fairness is assured. Timothy McVeigh is convicted and sentenced to death for the bombing of the Oklahoma City Federal Building in 1995.

1998   On Thanksgiving Day, seven Texas death row inmates escape their cells, and one, Martin Gurule, makes it over the fence, triggering a massive manhunt. Gurule's body is found in a nearby river a week later.

1999   Journalism students at Northwestern University research and report on many cases in Illinois of innocent defendants being convicted and sentenced to death. Anthony Porter is freed from death row as a result.

The federal government finishes work on the new federal death row at the United States Penitentiary in Terra Haute, Indiana.

Arizona executes Karl LaGrand by lethal injection. Arizona executes his brother, Walter LaGrand, in the gas chamber after the Supreme

Court holds, in *Stewart v. LaGrand*, that he has waived any claim that it is cruel and unusual punishment by choosing that as his method of execution.

Russia abolishes the death penalty. President Boris Yeltsin commutes approximately 700 death sentences to terms of imprisonment.

2000s   Public opinion shifts again, resulting in fewer executions, as concerns over the risk of executing the innocent and the high cost of capital punishment dominate debate.

2000   Professor James Liebman of Columbia University releases a study asserting that more than two-thirds of more than 4,500 death penalty cases between 1973 and 1995 were overturned at least once for serious trial error.

Frank Lee Smith dies of cancer after 14 years on Florida's death row. Postmortem DNA testing exonerates him of participation in the 1985 rape and murder of an 8-year-old girl.

Governor George Ryan declares a moratorium on executions in Illinois. Governor Jeanne Shaheen vetoes legislation that would have repealed the death penalty in New Hampshire. The move is symbolic only: New Hampshire's last execution was in 1939.

Governor Frank O'Bannon orders a commission to study Indiana's death penalty system to ensure innocent persons are not executed.

2001   On his last day in office, President Clinton commutes the federal death sentence of drug kingpin Ronnie Chandler to life imprisonment. On June 11, 2001, Timothy McVeigh becomes the first person executed under federal death penalty since 1963. Eight days later, Juan Raul Garza becomes the second.

2002   Ray Krone leaves an Arizona prison, the 100th person given the death penalty to be freed as innocent, after DNA testing establishes probable guilt of another person. He and Kirk Bloodsworth (see 1993) are invited to testify before the United States Senate.

The Supreme Court decides, in *Atkins v. Virginia*, that the Eighth Amendment forbids the execution of mentally retarded murderers.

Governor Parris Glendenning declares a moratorium on executions in Maryland.

Ohio executes Alton Coleman by lethal injection. Coleman had been on the death row of three states for a murder committed during a three-month spree in 1984, during which Coleman committed robberies, rapes, and seven murders in Illinois, Indiana, and Ohio.

A federal trial judge in New York City declares the Federal Death Penalty Act of 1994 unconstitutional because of the risk that innocent defendants might be executed. The Court of Appeals for the Second Circuit reverses his ruling five months later.

2003   On his last day in office, Governor George Ryan commutes to life imprisonment the death sentences of all 167 inmates on Illinois' death row.

On his first day in office, Governor Robert Ehrlich rescinds the moratorium on executions in Maryland.

A Virginia jury finds John Allen Muhammed should die for the first-degree murder of 10 persons killed in sniper attacks during three weeks in October 2002. A separate jury convicts his teenage accomplice, Lee Malvo, but declines to recommend the death penalty.

Economists Lawrence Katz, Steven Levitt, and Ellen Shustorovich publish *Prison Conditions, Capital Punishment, and Deterrence,* asserting that statistical studies show that the risk of death in prison from inmate violence and poor health care deters crime, while the death penalty is carried out so rarely that it has no additional deterrent effect. They note that only about 2 percent of death row prisoners are executed in a given year, only twice the death rate from accidents and violence among all American men.

Economists H. Naci Mocan and R. Kaj Gittings publish *Getting off Death Row: Commuted Sentences and the Deterrent Effect of Capital Punishment,* asserting that statistical studies show each death penalty execution carried out deters approximately five murders, while each commutation of a death sentence causes about five murders.

Economists Hashem Dezbaksh, Paul Rubin, and Joanna Sheperd publish *Does Capital Punishment Have a Deterrent Effect? New Evidence from Postmoratorium Panel Data,* asserting that statistical studies show that each death penalty execution carried out deters approximately 18 murders.

2004   Maryland executes Steven Oken for rape and murder during a 20-day spree in 1987 during which Oken murdered three women.

A California jury finds Scott Peterson should die for the first-degree murder of his pregnant wife. Peterson joins the nation's largest death row population in a state where more than 670 death sentences have been imposed but only 13 executions have been carried out since *Gregg v. Georgia* in 1976.

New York's Court of Appeals decides, in *People v. LaValle,* that New York's death penalty statute is unconstitutional under the state constitution and that death penalty cases can be brought only as noncapital first-degree murder cases until the legislature enacts a different sentencing statute. No legislative solution has been forthcoming.

2005   President George W. Bush, in his State of the Union address, announces an expansion of federal efforts to use DNA evidence to prevent wrongful convictions.

The Supreme Court decides, in *Roper v. Simmons*, that the Eighth Amendment forbids the death penalty for murderers who commit their crimes before age 18.

The *Stanford Law Review* devotes an entire issue to discussion of modern studies addressing whether the death penalty is a deterrent to crime. Law Professor John Donohue and economist Justin Wolfers publish *Uses and Abuses of Empirical Evidence in the Death Penalty Debate,* asserting that after almost 40 years, Sellin's 1967 study is close to state of the art and that the only clear conclusion is that too few executions are carried out to determine the effect of the death penalty on the homicide rate.

Connecticut executes serial killer Michael Ross after he abandons all appeals. It is the first execution in New England in 45 years.

2006   Richard Moore, age 76, dies of old age after 26 years on Indiana's death row for the shotgun murders of his ex-wife, father-in-law, and a police officer responding to the crime.

Virginia executes Roger Keith Coleman for a rape and murder committed in 1981. In *Coleman v. Thompson* (1991), the Supreme Court held Coleman had no constitutional right to a competent attorney in a *habeas corpus* appeal that was filed three days late. Despite media claims asserting that executing Coleman risked killing an innocent man, postmortem DNA testing confirms that Coleman was in fact guilty.

Governor Richard Codey imposes moratorium on executions in New Jersey.

The Court of Appeals for the Ninth Circuit, in *Morales v. Hickman*, affirms a ruling that California can execute Michael Angelo Morales for the rape and murder of a 17-year-old girl, but only if an anesthesiologist is present to make sure California's lethal injection protocol does not result in Morales regaining consciousness and suffering pain during the execution. No anesthesiologist is found who will take part. As of 2011, Morales remains on death row.

Paul Zimmerman, an economist, publishes *Estimates of the Deterrent Effect of Alternative Execution Methods in the United States: 1978–2000,* asserting that statistical studies show that while the death penalty carried out by electrocution deters murder, other methods such as lethal injection do not.

2007   South Dakota executes Elijah Page by lethal injection for the robbery, torture, and murder of a teenager, Chester Allen Poage. It is

South Dakota's first execution in 60 years, made possible by Page's abandonment of all appeals.

The United Nations General Assembly votes 104–54 in favor of a nonbinding recommendation for a moratorium on the death penalty.

New Jersey repeals its death penalty statute, the first state to do so since *Gregg v. Georgia* in 1976.

2008   Nebraska's Supreme Court decides, in *State v. Mata*, that use of the electric chair is cruel and unusual punishment under the state constitution. The Court affirms Raymond Mata's death sentence in the event the legislature passes a constitutional method of execution. As of 2011, Mata remains on death row.

The Supreme Court decides, in *Baze v. Rees*, that the Eighth Amendment permits the use of three-drug method of lethal injection.

The Supreme Court decides, in *Kennedy v. Louisiana*, that the Eighth Amendment forbids the death penalty for rape of a child not resulting in death.

Texas executes Jose Ernesto Medellin, a Mexican national living in Texas since childhood, for his part in the gang rape and murder of two teenage girls in 1993. Medellin's case draws international attention after Texas refuses to schedule a new trial for Medellin despite a ruling by the International Court of Justice that Medellin and other Mexican citizens were denied information under the Vienna Convention about their right to contact the Mexican consulate. The Supreme Court, in *Medellin v. Texas*, decides that despite the United States' participation in the Vienna Convention, federal law does not require Texas to obey the decision of the International Court of Justice.

Law professor Jon Gould and attorney Lisa Greenman publish a study for the Judicial Conference of the United States examining the costs of defending federal death penalty cases in 119 cases in which the federal death penalty was authorized between 1998 and 2004. *Report on the Cost Quality and Availability of Defense Representation in Federal Death Penalty Cases* concludes that the median cost of defense when the prosecution seeks the death penalty is approximately $353,000, seven times the median cost when the death penalty is not sought.

2009   New Mexico repeals its death penalty statute, the second state to do so since *Gregg v. Georgia* in 1976.

Washington State's Supreme Court stays executions in that state pending a hearing on whether its lethal injection method inflicts cruel and unusual punishment.

2010   Ohio executes eight inmates, its highest number in sixty years. A panel appointed by the Texas Supreme Court dismisses a reprimand issued to Presiding Judge Sharon Keller of the Texas Court of Criminal Appeals, who had been accused of misconduct in refusing to allow an after hours appeal of the 2007 execution of Michael Richard.

2011   Ohio's Roman Catholic bishops call for Ohio to repeal the state's death penalty. Illinois Governor Pat Quinn signs repeal of death penalty, after that state's ten year moratorium on executions. The repeal provides that money saved is to be expended "for services for families of victims of homicide or murder and for training of law enforcement personnel." Reacting to limits on availability of sodium thiopental, states (Ohio, Arizona, Oklahoma, Texas, Alabama, and Mississippi) using lethal injection switch or consider switch to use of pentobarbital. Death penalty opponents decry use of pentobarbital because it is used in euthanizing animals, leading to new challenges in state and federal courts.

SOURCES

Capital Punishment Timeline at http://www.clarkprosecutor.org/html/death/timeline.htm (1 March 2009).
Congressional Quarterly Researcher, March 10, 1995 Volume 5, No. 9, as cited in "Frontline: Angel on Death Row," at http://www.pbs.org/wgbh/pages/frontline/angel/timeline.html (6 November 2008).
United States Supreme Court Reports.

NOTES

1. David F. Hawke, *Benjamin Rush: Revolutionary Gadfly* (Indianapolis, IN: Bobbs-Merrill Co., 1971), 364–66.

2. Scott W. Howe, "Reassessing the Individual Mandate in Capital Sentencing: Darrow's Defense of Leopold and Loeb," *Iowa Law Review* 79 (July 1994): 989, 994–1012.

3. *Nebraska Press Association v. Stuart*, 427 U.S. 539, 549 (1966).

4. Dane Drobny, "Death TV: Media Access to Executions Under the First Amendment," *Washington University Law Quarterly* 70 (Winter 1992): 1179, 1204.

5. Thorsten Sellin, "Homicides in Retentionist and Abolitionist States," 135–38, "The Death Penalty and Police Safety," 138–54, and "Prison Homicides," 154–66, from *Capital Punishment*, Thorsten Sellin, ed. (New York: Harper & Row, 1967); Thorsten Sellin, *The Death Penalty* (Philadelphia: Lippincott, 1959).

6. Thorsten Sellin, "Executions in the United States," from *Capital Punishment*, Thorsten Sellin, ed. (New York: Harper & Row, 1967), 31–35.

7. Arthur J. Goldberg, "Memorandum to the Conference Re: Capital Punishment," *South Texas Law Review* 27 (1986): 493–506.

8. John D. Bessler, *Kiss of Death: America's Love Affair With the Death Penalty* (Boston: Northeastern University Press, 2003), 1–7.

9. Steven A. Blum, "Public Executions: Understanding the Cruel and Unusual Punishments Clause," *Hastings Constitutional Law Quarterly* 19 (Winter 1992): 413, 416.

10. Daniel. Hudson, *Managing Death Sentenced Inmates: A Survey of Practices* (Lanham, MD: American Correctional Association, 2000), 82–83.

11. Hudson, *id.*

12. Testimony of Kirk Bloodsworth to the Maryland Commission on Capital Punishment, September 8, 2008, available at http://www.thejusticeproject.org/kirk/testimony-to-maryland-commission-on-capital-punishment/ (1 March 2009).

Appendix 3

Bibliography and Selected Resources

We hope you will take the time to read the endnotes to the chapters and are curious enough to read some of the references cited there. We believe a bibliography should provide the reader with a selection of useful sources for furthering your study of this field and not repeat our endnotes. Now that we have entered the age of search engines, you can easily generate thousands of references yourself simply by typing "capital punishment" into your computer. And that brings us to our first bibliographic choice: because twenty-first-century readers are, on average, more likely to go to the Internet than to the library, we begin by presenting some online resources. Given the speed with which the Internet changes, we cannot guarantee all sites are current, but all were operating through the end of the Supreme Court's 2009 term on June 30, 2010, and most of these sites will have staying power.

Because the Supreme Court is the final authority on the interpretation of the Eighth Amendment, you should start by going to the Supreme Court's site, http://www.supremecourtus.gov/. The full text of opinions is posted there within hours of issuance. Opinions since 2005 are posted on the Supreme Court's site itself, and the Supreme Court makes the text of its opinions available to several online services that, for a fee, provide the text of all or most Supreme Court opinions. Especially useful is the free site maintained by the Cornell University Law School at http://supct.law.cornell.edu/supct/index.html containing historic decisions indexed by topic.

The decisions of lower federal courts are available for a fee on PACER (Public Access to Electronic Court Records), which you can access from the websites of the federal court system, http://www.uscourts.gov/.

In the executive branch, the Department of Justice, Bureau of Justice Statistics, keeps current statistics on crime in general and capital punishment in particular at http://www.ojp.usdoj.gov/bjs/.

In 1939, Congress created the Administrative Office (AO) of the United States Courts, which manages the technology, personnel, and financial systems used by the federal judiciary. In 1967, Congress created the Federal Judicial Center (FJC) to act as the educational arm of the federal judiciary. The AO maintains a website at http://www.uscourts.gov/adminoff.html, which provides a well-written guide to understanding the federal court system called, originally enough, *Understanding the Federal Courts*. The FJC maintains a website at http://www.fjc.gov/ that contains many useful documents written specifically for federal judges, most notably *Resource Guide for Managing Capital Cases Volume I: Federal Death Penalty Trials* (2004) and *Resources for Managing Capital Cases Volume II: Habeas Corpus Review of Capital Convictions* (2004). If you want to see the nuts and blots of death penalty procedures, visit this site.

To find out what federal prosecutors read on the subject, go to the Department of Justice site at http://www.usdoj.gov/. There, you can find the manual used by the United States Attorneys to decide when and how to seek the death penalty. Look for the *United States Attorney's Manual*, Chapter 9, section 10.

To get the federal defense perspective, visit http://www.capdefnet.org, the home of Federal Death Penalty Resource Counsel, a working group of the federal public defenders. Their site contains its own bibliography of news articles and scholarly essays opposed to the death penalty.

The Death Penalty Information Center maintains a deservedly acclaimed website with information about the death penalty in United States and internationally at http://www.deathpenaltyinfo.org/. Article topics include *alternatives, arbitrariness, capital juries, clemency, constitutionality, costs, deterrence, due process, federal death penalty, federal habeas corpus, foreign nationals, general, innocence, juveniles, mental retardation, mitigation, moral issues, opinions/views, politics, race, religion, representation, state habeas review, state specific, Supreme Court, women,* and *studies and additional resources.* Of particular value is the "Espy File," representing an attempt by historian M. Watt Espy to document every one of more than 15,000 executions in the United States.

The overwhelming majority of capital punishment cases arise under state law. To look at literature concerning them, go to the website maintained by the American Bar Association. Founded in 1878, the ABA has approximately 400,000 members and is the largest association of lawyers in the world. It has officially called for a moratorium on executions and has published standards for assuring the effective representation of counsel for capital defendants. The website of its Death Penalty Moratorium Implementation Project is http://www.abanet.org/moratorium/home.html. It contains not only news updates but also the text of studies commissioned by legislatures of several states that have changed or are studying changes in death penalty legislation, including California, Illinois, Maryland, and New Jersey. There are assessments of the effectiveness (from a defense attorney's point of view) of the adequacy of death penalty representation in Alabama, Arizona, Florida, Georgia, Indiana, Ohio, Pennsylvania, and Tennessee. Most assessments contain well-chosen bibliographies of news articles and law journal essays in opposition to the death penalty.

For pro–death penalty resources, the office of the prosecutor for Clark County, Indiana, maintains http://www.clarkprosecutor.org/html/death/death.htm, which contains more than 3,000 links to other websites.

Since 1994, Professor Lawrence Hinman of the University of San Diego has edited the Ethics Updates—Punishment and the Death Penalty website at http://ethics.sandiego.edu/Applied/DeathPenalty/index.asp. In addition to original material and a good short bibliography of its own, it contains links to the full text of 1990s-era radio broadcasts, speeches, and classic essays on capital punishment (for example, John Stuart Mill, "Speech In Favor of Capital Punishment," Hugo Bedau, "The Case Against Capital Punishment," and John Rawls, "Two Concepts of Rules").

Turning to nonelectronic resources, in 2005, the State University of New York at Albany's School of Criminal Justice opened the National Death Penalty Archive. In addition to unpublished works of historical interest, such as the originals of clemency petitions, the archive contains the original papers of the Espy File, as well as the papers of two of the United States' most prominent writers about the death penalty, Hugo Bedau (against) and Ernest van den Haag (for). Contact the M. E. Grenander Department of Special Collections and Archives at SUNY Albany to find what resources are available. The NDPA's website is http://library.albany.edu/speccoll/ndpa.htm.

To gather information about the death penalty, the above resources are more than adequate. To actually gain understanding of the death penalty itself, however, one needs to read about the lives and times of persons involved in the making of the law. Whether you believe that history is the product of the efforts of great men and women or that inexorable forces of history thrust persons along its path, we believe both biographical resources and histories of ideas are indispensable. Do not expect a book or even a chapter on George Washington and capital punishment, because part of understanding the history of capital punishment, in part, is learning why our forebears did not think about the issue as we do.

For original source documents relevant to the Eighth Amendment, the Supreme Court, and its role in constitutional law, see:

Adler, Mortimer, ed. 1976. *The Annals of America, 1493–1754*, vol. 1. Chicago: Encyclopedia Britannica.

American Law Institute. 1980. *Model Penal Code and Commentaries, Part II*. 3 vols. Philadelphia: American Law Institute.

Beccaria, Cesare. 1963 [1764]. *On Crimes and Punishments*. Englewood Cliffs, NJ: Prentice Hall. Henry Paolucci, translator.

Blackstone, William. 1979 [1765–69]. *Commentaries on the Laws of England*. 4 vols. Chicago: University of Chicago Press.

Cogan, Neil H., ed. 1997. *The Complete Bill of Rights*. New York: Oxford University Press.

Elliot, Jonathan, ed. 1937 [1836]. *Debates in the Several State Conventions on the Adoption of the Federal Constitution*. 5 vols. Philadelphia: J. B. Lippincott Company.

Ford, Paul L., ed. 1968. *Pamphlets on the Constitution of the United States*. New York: Da Capo Press.

Goldberg, Arthur J. 1986. "Memorandum to the Conference Re: Capital Punishment," *South Texas Law Review* 27: 493.

Kaminski, John P., ed. 2008. *The Founders on the Founders: Word Portraits from the American Revolutionary Era*. Charlottesville: University of Virginia Press.

Kenyon, J. P., ed. 1966. *The Stuart Constitution 1603–1688: Documents and Commentary*. London: Cambridge University Press.

Schwartz, Bernard, ed. 1980. *The Roots of the Bill of Rights*. Five vols. New York: Chelsea House.

Story, Joseph, with introduction by Ronald D. Rotunda and John E. Nowak. 1987. *Commentaries on the Constitution of the United States*. Durham, NC: Carolina Academic Press.

United States Department of Justice. 2000. *Survey of the Federal Death Penalty System 1988–2000*. Washington, DC: Department of Justice.

For American constitutional law, the history of ideas, and the transformation of American legal thinking, see:

Abraham, Henry J. 1993. *The Judicial Process (6th edition)*. New York: Oxford University Press.

Bailyn, Bernard. 1992. *The Ideological Origins of the American Revolution (enlarged edition)*. Cambridge, MA: Belknap Press of the Harvard University Press.

Berger, Raoul. 1977. *Government by Judiciary: The Transformation of the Fourteenth Amendment*. Cambridge, MA: Harvard University Press.

Berkin, Carol. 2003. *A Brilliant Solution: Inventing the American Constitution*. Orlando, FL: Harcourt, Inc.

Bork, Robert H. 1996. "Our Judicial Oligarchy," *First Things* 67 (November): 21.

Brant, Irving. 1965. *The Bill of Rights: Its Origin and Meaning*. Indianapolis, IN: Bobbs-Merrill Company.

Cardozo, Benjamin N. 1921. *The Nature of the Judicial Process*. New Haven, CT: Yale University Press.

Clinton, Robert. 1999. "How the Court Became Supreme," *First Things* 89 (January): 13.

Closen, Michael L., and Robert J. Dzielak. 1996. "The History and Influence of the Law Review Institution," *Akron Law Review* 30 (Fall): 15.

Corwin, Edward S. 1958. *The Constitution and What it Means Today*. Princeton, NJ: Princeton University Press.

Cover, Robert M. and T. Alexander Aleinikoff. 1977. "Dialectical Federalism: Habeas Corpus and the Court," *Yale Law Journal* 86: 1035.

Douglas, William O. 1961 *A Living Bill of Rights*. New York: Doubleday.

Fairman, Charles. 1949. "Does the Fourteenth Amendment Incorporate the Bill of Rights?" *Stanford Law Review* 2 (December): 5.

Frankfurter, Felix. 1958. "The Supreme Court in the Mirror of Justices" *ABA Journal* 44: 723.

Friedman, Lawrence M. 1973. *A History of American Law*. New York: Touchstone Books, Simon & Schuster.

Gunther, Gerald. 1964. "The Subtle Vices of the 'Passive Virtues': A Comment on Principle and Expediency in Judicial Review," *Columbia Law Review* 64: 1.

Holmes, Oliver Wendell, Jr. 1881. *The Common Law*. Boston: Little, Brown and Company.

Maine, Henry S. 1970 [1861]. *Ancient Law: Its Connection with the Early History of Society and its Relation to Modern Ideas*. Gloucester, MA: Peter Smith.

Maitland, F. W. 1908 (H.A.L. Fisher, editor). *The Constitutional History of England*. Cambridge, UK: Cambridge University Press.

Melusky, Joseph. 2000. *The American Political System: An Owner's Manual*. Boston: McGraw-Hill.

O'Brien, David M. 2005. *Storm Center: The Supreme Court in American Politics (7th edition)*. New York: W. W. Norton & Company.

Posner, Richard A. 2008. *How Judges Think*. Cambridge, MA: Harvard University Press.

Pound, Roscoe. 1957. *The Development of Constitutional Guarantees of Liberty*. New Haven, CT: Yale University Press.

Pound, Roscoe. 1999 [1921]. *The Spirit of the Common Law*. New Brunswick, NJ: Transaction Publishers.

Rehnquist, William H. 2001. *The Supreme Court*. New York: Alfred A. Knopf.

Silverstein, Mark. 1994. *Judicious Choices: The New Politics of Supreme Court Nominations*. New York: W. W. Norton & Company.

Stannard, David E. 1977. *The Puritan Way of Death*. New York: Oxford University Press.

Sutherland, Arthur E. 1965. *Constitutionalism in America*. New York: Blaisdell Publishing Company.

Watson, Bradley C. S. 2009. *Living Constitution, Dying Faith: Progressivism and the New Science of Jurisprudence*. Wilmington, DE: ISI Books.

For treatment of the death penalty in and the problem of crime and punishment in general:

Allen, Francis A. 1981. *The Decline of the Rehabilitative Ideal.* New Haven, CT: Yale University Press.

Banner, Stuart. 2002. *The Death Penalty: An American History.* Cambridge, MA: Harvard University Press.

Bedau, Hugo A., ed. 1982. *The Death Penalty in America (3d edition).* New York: Oxford University Press.

Berns, Walter. 1979. *For Capital Punishment: Crime and the Morality of the Death Penalty.* New York: Basic Books.

Carrington, Frank. 1978. *Neither Cruel Nor Unusual.* New Rochelle, NY: Arlington House.

Cohen, Bernard L. 1970. *Law Without Order: Capital Punishment and the Liberals.* New Rochelle, NY: Arlington House.

Cohen, Morris R. 1940. "Moral Aspects of the Criminal Law," *Yale Law Journal* 49 (April): 987.

Coyne, Randall and Lyn Entzeroth. 2006. *Capital Punishment and the Judicial Process (3rd edition).* Durham, NC: Carolina Academic Press.

DeGrandis, Michael P. 2003. "*Atkins v. Virginia*: Nothing Left of the Independent Legislative Power to Punish and Define Crime," *George Mason Law Review* 11 (Summer): 805.

Demleitner, Nora V. 2005. "Is There a Future for Leniency in the U.S. Criminal Justice System?" *Michigan Law Review* 103 (May): 1231.

Dershowitz, Alan M. 2004. *America on Trial: Inside the Legal Battles that Transformed Our Nation.* New York: Warner Books.

Dezhbaksh, Hashem, Paul H. Rubin, and Joanna Shepherd. 2003. "Does Capital Punishment Have a Deterrent Effect? New Evidence from Postmoratorium Panel Data," *American Law and Economics Review* 5 (August): 344.

Donohue, John J. and Justin Wolfers. 2005. "Uses and Abuses of Empirical Evidence in the Death Penalty Debate," *Stanford Law Review* 58 (December): 791.

Douglas, Davison M. 2000. "God and the Executioner: The Influence of Western Religion on the Death Penalty," *William and Mary Bill of Rights Journal* 9 (December): 137.

Dubber, Markus D. 1998. "The Right to be Punished: Autonomy and Its Demise in Modern Penal Thought." *Law and History Review* 16 (Spring): 113.

Dulles, Avery. 2001. "Catholicism and Capital Punishment," *First Things* 112 (April): 30.

Garland, David. 2010. *Peculiar Institution: America's Death Penalty in an Age of Abolition* (Cambridge, MA: The Belknap Press of the Harvard University Press).

Greenberg, Jack. 1986 "Against the American System of Capital Punishment," *Harvard Law Review* 99 (May): 1670.

Greenlee, Harry and Shelia P. Greenlee. 2008. "Women and the Death Penalty: Racial Disparities and Differences," *William and Mary Journal of Women and the Law* 14 (Winter): 319.

Grossman, Mark. 1998. *Encyclopedia of Capital Punishment*. Santa Barbara, CA: ABC-CLIO.

Hoeflich, M. H. 1986. "Law and Geometry: Legal Science from Leibniz to Langdell," *American Journal of Legal History* 30 (April): 95.

Hood, Roger and Carolyn Hoyle. 2008 (4th edition). *The death Penalty: A World-wide Perspective* (Oxford: Oxford University Press).

Ignatieff, Michael. 1978. *A Just Measure of Pain: The Penitentiary in the Industrial Revolution 1750–1850*. New York: Pantheon Books.

Jackson, Bruce and Diane Christian. 1980. *Death Row* Boston: Beacon Press.

Jackson, Jesse. 1996. *Legal Lynching: Racism, Injustice and the Death Penalty*. New York: Marlowe & Company.

Joyce, James A. 1961. *Capital Punishment: A World View*. New York: Thomas Nelson & Sons.

Katz, Lawrence, Steven D. Levitt, and Ellen Shustorovich. 2003. "Prison Conditions, Capital Punishment, and Deterrence," *American Law and Economics Review* 5 (August): 318.

Kearns, Timothy S. 2005. "The Chair, the Needle and the Damage Done: What the Electric Chair and the Rebirth of the Method-of-Execution Challenge Could Mean for the Future of the Eighth Amendment," *Cornell Journal of Law and Public Policy* 15 (Fall): 197.

Kirchmeier, Jeffrey L. 2002. "Another Place Beyond Here: The Death Penalty Moratorium Movement in the United States," *University of Colorado Law Review* 73 (Winter): 1.

Kozinski, Alex and Sean Gallagher. 1995 "Death: The Ultimate Run-On Sentence," *Case Western Reserve Law Review* 46 (Fall): 1.

Kronenwetter, Michael. 1993. *Capital Punishment*. Santa Barbara, CA: ABC-CLIO.

Lanier, Charles S., William Bowers, and James R. Acker, eds. 2008. *The Future of America's Death Penalty: An Agenda for the Next Generation of Capital Punishment Research*. Durham, NC: Carolina Academic Press.

Laurence, John. 1960. *A History of Capital Punishment*. New York: Citadel Press.

Ledewitz, Bruce, and Scott Staples. 1993. "No Punishment Without Cruelty," *George Mason University Civil Rights Law Journal* 4 (Winter): 41.

Lee, Robert W. 1990. "Deserving to Die," *The New American*, (13 August). Reprinted in George McKenna and Stanley Feingold, Taking Sides: Clashing Views on Controversial Political Issues (McGraw Hill, 2007, 142–49).

Liebman, James S., Jeffrey Fagan, Valerie West, and Jonathan Lloyd. 2000. "Capital Attrition: Error Rates in Capital Cases, 1973–1995," *Texas Law Review* 78 (June): 1839.

Lifton, Robert J. and Greg Mitchell. 2000. *Who Owns Death? Capital Punishment, the American Conscience, and the End of Executions*. New York: HarperCollins Publishers.

Lindgren, James. 1996. "Why the Ancients May Not Have Needed a System of Criminal Law," *Boston University Law Review* 76 (February/April): 29.

Little, Rory K. 1999. "The Federal Death Penalty: History and Some Thoughts about the Department of Justice's Role," *Fordham Urban Law Journal* 26 (March): 347.

Mocan, H. Naci and R. Kaj Gittings. 2003. "Getting Off Death Row: Commuted Sentences and the Deterrent Effect of Capital Punishment," *Journal of Law and Economics* 46 (October): 453.

McCafferty, James A. 1972. *Capital Punishment.* Chicago: Aldine-Atherton.

McClellan, Grant S., ed. 1961. *Capital Punishment.* New York: H. W. Wilson.

Mencken, H. L. 1926. "The Penalty of Death," in *Elements of Argument*, 394–96, Annette T. Rottenberg, ed. 1985. New York: St. Martin's Press.

Packer, Herbert L. 1964. "Making the Punishment Fit the Crime," *Harvard Law Review* 77 (April): 1071.

Pope John Paul II. 1995. *Evangelium Vitae (The Gospel of Life),* in Joseph G. Donders, ed. 1997. *John Paul II: The Encyclicals in Everyday Language.* Maryknoll, NY: Orbis Books.

Presser, Stephen B. 1982. *Studies in the History of the United States Courts of the Third Circuit.* Washington, DC: Government Printing Office.

Radelet, Michael and Marian T. Borg. 2000. "The Changing Nature of the Death Penalty Debates," *Annual Review of Sociology* 26: 43.

Roleff, Tamara, ed. 1999. *Crime and Criminals: Opposing Viewpoints.* San Diego, CA: Greenhaven Press.

Sellin, Thorsten, ed. 1967. *Capital Punishment.* New York: Harper & Row.

Sellin, Thorsten. 1959. *The Death Penalty.* Philadelphia: Lippincott.

Shapiro, Barbara J. 1969. "Law and Science in Seventeenth-Century England," *Stanford Law Review* 21 (April): 727.

Skelton, Meghan S. 1997. "Lethal Injection in the Wake of Fierro v. Gomez," *Thomas Jefferson Law Review* 19 (Spring): 1.

Smith, Bruce P. 2005. "The History of Wrongful Execution," *Hastings Law Journal* 56 (June): 1185.

Stack, Steven. 1987. "Publicized Executions and Homicide," *American Sociological Review* 52 (August): 532.

Standen, Jeffrey. 2005. "The New Importance of Maximum Penalties," *Drake Law Review* 53 (Spring): 575.

Stephenson, D. Grier. 1994. "Justice Blackmun's Eighth Amendment Pilgrimage," *BYU Journal of Public Law* 8: 271.

Stinneford, John F. 2008. "The Original Meaning of "Unusual": The Eight Amendment as Bar to Cruel Innovation," *Northwestern University Law Review* 102 (Fall): 1739.

Stras, David R. 2007. "The Supreme Court's Gatekeepers: The Role of Law Clerks in the Certiorari Process." *Texas Law Review* 85 (March): 947.

Student Note. 1910. "What is Cruel And Unusual Punishment," *Harvard Law Review* 24: 54.

Student Note. 1966. "The Cruel And Unusual Punishment Clause and the Substantive Criminal Law," *Harvard Law Review* 79: 635.

van den Haag, Ernest and John P. Conrad. 1983. *The Death Penalty: A Debate.* New York: Plenum Press.

Wekesser, Carol, ed. 1991. *The Death Penalty: Opposing Viewpoints.* San Diego, CA: Greenhaven Press.

Wiener, Scott. 1996. "Popular Justice: State Judicial Elections and Procedural Due Process," *Harvard Civil Rights-Civil Liberties Law Review* 31 (Winter): 187.

Zimmerman, Paul R. 2006. "Estimates of the Deterrent Effect of Alternative Execution Methods in the United States: 1978–2000," *American Journal of Economics and Sociology* 65 (October): 909.

For personal accounts:

Bennett, James V. 1970. *I Choose Prison.* New York: Alfred Knopf.

Bessler, John D. 2003. *Kiss of Death: America's Love Affair With the Death Penalty.* Boston: Northeastern University Press.

Bright, Stephen B. 1996. "The Electric Chair and the Chain Gang: Choices and Challenges for America's Future," *Notre Dame Law Review* 71 (July): 845.

Bright, Stephen B. 1999. "Death in Texas," *The Champion* 23 (July): 16.

Dow, David R. 1996. "The State, The Death Penalty, and Carl Johnson," *Boston College Law Review* 37 (July): 691.

Greenhouse, Linda. 2005. *Becoming Justice Blackmun: Harry Blackmun's Supreme Court Journey.* New York: Times Books.

Hawke, David F. 1971. *Benjamin Rush: Revolutionary Gadfly.* Indianapolis, IN: Bobbs-Merrill Co.

Lawes, Lewis E. 1969 [1924]. *Man's Judgment of Death.* Montclair, NJ: Patterson Smith.

Margulies, Joseph. 2002. "Memories of an Execution," *Law and Inequality: A Journal of Theory and Practice* 20 (Winter): 125.

Nygaard, Richard L. 1988. "Crime, Pain, and Punishment: A Skeptic's View," *Dickinson Law Review* 102 (Winter): 355.

Prejean, Sister Helen. 1993. *Dead Man Walking: An Eyewitness Account of the Death Penalty in the United States.* New York: Vintage Books/Random House.

Prettyman, Barrett, Jr. 1961. *Death and the Supreme Court.* New York: Harcourt, Brace & World.

Williams, Daniel E. 1993. *Pillars of Salt: An Anthology of Early American Criminal Narratives.* Madison, WI: Madison House Publishers, Inc.

Index

About the Authors

Dr. JOSEPH A. MELUSKY, professor of political science, director of the SFU Center for the Study of Government and Law, and Coordinator of Public Administration/Government Service, has been a full-time member of the teaching faculty at St. Francis University since 1980. He has received a number of teaching awards, including the Swatsworth Award, the Honor Society Outstanding Faculty Award, and the Alumni Association's Distinguished Faculty Award. He has served as Interim Vice President for Academic Affairs, Chair of the Department of History and Political Science, Chair of the Education Department, and Dean of General Education. He is a former president and vice president of the Pennsylvania Political Science Association, former president, vice president, and executive director of the Northeastern Political Science Association, and former member of the Executive Council of the Pennsylvania Humanities Council. He serves as Director of Employment Services of the NPSA and Judge of Elections for Blair Township, Hollidaysburg East. He has published numerous papers and several books. He earned his M.A. and Ph.D. in political science from the University of Delaware and has done postgraduate work at the Universities of Delaware and Michigan and at Carnegie-Mellon University.

KEITH ALAN PESTO received a B.A. in political economy from Johns Hopkins University (1980) and a J.D. from the University of Pennsylvania Law School (1983). Since 1994, he has been the United States Magistrate Judge for the Johnstown Division of the United States District Court, Western District of Pennsylvania. He has also been a lecturer at St. Francis University, Loretto, PA, and Juniata College, Huntingdon, PA. With Joseph Melusky, he is co-author of *Cruel and Unusual Punishment: Rights and Liberties Under Law* (ABC-CLIO, 2003).